The Greatest of Their Time

To Joanna, William and Oliver

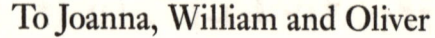

The Greatest of Their Time

Benedict Bermange

WHITE OWL
AN IMPRINT OF PEN & SWORD BOOKS LTD.
YORKSHIRE – PHILADELPHIA

First published in Great Britain in 2022 by
Pen & Sword White Owl
An imprint of
Pen & Sword Books Ltd
Yorkshire - Philadelphia

Copyright © Benedict Bermange, 2022

ISBN 978 1 39900 886 0

The right of Benedict Bermange to be identified as the Author of this work has been asserted by him in accordance with the Copyright, Designs and Patents Act 1988.

A CIP catalogue record for this book is available from the British Library.

All rights reserved. No part of this book may be reproduced or transmitted in any form or by any means, electronic or mechanical, including photocopying, recording or by any information storage and retrieval system, without permission from the Publisher in writing.

Printed and bound in England
By CPI (UK) Ltd.

Pen & Sword Books Ltd. incorporates the Imprints of Pen & Sword Archaeology, Atlas, Aviation, Battleground, Discovery, Family History, History, Maritime, Military, Naval, Politics, Railways, Select, Transport, True Crime, Fiction, Frontline Books, Leo Cooper, Praetorian Press, Seaforth Publishing, Wharncliffe and White Owl.

For a complete list of Pen & Sword titles please contact

PEN & SWORD BOOKS LIMITED
47 Church Street, Barnsley, South Yorkshire, S70 2AS, England
E-mail: enquiries@pen-and-sword.co.uk
Website: www.pen-and-sword.co.uk

or

PEN AND SWORD BOOKS
1950 Lawrence Rd, Havertown, PA 19083, USA
E-mail: uspen-and-sword@casematepublishers.com
Website: www.penandswordbooks.com

Contents

Foreword by Damon Hill OBE ... viii

Introduction ... 1
William Bedle (England) 1700–1721 ... 2
Flying Childers (England) 1721–1723 ... 4
James Figg (England) 1723–1734 ... 6
Jack Broughton (England) 1734–1750 ... 9
Clergé the Elder (France) 1750–1765 ... 11
Bill Darts (England) 1765–1769 ... 13
Eclipse (England) 1769–1770 ... 15
John Small (England) 1770–1778, 1779–1787 ... 17
Highflyer (England) 1778–1779 ... 19
William Beldham (England) 1787–1805 ... 21
Frank Buckle (England) 1805–1824 ... 23
Jem Robinson (England) 1824–1839 ... 25
Crucifix 1839–1840 ... 27
William Scott (England) 1840–1843 ... 30
Fuller Pilch (England) 1843–1850 ... 33
John Wisden (England) 1850–1859 ... 36
Donald Dinnie (Scotland) 1859–1868 ... 39
Young Tom Morris (Scotland) 1868–1875 ... 42
Matthew Webb (England) 1875–1876 ... 45
W. G. Grace (England) 1876–1896 ... 48
Bob Fitzsimmons (England) 1896–1903 ... 51
C. B. Fry (England) 1903–1908 ... 54

Jack Johnson (USA) 1908–1912, 1913–1915	57
Jim Thorpe (USA) 1912–1913	60
Ty Cobb (USA) 1915–1919	63
Jack Dempsey (USA) 1919–1923	66
Babe Ruth (USA) 1923–1930	69
Bobby Jones (USA) 1930	72
Don Bradman (Australia) 1930–1936, 1936–1939, 1946–1948	75
Jesse Owens (USA) 1936	79
Joe DiMaggio (USA) 1939–1942	82
Joe Louis (USA) 1942–1946	85
Fanny Blankers-Koen (Netherlands) 1948	89
Sugar Ray Robinson (USA) 1948–1951	93
Emil Zatopek (Czechoslovakia) 1951–1953	97
Ben Hogan (USA) 1953–1954	101
Roger Bannister (England) 1954	105
Juan Manuel Fangio (Argentina) 1954–1958	108
Pelé (Brazil) 1958–1962, 1967–1970	112
Rod Laver (Australia) 1962–1963	116
Jim Clark (Scotland) 1963–1964	119
Muhammad Ali (USA) 1964–1967, 1970–1972, 1974–1978	122
Mark Spitz (USA) 1972	126
Johan Cruyff (Netherlands) 1972–1974	129
Björn Borg (Sweden) 1978–1980	133
Martina Navratilova (USA) 1980–1984	137
Carl Lewis (USA) 1984–1986	140
Diego Maradona (Argentina) 1986	144
Mike Tyson (USA) 1986–1987, 1988–1990	148
Ben Johnson (Canada) 1987–1988	151
Steffi Graf (Germany) 1988	155

Ayrton Senna (Brazil) 1990–1991	158
Michael Jordan (USA) 1991–1993	162
Pete Sampras (USA) 1993–1996	166
Ronaldo (Brazil) 1996–1999	169
Tiger Woods (USA) 1999–2002	173
Michael Schumacher (Germany) 2002–2004	177
Roger Federer (Switzerland) 2004–2008, 2017–2018	181
Michael Phelps (USA) 2008	184
Usain Bolt (Jamaica) 2008–2010, 2012–2013	188
Lionel Messi (Argentina) 2010–2012, 2013–2015, 2021–2022	192
Serena Williams (USA) 2015	196
Cristiano Ronaldo (Portugal) 2015–2017, 2018–2021	200
Rafael Nadal (Spain) 2022	204

Foreword by Damon Hill OBE

People love to have a name they can quote as being the epitome of excellence. It shows they know at least something about a subject. Everyone knows Einstein is the most famous scientist. But was he any good? Well, yes, he probably was. But, actually, I have no idea. And how do you measure that anyway? Thankfully sport is easier to measure. You are either a winner or you're not. But even then, we argue about who the 'Greatest' of their time was.

One obvious 'Greatest' that springs to my mind is Muhammad Ali. But he didn't exactly leave anyone in any doubt that he was 'The Greatest of All Time', or GOAT. He virtually coined the phrase himself! And I don't know enough about boxing to argue the case.

Thankfully, there are people like Benedict who care enough to delve a little deeper into the facts and the statistics. For unlike, say, art, sport is lucky. It's riddled with statistics. It is the statistician's dream. And it needs numbers like a clock needs cogs. But even then, do the numbers tell the whole story? Was it easier to go around Augusta four under par in 1950, or today? Was it easier to get runs in cricket in 1890 or 1960? Did Roger Bannister break the four-minute mile because he had better plimsolls than those before? And maybe the reporting was slightly skewed from time to time and lauded the more favoured sportsperson? Heaven forbid!

This book addresses those questions and seeks to reveal more about the Greatest of Their Time. Sadly, I do not feature. But maybe Benedict will do a book on the merely 'Really Good' next time? I can't wait!

Introduction

For a great deal of the 1930s, Don Bradman was considered the most famous sportsman in the world. By any measure – statistics, acclaim – it appeared to be a straightforward decision. The same could be argued for Lionel Messi in the 2010s. But when, exactly, did they take their titles, from whom, and when did their reigns come to an end? For boxers it might be possible to narrow it down to the actual date, but for other sportsmen – and women – it is more difficult.

Athletes had been feted for their sporting prowess since ancient times, and since the advent of professional sport in the early eighteenth century there have been champions acclaimed throughout the world. This book aims to give a clearer idea of who was – at any point in time – the greatest athlete in the world – even if the world was unaware of it at the time.

In some cases, these athletes have managed to reclaim their position at the top of the tree, as can be seen from the list of dates. And Muhammad Ali – being Ali – reclaimed the title twice – just as he did with the World Heavyweight title.

William Bedle (England) 1700–1721

Cricket was a very different game in its early prehistory. The game itself probably originated in south-east England, with the first definite reference coming in 1598 from 59-year-old John Derrick of Guildford, who testified that he had played cricket as a boy while attending the Free School. This would imply that the game was being played as early as the 1550s – in the reign of 'Bloody' Mary.

Believed to have been played exclusively by children at the outset, it was only taken up by adults after several generations. Records of the game spread through the country over the next hundred years, developing from its traditional heartland of The Weald – the area of south-east England between the chalk hills of the North and South Downs. Derived from the Old English 'weald', meaning forest, the area was used both for agriculture and industry. The traditional industries of cloth-making and iron-working were in decline though, as large areas of oak forest had been cleared to make room for the rearing of cattle.

The equipment was different too. The cricket bat of the early eighteenth century bore more resemblance to a modern hockey stick, with a curved end, as that was the most effective method of striking a ball that had been skimmed along the ground underarm. The previous century had seen two cricketing fatalities when Jasper Vinall and Henry Brand both died having been struck by such a curved bat while the batsman had attempted to strike the ball a second time to avoid being caught.

Dartford Cricket Club in Kent is one of the oldest such establishments in the world, able to trace its history back to the very earliest days of the eighteenth century, if not even earlier. The town nestled between the North Downs and the River Thames and had a population of only a thousand or so, but its cricket team was sufficiently strong to frequently represent Kent as a county.

In 1723, the prominent Tory politician Robert Harley, Earl of Oxford recorded in his journal:

> At Dartford upon the Heath as we came out of the town, the men of Tonbridge and the Dartford men were warmly engaged at the sport of cricket, which of all the people of England the Kentish folk are the most renowned for, and of all the Kentish men, the men of Dartford lay claim to the greatest excellence.

Their claim as the most successful team in England was only rivalled at the time by the London Cricket Club, and the jewel in Dartford's crown was William Bedle – the earliest-known cricketing superstar.

Bedle was born in 1679 in Bromley but spent the majority of his life near Dartford, where his primary occupation was as a farmer and grazier, and he became quite wealthy.

Freedom of the Press in Great Britain was established in 1695 and newspapers of the time gradually started to incorporate coverage of sports, predominantly from a betting perspective. However, even if written reports of Bedle's feats on the field were few and far between, his reputation was well known, and he was in his prime in the first twenty years of the eighteenth century.

Cricket is blessed to have better records than most sports and details of six matches involving Dartford or Kent against London or Surrey in the first quarter of the eighteenth century still survive. The earliest-known inter-county match took place in 1709 between Kent and Surrey on Dartford Brent. The result is not known, but it was played for a £50 stake.

London hosted Kent at White Conduit Fields in August 1719 and July 1720, Kent winning the first match and London the second. There were London v Dartford fixtures in July 1722 and then two in June 1724. Of the two 1724 matches, the second one was the earliest-known match at Kennington Common, near where The Oval is now situated. Alas, even for a sport so rich in its statistics, the details of the individual feats of these early matches do not exist, even if the match results do.

Bedle's name appears on a tablet in Dartford Parish Church listing the bellringers of 1749. He died at his home near Dartford on 3 June 1768, aged 88. His obituary appeared in *Lloyd's Evening Post* the following week and described him as 'formerly accounted the most expert cricket player in England' – surely the first person to be accorded that honour.

Flying Childers (England) 1721–1723

If you ever find yourselves heading north on the M1, you might fancy a stop-off at one of three pubs – at Melton Mowbray, Stanton in Peak or Doncaster. All three pubs share a name, that of 'Flying Childers', who is considered the first truly great thoroughbred racehorse, and the first to receive universal acclaim from the public.

Flying Childers was bred by Colonel Leonard Childers of Cantley Hall, near Doncaster in Yorkshire, and was sired by Darley Arabian, who was one of three dominant foundation sires of modern thoroughbred horse-racing bloodstock. This bay Arabian horse was bought in Aleppo, Syria, by Thomas Darley in 1704 and shipped back to England. The horse was kept primarily as a private stallion at Aldby Park in Yorkshire but accepted a few outside mares, including Childers' mare Betty Leedes.

His maternal grandsire, Careless, was considered the best racehorse in England at the end of the seventeenth century, while Careless' sire, Spanker, was one of the best during the reign of Charles II.

In 1715, Betty Leedes gave birth to a bright bay colt with a blaze and four white stockings. He grew to about 15 hands, which was considered tall for his time, although about the same size as his own sire. Carrying the name of his breeder, he was purchased as a youngster by William Cavendish, the 2nd Duke of Devonshire, for whom he raced.

He first raced at the age of 6, competing in three races and winning them all. The first was on 26 April 1721 at Newmarket where he defeated the Duke of Bolton's Speedwell in a 500-guineas race over 4 miles on the Beacon Course. The previous year, Speedwell had beaten the Duke of Rutland's famous Coneyskins in a 4-mile race.

The second race, also at Newmarket, was in October, where he won in a walk over and collected a 500-guinea forfeit from Speedwell. In his third race of the year, he defeated Almanzor, also by Darley Arabian, and a mare, Brown Betty, in a three-horse race. Childers carried 9st 2lbs and covered the Round Course, measured at 3 miles 4 furlongs and 187 yards, in six minutes and forty seconds.

It was not just the victories which stunned the spectators, but the manner of them. It is claimed that he covered nearly a mile in a minute during his match with Almanzor and Brown Betty, and also covered the Beacon Course at Newmarket, then measured at 4 miles 1 furlong 138 yards, in seven minutes and thirty seconds, with each stride covering 25 feet.

The following year, Flying Childers raced only once, winning at Newmarket on 22 October, defeating Lord Drogheda's Chaunter in a 1000-guineas match over 6 miles. Each horse carried 10 stone. Although 12 years old at the time, Chaunter had beaten the best horses of his day.

The same year, he defeated the celebrated runner, Fox, in a trial at York by a quarter of a mile, while conceding a stone in weight. In 1723, as an 8-year-old, he won both his scheduled starts by walk over. He received 50 guineas forfeit from both the Duke of Bridgewater's Lonsdale Mare and Lord Milsintown's Stripling when they withdrew from a 300-guineas match. In November, he collected a forfeit of 100 guineas from Lord Godolphin's Bobsey when the challenge of a 200-guineas race was declined.

The Duke of Devonshire received many lucrative offers for the horse, including one reputedly of the horse's weight in gold crowns, which he refused. Flying Childers retired, unbeaten and untested, to the duke's famous stud at Chatsworth House in Derbyshire, and was used there as a private stallion.

He was a Champion Sire in both 1730 and 1736, but was not quite as successful at stud as he was on the turf. Nevertheless, he sired the Champion Sires Blacklegs and Blaze, with Blaze's male line surviving to this day, albeit through non-thoroughbred descendants Messenger (in Standardbreds) and Shales (in Hackneys). Snip, Second and Hampton Court Childers were also very good stallions.

He died at the duke's stud at Chatsworth in 1741.

James Figg (England) 1723–1734

Although boxing as a sport started in England about forty years before his rise to stardom, James Figg is considered to have been the first English bare-knuckle boxing champion. He was also the first to teach and promote boxing both as a skill and a competitive sport.

James Figg was born the youngest of seven children into a poor farming family in Thame, Oxfordshire in 1684. He learned to fight in local fairs, offering challenges to more established fighters across the Midlands and grew equally adept at both armed and unarmed combat, becoming especially proficient at fencing.

He was spotted by the Earl of Peterborough, who enjoyed sport and gambling to an equal degree. A former military leader, he took Figg to London where he would fight anyone brave enough to enter the ring against him. In 1719, Figg's claim to the bare-knuckle Championship of England was secured, and he opened a fighting academy. Located just north of Oxford Street, it accommodated more than 1,000 people and it became a place where he and his students could teach and demonstrate their skills. His business card – designed for him by the artist William Hogarth – described him as 'master of the noble science of defence'. He taught boxing and fencing to the sons of the nobility, as well as tutoring a number of prize-fighters.

The technique of boxing that Figg popularised was dramatically different from the boxing of today. Although hitting with fists was emphasised, a boxer could also grab and throw his opponent and then either hit him when he was down or continue to grapple while on the ground.

The sport of prize-fighting was on the rise in the early years of the eighteenth century, and Figg's Amphitheatre was one of several London venues devoted to the sport. The traditional 'ring', previously formed by the spectators, was replaced by the elevated square platform we see to this day.

Prize-fighting was a brutal affair, consisting of three rounds. The first round was fought with short-swords, the second with fists, and the third with the quarter-staff, which consisted of a shaft of hardwood with a metal spike attached to each end. Figg's greatest rival in the sport was a pipe-maker from Gravesend by the name of Ned Sutton, and the two fought three times, with as much as £3,000 wagered on the outcome of each bout.

In the pair's first encounter in 1725, Sutton defeated Figg and claimed the English title. Figg demanded a rematch, and the second clash took place in June 1727 at the famed Adam and Eve venue, on the road heading north from London. The venue was filled to capacity, with standing room only and Prime Minister Robert Walpole among the assembled crowd.

In the opening round, Sutton drove Figg back, and forced him to slice himself on the arm with his own blade. Figg then drew blood with a wound to Sutton's shoulder. The two traded throws in the second round before Sutton knocked Figg out of the ring with a hard punch to his body. However, as time passed, Figg slowly gained the upper hand until Sutton was forced to submit. Refreshed by an inter-round ale, Figg wasted little time in the final round and reclaimed his title by injuring Sutton's knee. The pair fought once more, which again Figg won, hastening Sutton's retirement from the sport.

Since bare-knuckle exhibitions were also tremendously popular with the working classes, Figg continued to make appearances in public, often at London's Southwark Fair, in a boxing booth where he would take on all-comers. Fighting infrequently in formal matches, Figg retained the championship until his retirement in 1730 with a record of 269 wins and just one solitary defeat. Having trained a number of proteges, such as Jack Broughton, George Taylor and Bob Whitaker, he could sit back and rely on them to help attract the spectators and bring in the cash, while still maintaining his position as the most well-known person in the sport.

Figg, who socialised with the Prince of Wales and other members of the royal family, died in 1734. Although some considered him a better swordsman than boxer, his role in popularising and teaching the sport gave him the title of the 'Father of Boxing' – although some now attribute that honour to Figg's successor, Broughton.

The former Greyhound Inn in Thame – now named after Figg – is traditionally held to have been his headquarters in his early days. His portrait hung over the bar there long after his death; these verses were inscribed below it:

The Mighty Combatant the first in fame,
The lasting Glory of his native Thame,
Rash and unthinking Men at length be wise,
Consult your safety and Resign the Prize,
Nor tempt Superior Force, but Timely Fly
The Vigour of his Arm, the quickness of his eye.

Jack Broughton (England) 1734–1750

Jack Broughton was born in the village of Baunton, near Cirencester in 1704. His mother died when he was young, and – in response to his new stepmother's cruelty – he left home with his 10-year-old sister and headed on foot to Bristol.

Jack managed to find work at the waterside and soon became popular due to his generosity. His sister attracted a number of suitors, before marrying a wealthy mechanic at the age of 18. With his sister's future secure, Jack could try to expand his horizons beyond the waterside in Bristol and when he attended a fair in 1725, opportunity knocked in an unusual manner.

During one of the boxing contests at the fair, Broughton took exception to the disparity in physical stature between the two pugilists. He expressed his feeling to the bully, whereupon the two men were invited on to the stage to settle the matter under the eye of James Figg, who was presiding over the boxing matches at the fair. Broughton won the resulting fight convincingly and impressed the watching Figg enough to receive an invitation to London.

Once in the capital, he studied boxing as both an art and science. Whereas in the past boxing had been more brawn than brain, he became the first student of boxing as a tactical battle. Soon his skill was noticed by the noblemen and gentlemen who frequented Figg's establishment, and he was much sought after as a tutor – even before he had achieved much in the ring.

Upon the death of Figg in 1734, George Taylor claimed the Championship of England, but he met his match when he faced Broughton two years later. By that time, Broughton had attracted the patronage of the Duke of Cumberland and was considered the greatest draw in the country. Taylor attempted to end the bout quickly, but Broughton had, by now, perfected the art of defence and was able to absorb the blows. Taylor had punched himself out and was defeated within twenty minutes.

However, the bout that changed Broughton's life – and changed boxing irrevocably – occurred on 17 February 1741 in a fairground booth on Tottenham Court Road. Broughton won the fight and inflicted such punishment on

George Stevenson that he died a few days later. Broughton immediately retired from the ring and set himself the challenge to put together a set of rules to be followed in all bare-knuckle contests.

Broughton's set of seven basic rules were regarded as definitive for around a century, and were later incorporated into the London Prize Ring rules. They introduced measures that remain in effect in professional boxing to this day and are widely regarded as the foundation of the modern sport, prior to the development of the Marquess of Queensberry rules in the 1860s.

Broughton also was the inventor of the first boxing gloves, known as 'muffles', which were used in his boxing academy by his students to 'prevent the inconvenience of black eyes, broken jaws and bloody noses …' They were never used in the professional prize ring as fights were still all bare-knuckle, but they were a convenient way to prevent serious damage to his aristocratic patrons!

In 1743, he came out of retirement and opened his own amphitheatre, which also hosted events such as bear baiting and fights with weapons. The following year he retired again and devoted his time to training future generations of fighters.

As with so many boxers, he was coaxed out of retirement again, and in 1750 made the mistake of fighting a younger man by the name of Jack Slack – the 'Norfolk Butcher'. They met at Broughton's Amphitheatre, with Broughton the heavy favourite. The Duke of Cumberland bet £10,000 on Broughton to win, but the fight lasted only fourteen minutes. Broughton was temporarily blinded by a punch between his eyes which, despite the duke imploring his man to carry on fighting even when he was unable to see, hastened the end of the contest.

A bad loser, the Duke of Cumberland went to Parliament and promptly closed Broughton's premises, after which prize-fighting was made illegal. Broughton turned the amphitheatre into an antiques dealership, and he would prove successful in that role. Later in life, he became a Yeoman of the Guard and after his death in 1789 was buried in Westminster Abbey – the only boxer to have been afforded that honour.

Clergé the Elder (France) 1750–1765

Real Tennis has its origins in Europe and there are references in the Classics to a game that was played in a stone court. The game developed as a form of handball played by monks in the cloisters of French and Italian monasteries in the eleventh century. The monastic-style buildings of the Middle Ages lent themselves to games played within the quadrangles, utilising the walls. The balls were made from the monks' discarded robes.

Louis X of France was a keen practitioner of *jeu de paume* – game of the palm – and was the first known player by name. He disliked playing outside and so decided to build indoor, enclosed courts. The game literally became the death of him: after a game in 1316 he became dehydrated, drank too much chilled white wine, and died shortly afterwards from pneumonia.

The shape of the court, as we know it today, evolved slowly over the Middle Ages, but by the end of the fifteenth century, approximate dimensions had been agreed: an overall length of 90ft and a width of 30ft. Players began to protect their hands with a leather glove. Later this glove acquired gut strings in the style of a guitar. Finally, a short handle came to be added to it. The first rules of tennis ever published – Hulpeau's *Ordonnance du Royal et honourable Jeu de la Paume*, Paris, 1592, began:

'You gentlemen who desire to strive with another at tennis must play for the recreation of the body and the delectation of the mind, and must not indulge in swearing or in blasphemy against the name of God.'

Among the English kings, Henry VII, Henry VIII, Charles I, Charles II and James II are all known to have played. Most famously, Henry VIII was responsible for The Royal Tennis Court at Hampton Court Palace in England. The world's oldest court still in use is at Falkland Palace Scotland, built for James V of Scotland in 1539, and is unique in being the only current Real Tennis court without a roof.

Interest in the game spread to Australia and North America in the nineteenth century. A court was built in Hobart, Tasmania in 1875 and in Boston in the US just one year later. The Melbourne Tennis Club was subsequently established in Exhibition Street, Melbourne in 1882. Recently, there has been a resurgence of interest in the game and there have been new courts built at Radley College, Wellington College, Bordeaux and Chicago.

The Real Tennis World Championship can lay claim to being the longest-running continuous world championship of any sport, with the first champion being Clergé The Elder who held the title for a quarter of a century from 1740 to 1765.

What was remarkable about the Frenchman was the power of his serve, which he was able to combine with great precision. He was equally adept on both forehand and backhand sides and was a proficient volleyer.

Not only was he a champion in singles play, he was also the finest doubles player in the world. He would be sure to only play his own strokes, sticking to the rules and advising his partner – whether a weak or strong player – how to take theirs. When receiving serve, he would defend the galleries (the window-like openings that can offer the chance to win the point instantly) with his volleys and return each shot that had bounced off the 'tambour' – the buttress projecting out from the wall of the court.

He would leave the ball to his partner rather than move away from his preferred position on the court. This was in marked contrast to other players of the day, who would attempt to play every ball within their reach and be quick to criticise their partners.

It was not just the quality of his play that marked out Clergé from his peers in the eighteenth-century Real Tennis world. He was renowned for being of the highest possible character, as admirable off the court as on it, a perfectly honourable and honest man, who would never play for money.

Bill Darts (England) 1765–1769

Following the defeat of Jack Slack to Bill Stevens in 1760 and the end of his ten-year reign as the undisputed champion, the sport of prize-fighting entered an era known as the 'Black Period'. The aristocracy had lost their interest in the ring, preferring to attend the racecourse and when George II died four months after Slack's defeat, the sport lost its royal patronage too.

Whereas noblemen such as the Earl of Eglinton, the Duke of Queensberry (then Earl of March), and the Duke of Cumberland previously acted as patrons of fighters, they now turned their attention to horse racing, where they could also indulge their gambling habits.

After the golden era of Figg, Broughton and Slack, the period that followed saw many inferior fighters attempting to assert their ascendancy and challenge for the Championship of England. But fixed fights were rife and there was more evidence of the title being 'bought' rather than won in the ring.

Bill Darts was born in Spitalfields in London in 1741 and was blessed with a hard punch in either hand, coupled with no small measure of skill. After several fights around the country, he fought and defeated George Meggs at Shepton Mallet in June 1764. Meggs was no mean fighter; he had learned the arts from Jack Slack, who now split his time between running a butcher's shop and training fighters.

Around the same time, there was another claimant to the throne by the name of Tom Juchau – who defeated George Millsom at Colney, near St Alban's in a contest lasting seventy minutes in August 1765. With both Darts and Juchau backed by the Duke of Richmond, a huge sum of 1,000 guineas was raised to bring the two rivals together for a fight.

It took place near Guildford on 21 May 1766 and it was the first major bout to have taken place in the open air, with all the former major contests having taken place within amphitheatres. A huge grandstand was erected as well as an additional scaffold which was able to accommodate 600 people. With no money being charged for admission, a vast throng assembled to try to catch a glimpse of the two protagonists.

However, the event itself failed to live up to the billing. It had been hoped that this fight would lift the sport from the dishonesty that was plaguing the era, but the two did not fight fairly. Paying scant attention to the rules established by Broughton, Juchau repeatedly struck foul blows, and despite protests from Darts, the fight was allowed to continue. After forty minutes, and in the seventeenth round, Darts responded in kind with a low blow which connected with Juchau's abdomen, putting an end to the bout.

Darts was proclaimed champion and fought twice the following year, retaining his title and winning 100 guineas each time. In July, he defeated Doggett, the Bargeman at Melksham in a fight lasting an hour. He then headed east to Epping Forest, where he fought Swansey the Butcher on 13 October. This was an easier fight, and he won in fifteen minutes.

He was to meet his match on 27 June 1769, however, when he fought Tom Lyons, the Waterman at Kingston. Lyons was a tough man who had grown up no stranger to street fights. A powerful hitter, he had an enormous capacity for taking punishment. Despite that, Lyons entered the fight as a 10 to 1 outsider and for the first half hour those odds seemed accurate, as Darts had very much the upper hand, knocking Lyons over in nearly every round. Lyons managed to absorb all this pressure, safe in the knowledge that it would only need one perfectly located punch to bring him victory and the championship. After forty-five minutes, a chance blow sent Darts to the floor and ended the fight.

After his defeat, Darts fought and defeated Steven Oliver at Putney in March 1770, before losing to Irishman Peter Corcoran at Epsom the following year, in just seven minutes. That fight was marred by allegations that it was fixed; either way, Darts never fought again and died in 1781.

Eclipse (England) 1769–1770

On 1 April 1764, Europe was treated to an annular solar eclipse, with the maximum effect best seen in south-east England and northern France. Viewing conditions were not ideal in London, which led potential observers to travel as far as Edinburgh in order to avoid cloud cover and obtain the best view. The time of maximum eclipse was at 10:17 a.m. and during the eclipse arguably the most valuable and influential horse in history was foaled.

His place of birth was at the Cranbourne Lodge Stud belonging to his breeder, the Duke of Cumberland – third son of George II – in Windsor Park. His male-line great-great-grandsire was the famous Darley Arabian.

A bright chestnut horse with a narrow blaze running down the length of his face ending between his nostrils, he had a white stocking on his right hind leg. He grew into a big horse, measuring more than 16 hands; he was also incredibly strong and fast.

The duke died in 1765 and Eclipse was bought for 75 guineas by William Wildman, a sheep dealer from Smithfield. At the time, there was a fear that Eclipse's temperament would make him impossible to race, but several years of hard riding proved to be more than enough schooling for the unruly colt.

His first race came at the age of 5, by which time he was fully mature. On 3 May 1769, he won a £50 plate at Epsom in a race for horses who had never previously won, defeating Gower, Chance, Trial and Plume. Before a second victory later that month at Ascot, in which he defeated Crème de Barbade, Irish owner and breeder Dennis O'Kelly famously predicted the result, saying: 'Eclipse first, the rest nowhere.' Suitably impressed, O'Kelly promptly purchased half of Eclipse for 650 guineas.

The rest of 1769 proved to be a procession of victories. He won a King's Plate at Winchester over 4 miles, then he gained walk overs for a City Plate at Winchester and a King's Plate at Salisbury. He won the City Silver Bowl over 4 miles at Salisbury at the end of June, then three more King's Plates, at Canterbury (a walk over), Lewes, and Lichfield. His jockey, Jack Oakley, habitually let Eclipse run as he pleased, and made few attempts to hold him back.

The same was to occur the following year. O'Kelly bought out Wildman's remaining half share in the horse in April, this time for 1,100 guineas and the same month Eclipse defeated Bucephalus over the Beacon Course at Newmarket in what was to prove his toughest outing. Just two days later at the same meeting, he won the Newmarket King's Purse, easily beating Pensioner, Diana and Chigger 'out of sight'.

On 23 August 1770, he won the Great Subscription at York, run in a single 4-mile 'dash', followed by another King's Plate at Lincoln – again via a walk over. At the Newmarket meeting, he won two races in two days, including the King's Plate in a walk over.

And just like that his racing career was over, with an unblemished record of eighteen victories in eighteen races. He had proved himself superior to all his contemporaries, and by a wide margin, and was declared the greatest racehorse since Flying Childers half a century earlier. The lack of any suitable opposition – with Eclipse setting out at 70 to 1 on in his final race – was the main reason he was hastened into retirement.

Eminent writer Sir Theodore Cook wrote of him:

> His excellence was not only owing to the races he won, but even more clearly to the astonishing ease with which he won them, and to the fact that in addition to his undoubted speed and stride, he possessed sound wind, an ability to carry heavy weight, and an endurance over long distances which could never be thoroughly tested, for its limit was never reached.

Eclipse retired to O'Kelly's Clay Hill Stud, near Epsom in 1771 and became one of the leading sires of his era. In all, he sired 344 winners, including the Derby victors Young Eclipse, Saltram, Volunteer, and Sergeant. It is estimated that among all living thoroughbreds, at least 95 per cent can trace their direct tail male line back to Eclipse, mainly through his two sons Pot-8-os and King Fergus. One of his daughters, Annette, was also a Classic winner, triumphing in the Oaks of 1787.

In 1788, he was moved, by carriage, to O'Kelly's Cannons Park stud in Stanmore, Middlesex and it was there that he died of colic on 26 February 1789 at the age of 24. He has been immortalised after death in the Eclipse Awards in the US, which honour the champions of the sport, and in the Eclipse Stakes, a Group 1 race at Sandown Park.

John Small (England) 1770–1778, 1779–1787

Nobody can be certain when cricket was first played on Broadhalfpenny Down in Hambledon, Hampshire, but it seems certain to have been in the first half of the eighteenth century. The name 'Broadhalfpenny' came from the fact that the open space was where local people had met and traded, and they would pay halfpenny for the privilege of trading there for a day.

Richard Nyren was the original driving force behind the development of the Hambledon cricket team, which benefited from its close-knit community and its ability to attract talented cricketers from neighbouring counties. However, the star of the first great Hambledon team was John Small, a batsman who was the first to combine the traditional aggression with concentration and defence: crucial talents required to build an innings and the foundations upon which modern batting is based.

John Small was born on 19 April 1737 in Empshott but moved with his family to Petersfield at the age of 6, where he remained for the rest of his life. He started off as a shoemaker, but, after playing in his first major match in 1755 at the age of 18, gave up his trade to concentrate on cricket.

Unfortunately, many of his early feats of scoring have not been recorded, but he scored 140 runs across his two innings against Kent in 1768 and four years later made 112 of Hambledon's total of 225 against England. Following his unbeaten innings of 136 against Surrey in 1776, the *Kentish Gazette* proclaimed him as 'the best cricketer the world ever produced'. He was the bedrock upon which the Hambledon batting was founded for many years.

Hambledon became the sole source for decisions surrounding the laws of the game and the club found itself taking responsibility for dealing with any new issues which arose. One such issue came about on 23 September 1771 when Thomas White arrived at the crease with a bat the same width as the stumps. Two days later, a law was passed limiting the width of the cricket bat to 4¼ inches. One of the signatories was John Small, and a copy of the minutes of the discussions still survives.

Another issue was the nature of the stumps. On 22 May 1775, Hambledon were playing Kent at the Artillery Ground in London for the considerable sum of 50 guineas. Edward 'Lumpy' Stevens of Kent bowled a ball through John Small's two stumps on three separate occasions but each time failed to dislodge a bail. Despite the fact that Hambledon went on to win that match, it was agreed that something had to be done, and a third stump was introduced two years later.

Once he had made his reputation, he returned to working with leather, this time making cricket balls as well as bats. If you were in the market for some cricket equipment, it was easy to find his house and workshop in Dragon Street, Petersfield as there was a sign outside proclaiming:

> Here lives John Small,
> Makes bat and ball,
> Pitches a wicket, plays at cricket
> With any man in England.

After the addition of the third stump, it became even more important to play with a straight bat, and Small played a major part in the reshaping of the traditional curved cricket bat into the straighter form so familiar nowadays. The new shape would not only be able to strike a bouncing delivery better, but would also enable the batsman to pull and drive the ball to greater effect.

Small was blessed with a keen eye, as he was among the first batsmen to run quick singles, eagerly looking for gaps in the field while possessing an ability to judge the time it would take to make his ground successfully at the other end. He was a fine stroke-maker and could move his feet quickly and pierce the field with powerful strokes from his strong wrists. Over his many years playing, he developed a deep insight into the game and became an expert in the laws. He was a good enough batsman to play at county level for many years and his last recorded match was at Lord's Old Ground in August 1798 when he was 61.

After finally retiring from playing, he worked as a gamekeeper and concentrated on his bat- and ball-making business, with both being very much in demand. A talented musician, he was able to devote more time to playing the violin and double bass and he was a member of the church choir for all his adult life. He died in 1826.

Highflyer (England) 1778–1779

Highflyer was bred by Sir Charles Bunbury, the 5th Baronet, who, upon the death of his father Sir William Bunbury in 1764, had inherited the title and family estates at Mildenhall and Great Barton Hall in the eastern county of Suffolk. Highflyer's sire, Herod, spent his entire career at Nether Hall Stud, near Bury St Edmunds just east of Newmarket. It was at Great Barton, just north-east of Bury St Edmunds, that Highflyer was foaled in 1774 in a paddock where some highflyer walnut trees stood; he was named as such by his next owner, Frederick St John, 2nd Viscount Bolingbroke.

Highflyer went into training with Thomas Robson and was supposed to be well short of peak fitness when he turned out for his debut. His racing career coincided with an important shift in racing at the time, since only a few years earlier, the trend had been to wait until a horse was 5 years old before racing. but it was as a 3-year-old that he made his debut. Starting third favourite in a field of five over 2 miles of the Ditch In Course at Newmarket on 2 October 1777, he came home an impressive winner.

That was his only race in 1777 and when he reappeared as a 4-year-old the following year it was in the name of Bolingbroke's betting confederate Henry Compton. All his races were over the Beacon Course at Newmarket and he always proved far too good for his rivals. He started by winning a valuable sweepstakes before winning the Grosvenor Stakes in July. His most important win that year came on 1 October in the 1,400 Guineas Stakes for 4-year-olds, one of the most important races of the second half of the eighteenth century. Rounding off the season, he defeated 5-year-old Dictator in a 500-guineas match race, probably the best horse to oppose him, as Dictator had already won six races that year.

Highflyer turned 5 in 1779 and started the year with two more victories before Lord Bolingbroke was made an offer he could not refuse. Even Highflyer's ability to earn good money was not enough for the compulsive gambler Bolingbroke and Highflyer's ever-shortening odds were never going to hold any kind of value proposition for him. Possibly needing to raise some capital to pay off gambling debts, he sold his prize asset to Richard Tattersall for £2,500. A week after completing the sale in April 1779, Highflyer ran and defeated Magog over the Beacon Course at Newmarket.

Tattersall was a Yorkshireman and had served as Master of Horse for the Duke of Kingston. At the time, he was more astute as a businessman than as a racehorse owner, but he later became deeply involved in the art of horse-selling and an expert at handling the dispersal of bloodstock from various noble estates.

All opposition to Highflyer in the Great Subscription Purse at York in August 1779 disappeared, leaving him with a walk over victory and he added a further victory the following day, defeating Venetian at odds of 20 to 1 on. His final race was at Lichfield in September in the King's Plate, where he beat two others in 3-mile heats.

Just like Eclipse before him, Highflyer had defeated every horse put up against him. The only regret was that he was never tested against the other two stars of his day – Pot-8-os and Woodpecker – who were also in action on the same occasion as his final race at Newmarket – but in different races.

Highflyer was the Leading Sire for fifteen years, during which time he produced 469 winners, including three Derby winners, three St Leger winners, and an Oaks winner. Tattersall was not ashamed to credit the stallion with the financial success with which he built a mansion named 'Highflyer Hall'. While Eclipse is renowned as the male-line ancestor of 95 per cent of the thoroughbreds in the twenty-first century, Highflyer was the dominant sire of the eighteenth century, but his bloodline is virtually extinct now.

When Highflyer died on 18 October 1793, he was buried in his paddock, and his owner gave the great horse the epitaph:

> Here lieth the perfect and beautiful symmetry of the much-lamented Highflyer, by whom and his wonderful offspring the celebrated Tattersall acquired a noble fortune, but was not ashamed to acknowledge it.

William Beldham (England) 1787–1805

William Beldham was born in Yew Street Cottage in Wrecclesham, near Farnham on 5 February 1766. He was the fourth of six children of a farmer and was already representing Farnham at cricket by the time he was 16, alongside his older brother George. Two years later, he faced Hambledon and scored 43 against an attack featuring David Harris, considered the pre-eminent bowler of the day.

One early spring day in 1785, William was working in the fields when he was approached by the Earl of Winchelsea – the most important cricketing patron of the time – who had watched his innings the previous year. The earl managed to persuade the farmer to grant Beldham the time off required for him to represent Hampshire (or Hambledon as it was in fact) against England at the new cricket ground in White Conduit Fields. At that time, it was commonplace for players to be loaned out to assist other teams.

Beldham stood about 5 feet 8½ inches and was known as 'Silver Billy' due to his light-coloured hair and fair complexion. Agriculture was still the priority for him and he continued to work on the family farm, but each weekend, William, together with brother George and a couple of other boys from the town would ride on horseback to play for Hambledon. He was paid 5 guineas if the team won, but only 3 guineas if they lost. In the summer of 1788, he earned 42 guineas from playing cricket, far more than he would have earned in a year on the farm. It was good money, but still a far cry from the sums the watching aristocrats could earn from betting on the results of the games.

Beldham was possibly the first batsman who emphasised style as a key component of his art. His defence was rock solid but he could also be a brilliant hitter, making use of his excellent eye and exquisite timing. In an era of difficult pitches, he averaged more than forty runs per match between 1788 and 1800 when most of his peers struggled to reach twenty runs. In June 1794 he scored 72 and 102 as Surrey defeated England by 197 runs at Lord's Old Ground and in the same fixture in July 1801, he made 82 out of his team's total of 109 all out, an innings in which no other batsman reached double figures.

At his peak, the only bowler who consistently troubled him was David Harris, with whom he had some memorable duels. Beldham's response to Harris's bowling was to move down the pitch to try to intercept the ball just after it had bounced. Other players also adopted this technique of playing forward, but Beldham was, without doubt, the most adept.

He was an excellent judge of a run and was a fine fielder with a good knowledge of the game. He operated as a change bowler but was effective enough to be considered to be an all-rounder and took a total of 217 wickets in his 189 first-class matches of which we have details.

The last decade of the eighteenth century saw a decline in Hambledon cricket and shifting of the power base from Hampshire and other rural teams to London. It also saw an increase in betting, and match-fixing became rife. There had been plenty of betting on the Hambledon matches, but once the century turned, the bookmakers discovered how to reach the players and, in that way, they could attempt to influence the results of the matches.

Even with earning a match fee of up to 5 guineas, which was a far cry from the 10 shillings a week which could have been earned from working on the farm, the players were more than willing to give in to the bookies in return for a drink at the Green Man and Still pub on Oxford Street. Many matches were bought and sold in this manner, but Beldham managed to separate himself from these practices on the whole.

He was noted for his integrity and fair play and was subsequently shocked to discover ten years after the event that a match in which he had played in 1807 had been fixed. Beldham claimed that the only blots on his copybook were when he had rubbed mud and sawdust on the ball in a match at Lord's in June 1806 and when he had helped fix a match at Nottingham with the sole purpose of recouping £10 he felt he had been cheated out of by the same players in a previous match.

He finally retired from cricket in 1821 and moved to Tilford where he became the landlord of the Barley Mow pub, remaining there for twenty years before moving to the cottage next door, where he placed his cricket bat above the mantelpiece. He remained active well into old age, walking 7 miles at the age of 86 to see Godalming play England.

When he died at the age of 96 it was truly the end of an era as he was the last of the Hambledon immortals and the earliest cricketer of whom a photograph survives. He had been born just before the height of the club's fame and he lived long enough to witness the establishment of the first-class county system, and a team representing England had already toured North America. Cricket was well on its way to becoming the international sport it is now.

Frank Buckle (England) 1805–1824

The son of a Newmarket saddler, Frank Buckle was born on 18 July 1766. His father died when young Frank was just 12, and the six children came under the guardianship of his uncle, who apprenticed Frank to a saddler so that he could continue in the family business.

However, Frank had no intention of following that route, and frequently absconded from his master, showing far more interest in horses and stables. He had started to ride and exercise in the stables of the Earl of Grosvenor at the age of 9, and there was nothing his guardian could do to try to steer him from what was to prove his chosen course in life.

He became an apprentice to the Honourable Richard Vernon, who successfully combined horse breeding and training with a 36-year career in the House of Commons. Buckle studied the best jockeys of the day and made his debut on the track as a 16-year-old on 17 May 1783 at Newmarket. Wearing Vernon's colours and carrying a mere 3 stone 13 pounds he rode a bay colt called Wolf.

At the end of his apprenticeship, he rode for Lord Grosvenor and achieved his first Classic victory on John Bull, who he regarded as the best horse he ever rode, in the 1792 Derby. He won a second Derby on Daedalus in 1794 and three successive Oaks on Niké (1797), Bellissima (1798) and Bellina (1799).

Following Lord Grosvenor's death in 1802, Buckle first rode for Newmarket trainer Robert Robson. In their first year together, he won the Derby on Tyrant and the Oaks on Scotia. He rode a waiting race on Tyrant, while he brought Scotia to victory with one final effort to win by a head. Those triumphs were great examples of his racing tactics.

Buckle was not just a skilful rider, but also a remarkably good judge of a horse. A great many of his victories can be attributed to the fact that he stayed so calm in the saddle. He hated making the running, much preferring to come from behind.

His tally of twenty-seven victories in the English Classics remained a record for 150 years. What makes it even more remarkable is that his career had already lasted for twenty years before the introduction of the 2,000 and

1,000 Guineas. He won the 2,000 Guineas five times, the 1,000 Guineas six times, the Derby five times, the Oaks nine times (which still remains the record), and the St Leger twice. It was not until Lester Piggott's victory on Commanche Run in the 1984 St Leger that the record was finally eclipsed.

His chief rival in the period was the Irish jockey Dennis Fitzpatrick, who won five Classic races of his own. It was against Fitzpatrick that the famous race between Buckle's Hambletonian and Fitzpatrick's Diamond took place on 25 March 1799 over the 4-mile Beacon Course at Newmarket. The race aroused enormous interest, and many travelled to Newmarket to support Hambletonian – who won by half a neck mainly due to Buckle's expert manoeuvring between the ditch and the turn. Hambletonian started at 5 to 1 on, and an estimated 300,000 guineas was wagered on the result.

Buckle's three sons were born in Long Orton, and soon afterwards he decided to settle on a farm in Peterborough rather than the racing Mecca that was Newmarket. Determined to give his sons the best possible start in life, he moved to Bury St Edmunds in 1822 so they could be educated at the grammar school there. Once that had been accomplished, he moved back to Peterborough in 1827.

He thought nothing of making the 90-mile round trip to ride in trials, always returning home by six o'clock – in time for supper. He quietly bred cattle, greyhounds, bulldogs and fighting cocks with some success. He also became well known for his dress and was always immaculately turned out in boots and breeches. Discussions on horse racing were banned at home and he actively dissuaded his sons from following him in the saddle. As it transpired, one became a solicitor, one a pharmacist and the other a brewer.

His last race was on Conservator on 5 November 1831 when he was 63 and had been riding for exactly half a century, having entered Vernon's stables on 5 November 1781. Only a few months later, he died and was buried in the Orton Longueville parish churchyard, beneath a tombstone carrying the inscription:

> No better rider ever crossed a horse;
> Honour his guide, he died without remorse.
> Jockeys attend – from his example learn
> The meed that honest worth is sure to earn.

Jem Robinson (England) 1824–1839

Jem Robinson was born on 22 June 1794 into the horse-racing establishment, being the son of John Robinson, a small trainer in Newmarket. As a boy, he had the good fortune to be apprenticed in the stable of Robert Robson, with whom he remained for thirteen years. While there, he impressed everyone and soon moved on from ordinary stable work and exercise to the more responsible practice of riding in private trials.

While in Robson's stables he encountered Frank Buckle, who gave him a great deal of advice and encouragement. It was ironic that one of his earliest races was on Conviction, riding against Buckle's Pigmy and Robinson came out on top, much to the senior jockey's frustration. 'Don't you come that trick over me again,' said Frank to his young rival. 'What trick, sir?' Jem is reported to have replied, to which all that Buckle could retort was 'Never you mind what, but I say don't.' The two had many battles on the track, memorably dead-heating in 1821 with Robinson aboard Ardrossan and Buckle riding Abjer.

Robinson's first major victory came in the 1817 Derby aboard a chestnut horse called Azor, owned by John Payne. The horse was a 50 to 1 outsider in a field of thirteen. Originally thought to have been included in the race merely to act as a pacemaker, the other jockeys allowed him to build up a huge lead, and he clung on to win, creating the greatest upset in the race up to that time.

Robinson was an innovator and rode in the crouching style that is so familiar among jockeys now, having been popularised by American jockey Ted Sloan some half a century after Robinson. This was the technique of distributing the jockey's weight in the ridge between the shoulder blades of the horse, rather than the earlier custom to sit bolt upright in the saddle. Riding in this style, Robinson used his whip underhand and sometimes quite vigorously, and it was not unknown for him to draw blood on the horses he rode, a fact that some of the horses remembered and caused them to react violently to him in their stables.

In those days, jockeys could bet on their own races to win, and in 1824 Robinson backed himself to win the Derby, the Oaks and get married all within the space of a week. Having piloted Cedric and Augusta to victory in the respective races, he collected his winnings by marrying Elizabeth Powell on the Saturday of the meeting at Epsom.

He won the Derby again the following year, this time on Middleton, and in 1827 on Mameluke. The 1828 race ended in a dead heat between Robinson's mount, Cadland, and Bill Scott's, The Colonel – the only such finish in the first century of the running of the race. Scott kept close to the front-running Cadland throughout the race, before challenging for the lead in the final straight. A furlong from the finish, he was briefly in the lead but Cadland fought back and the two horses crossed the line together. The official judge declared the result a dead heat, with a deciding heat to be run at the end of the afternoon. Scott repeated his earlier tactics by holding The Colonel back for a late challenge but was unable to overtake his rival and Robinson won by a neck for his fourth Derby triumph in five years.

Eight years would pass before Robinson's next Derby triumph, this time on Bay Middleton. The horse's trainer, James Edwards, met Robinson by chance in London, and having informed Robinson that his prospective horse for the Derby – Bay Middleton – was difficult to handle, begged for help. Robinson went to Edwards' stables and discovered that none of Edwards' stable hands were prepared to ride him. The first meeting of horse and jockey did not go well as the horse bolted as soon as Robinson was in the saddle. However, they gradually established a great understanding and Robinson rode him to victory in all six of his races, including the 1836 Derby.

In total, he rode twenty-four Classics winners, including nine victories in the 2,000 Guineas. His final two Classics victories came in that race at Newmarket, aboard Conyngham in 1847 and Flatcatcher the following year. He made a gallant effort to win the 1850 St Leger when his mount Russborough dead-heated with Voltigeur, but he lost the deciding run-off.

His racing career came to a sudden and painful end at the first spring meeting in 1852. Riding Lord Clifden's 2-year-old Feramorz, he was thrown to the ground just after the start of the race, breaking his left thigh, collar bone and several ribs. The accident left him with one leg several inches shorter than the other, and he never donned the silks again.

He set up his own stable yard in Newmarket but was less successful in retirement than he had been in the saddle, preferring to spend his time in London. He had earned a great deal of money over the course of his time riding, at one stage commanding 100 guineas for riding Ephesus in the 1851 St Leger, but most of his winnings disappeared over his retirement, and at the end he was reliant on annuities from the Dukes of Rutland and Bedford. He died in 1873 and was buried in Newmarket cemetery.

Crucifix 1839–1840

In the spring 1837 sale of Lord Chesterfield's stud, one lot of a 21-year-old mare and her lanky foal was bought for 54 guineas by Lord George Bentinck, who had previously bred the 1,000 Guineas winners Firebrand and The Flea. He could obviously spot something that he liked as the mare was Octaviana, and the foal Crucifix. There was no doubting the pedigree of the foal, as her sire was Priam, the 1830 Derby winner.

Crucifix made her first public appearance at the Newmarket July meeting in 1839, racing in the July stakes. Eight horses started, but five were soon off the pace, leaving the leading three to fight it out for victory. The Duke of Grafton's Currency led for the most part, but jockey John Day played the waiting game aboard Crucifix, finally moving ahead to take the race by two lengths, going away.

Her reward for victory was to be given an additional 9lbs to carry for the Chesterfield Stakes at the same meeting. After several false starts, the horses ran the full course and Crucifix finished second to Lord Albemarle's Iris. However, the steward, Lord Albemarle, decided that it was 'no race', and in the actual contest Crucifix reversed the result and won easily by two lengths.

Her reputation continued to grow, with victory in the Lavant Stakes at Goodwood, followed by winning the Molecomb Stakes at the same meeting before returning to Newmarket where she continued her winning ways.

In the October meeting, she won the Hopeful Stakes, a race plagued by seventeen false starts with the horses kept at the post for over an hour. The second October meeting saw her victorious in the Clearwell Stakes and Prendergast Stakes. She rounded off her year as a 2-year-old by running a dead heat with Gibraltar after another long delay at the starting post in the Criterion Stakes in the Houghton Meeting. Rather than a re-run, the two owners decided to split the winnings, as both horses were not fit to race again. Lord Bentinck presented John Day with a cheque for £100 'not for your riding but for keeping your temper'. It was pocket change for Bentinck, who had seen his horse complete her first season on the turf unbeaten in her nine races, having won £4,587, a lucrative return on the original outlay of 54 guineas.

Standing nearly 16 hands high, she was described as having a long neck with thin shoulders. Her chest was very narrow, and her fore and hind legs small. She was said to have been a shambling mover with a tendency to cross her legs, but she was incredibly active, and could reach top speed in just a few strides without any real effort.

A vast crowd gathered at Newmarket on the Tuesday of the first spring meeting in 1840 to watch the 2,000 Guineas, in which six horses came to the post. Lord Orford's grey, Angelo, made the early running before Lord Bentinck's other entrant Capote took the lead and stayed there for half a mile. When they reached the bushes, Crucifix moved up from the rear of the field and managed to take the lead by a length. Mr Houldsworth's horse Confederate moved into second place ahead of Angelo, but Crucifix never lost her lead and won by a length.

On Thursday at the same meeting, she triumphed in the 1,000 Guineas, setting off at 10 to 1 on, the shortest-price in the history of the race. She romped home, ahead of Bentinck's Rosablanca, Lord Albemarle's Spangle and Lord Exeter's Silistria.

Having won both Classic races, Crucifix was established as the firm favourite for the Oaks, but she was starting to feel the effects of so many races at such a tender age. Her trainer at the Danebury stable advised Bentinck that she would probably only be able to race once more, and the utmost care was taken to ensure she reached the post in as good condition as possible.

On 5 June, in the presence of both Queen Victoria and Prince Albert, Crucifix set off as the firm favourite in what was to be her last race. There were fifteen fillies in the field, but again the start was marred by false starts, this time sixteen of them delaying the start of the race for more than an hour. When they finally did get off, Lalla Rookh took an early lead with Crucifix right at the back of the field by two lengths. However, the pace was slow and so she had plenty of time to catch up and started to make the running and increased speed once they reached the top of the hill. Coming down the straight it was a close race between Crucifix, Welfare and Teleta, but it was the favourite who ended up in front, winning by half a length. Just after the finishing line, her jockey said with a sigh: 'That is well over.'

And so ended her racing career, unbeaten in her twelve races condensed over the same number of months. She had been backed strongly in the St Leger that year, but it was finally declared that she would run no more.

She retired to stud where she was successful, with many of her descendants winning races to this day. She was subsequently sold with her son – future Derby winner Surplice – to the Honourable Edward Mostyn for £10,000. In turn, he sold her to Henry Agar-Ellis Clifden, 3rd Viscount Clifden, and she died in 1858 at Danebury, near Stockbridge in Hampshire.

William Scott (England) 1840–1843

'**G**lorious' Bill Scott was born in Chippenham in 1797, the son of a former jockey, and so it was only natural that his father had him ride a horse as soon as he was old enough.

Bill and his brother John were both sent to apprentice in Newmarket under trainer James Edwards, with Bill continuing to graduate under James Croft at Hambleton. As he grew older, John gained too much weight to be a jockey and turned his attention to training. He did so with great success, frequently providing horses from his Malton stables that his brother turned into winners on the track. Bill, therefore, became the most famous north-based jockey ever known.

The two brothers could not have been more dissimilar. John was solid, steady and reliable. Bill, on the other hand, was highly strung, talkative, amusing and a great raconteur. During the winter months, when there was no racing, John and Bill Scott would go hunting together, so they were seldom out of the saddle.

His preferred style of riding was as a front-runner, rather than playing a waiting game, and as with many jockeys of the day, he could be harsh on his mounts. When he won his first Classic – the 1821 St Leger – his horse, Jack Spigot, had to be blindfolded before it was mounted due to its hatred of the jockey as a result of his ill treatment in previous races. Scott felt that he had not earned his fee unless he had pushed a horse to its limits, even if all chances of winning had gone.

Having dead-heated in the 1828 Derby aboard The Colonel with Jem Robinson's mount Cadland, he lost the subsequent run-off when he was a bundle of nerves, and he had to wait a further four years before he finally won the Derby when St Giles triumphed. He put his dead-heat experience behind him when – astonishingly – the 1839 St Leger also finished in that fashion. Making no mistake in the run-off this time, he led all the way aboard Charles the Twelfth and defeated Euclid, ridden by Patrick Conolly.

When on top form, he was peerless on the track, and was a superb judge of a horse and exactly what that horse could produce, never more in evidence than in the 1841 St Leger at Doncaster. The hot favourite was the Derby winner, Coronation, and so favoured was he to continue his unbeaten career that the race was considered a formality and attracted less interest than was customary.

Scott's mount Satirist went off at odds of 5 to 1 and Cuttonian made the early running before Coronation took the lead at the half-way point with Satirist just behind. When they neared the finish, it appeared that Coronation would add another Classic to her belt, but Satirist gained a slight advantage in the final strides and won by half a neck.

Scott loved nothing more than to tell stories over a bottle of port, and drink began to play a part in his decline. His style of riding and character started to become unpredictable and he suffered several alcohol-related falls on the track. In 1844, he had a violent quarrel with his brother John, and left to establish his own stables at his home at Highfield House, near Malton, with William Oates handling the training aspect.

Soon after setting up on his own, he paid £10 to a farmer called Hudson in Driffield for a young horse called Tibthorpe. His first race was as a 3-year-old in the 2,000 Guineas at Newmarket on 28 April 1846, starting at odds of 5 to 1 in a field of six runners. Scott rode perfectly to win a slowly run race. Allegations were made that the horse was in fact a year older than claimed but an inspection of his teeth confirmed his age. As a result of that triumph, the horse was made second favourite for the Derby and was renamed after Sir Tatton Sykes.

At Epsom on 27 May, Sir Tatton Sykes started at 10 to 1 for the Derby in a field of twenty-seven runners. However, having backed the horse handsomely to win, Scott then spent the morning of the race with a bottle of brandy. He then proceeded to have a long argument with the starter, causing him to fall many lengths behind the rest of the field when the race eventually started. It says something for the quality of his horsemanship that he managed to make up the lost ground and challenge for the lead in the closing stages. But he was unable to mount a strong finish and was beaten by Pyrrhus the First.

At Doncaster in September, twelve horses ran in the St Leger Stakes, with Sir Tatton Sykes as joint favourite. Fearing a repetition of what had transpired at Epsom, Scott's friends scarcely let him out of their sight in the build-up to the race and William Oates was even prepared to ride in Scott's place, but they were relieved when he turned up for the race fully sober.

Scott followed the early leaders and then moved forward to contest the lead with Iago, from the stable of his brother John. The two horses drew clear, and Sir Tatton Sykes emerged victorious by half a length. It was a memorable final Classic triumph, but due to Scott's drunkenness before the Derby, Sir Tatton Sykes missed out on becoming the first winner of the English Triple Crown consisting of the 2,000 Guineas, the Derby and the St Leger.

Scott won nineteen English Classics in all, including nine St Leger victories, which remains a record to this day for that race. He added four victories in the Derby and three each in the Oaks and 2,000 Guineas. His last ride was in the 1847 Derby and he died the following year at the age of 51.

Fuller Pilch (England) 1843–1850

The man dubbed 'the greatest batsman ever known until the appearance of W. G. Grace' was born on 17 March 1803 in Horningtoft, Norfolk, the son of Nathaniel Pilch – a tailor – and Frances Fuller. He moved north at an early age and had his formative cricketing education in Sheffield, alongside his two older brothers Nathaniel and William – both of whom would also become cricketers. Moving back south, he was asked to represent his native county against the MCC at Lord's in 1820 at the age of 17. It was a memorable match for all the wrong reasons for the young man, as William Ward set a record with an innings of 278 for the MCC and Norfolk were defeated by a massive 417 runs.

Fuller Pilch did contribute with the ball, taking one wicket in MCC's first innings and the last three in their second, and despite innings of just 0 and 2, he did draw a comment from the triumphant Ward, who said 'If that young Pilch goes on in his play there is much promise in him.' Prophetic words indeed, but no one at the time could possibly have foreseen that he would go on to become the leading batsman in the country and hold that position for the best part of two decades.

He was a tall man for the times – growing to just over 6 feet in height and weighing nearly 13 stone – and used every inch of his height to play his forward defensive stroke back down the wicket. Nicknamed 'Pilch's Poke', it required great skill and bravery to play against the era's fast round-arm bowlers on pitches which bore little resemblance to those of today, often being quite uneven. He was equally adept off the back foot, able to cut the ball powerfully either side of point on the off side, as well as striking effectively through the leg side.

Following the 1820 match, he spent six seasons at Bury St Edmunds before returning to Norwich, where he became the lessee of the Norwich cricket ground and ran a local pub on Bracondale Hill. By 1827, news of his batting prowess had spread and he was in great demand, returning to first-class cricket that year and immediately top-scoring for England against Sussex at Sheffield. From then onwards, he was a regular in top-flight cricket.

His fame hit its heights in 1833 when he accepted the challenge from Thomas Marsden of Sheffield to play any man in England at a single-wicket contest. Marsden had previously made his name by scoring 227 against the Nottingham club back in 1826. The first match was to be played in Norwich with the return in Marsden's home town of Sheffield.

On 18 July, Marsden won the toss in the first of the two games and chose to bat, but he struggled against Pilch's bowling. In attempting to play forward to his twenty-seventh delivery, Marsden missed it and his wicket fell, having scored just seven runs in thirty-six minutes at the crease. Pilch then played himself in against Marsden's bowling before becoming more aggressive, reaching 77 before a ball ricocheted off his leg on to the stumps.

Marsden then started his second innings, and he had faced seven balls from Pilch without scoring before he struck the ball straight back to the bowler, who completed the catch to win the match by an innings and seventy runs to the delight of the Norfolk fans.

The return match was set for the first week in August and more than 20,000 people attended over the course of the three days. On this occasion, Pilch scored 82 runs in his first innings and 108 in his second for a total of 190 runs. Marsden was dismissed for scores of 27 and 35 to give Pilch a second victory, this time by 128 runs.

In a time where single-wicket cricket was very much the norm, these two victories made Pilch a household name and his services were hugely marketable to the highest bidder. That value only increased in 1834 when he scored 87 not out and 73 as Norfolk defeated Yorkshire by 272 runs in a match advertised in the *Norfolk Chronicle* as 'The Great Match of Cricket'. He was not finished there, as he added 105 not out for England against Sussex at Lord's two weeks later, before rounding up his tremendous feats of scoring with a career-best, unbeaten 153 for Norfolk against Yorkshire in a five-day match at the Hyde Park Ground in Sheffield.

The following year, Kent signed him as player-manager on a salary of £100 per year, and he moved from Norwich to Town Malling, a few miles from Maidstone, where he ran a pub with a cricket ground attached. Pilch rewarded Kent with nineteen years of loyal service, and they gave him permission to represent the MCC in their major matches at the time.

He moved to Canterbury in 1842 and became the proprietor of the Saracen's Head pub as well as continuing his feats of high scoring. It was his batting which inspired his two older brothers to compile and publish the first batting averages, which were printed in a contemporary magazine entitled *Bell's Life*. In 1843 he scored 525 runs at an average of 23. The following year it was 592 runs at 14 and in 1845 he managed 657 runs at an average of 16 per innings. Those figures may not appear impressive in comparison with modern-day figures, but he was truly the dominant batsman of the day. Over the period between 1830 and 1850 he scored far more runs in first-class cricket than anyone else, with more hundreds and fifties too.

His form started to decline after that, however, and his struggles against the pace bowling of Harvey Fellows in the annual Gentlemen v Players match at Lord's in 1849 hastened him into retirement soon afterwards. In retirement he went back to his roots and opened a tailor's shop with his nephew William as well as acting as the first groundsman at the St Lawrence ground from its opening in 1847 until just two years before his death on 1 May 1870 at the age of 66.

John Wisden (England) 1850–1859

John Wisden was born at 15 Hampden Place in Brighton on 5 September 1826, the son of a local builder. He attended Middle Street School and first became interested in cricket when he was employed as 'longstop boy' at the local Montpelier Cricket Ground. He first represented Sussex at the age of 18, and made an immediate impact, taking six wickets for forty-six runs in the first innings of his debut against Kent at the Royal New Ground in Brighton. That good early start enabled him to maintain his position in the side for all five of their games in 1846 and the following year he was selected for William Clarke's All-England XI.

There have been many fast bowlers in the history of cricket, but of all of them, John Wisden was quite possibly the smallest. Standing just 5 feet 4 inches and tipping the scales at 7 stone, he earned the nickname 'Little Wonder' from the umpire Bob Thoms, after the 1840 winner of the Derby at odds of 50 to 1, which defeated the much-fancied Launcelot, under Bill Scott.

He played regularly alongside William Lillywhite, one of the leading bowlers of the first half of the nineteenth century, and learned much from him. Wisden started out with the sole aim to bowl as fast as he could, but he also developed his own technique, such as the ability to cut the ball in sharply from outside the off-stump, which was an unprecedented skill in those days of round-arm bowling.

He reached immortality in 1850 at the age of 23 playing for North against South at Lord's when he performed the feat – still unmatched to this day – of dismissing all ten of the opposition batsmen 'bowled'. Writing in *Wisden's Almanack*, Sir Spencer Ponsonby-Fane – one of his contemporaries – summed up his method as follows:

> He was a very fine and accurate bowler, perfect length, but with little work, except what the ground gave for it. He was a fast medium, but I think he was classed as a fast bowler – and played on that side in the match, Fast v Slow. He was a delightful bowler to play

against, but required very careful watching, for he was apt to send in occasionally a very fast shooter, then so fatal on Lord's Ground.

In 1852 he joined Harrow School as its cricket professional and spent four summers in the role. That same year, he joined forces with his Sussex teammate James Dean to establish the United All-England Eleven, who regularly played against William Clarke's All-England XI in major matches.

Alongside George Parr, in 1859 Wisden organised the first overseas tour made by England cricketers, a full eighteen years ahead of the first Test Match. Wisden's tour was to North America, and it proved to be a huge success. Four players were from Surrey, three from each of Nottinghamshire and Cambridgeshire, with the remaining two from Sussex. The tourists won all their matches and Wisden took a total of eighty-one wickets in nine matches, including figures of 16-18 and 13-44 in the tour finale against Twenty-Two of Canada.

He was no mean batsman, and was the leading all-rounder of his time. In an era of low scoring, he twice made centuries in first-class matches. His innings of 100 for Sussex against Kent at Tunbridge Wells in 1850 contained four sixes, and his career-best innings of 148 was made for Sussex against Yorkshire at Sheffield in 1855 against an attack featuring a quartet of fine bowlers: Ike Hodgson, Andrew Crossland, George Wright and George Chatterton.

He excelled at single-wicket cricket, which was so popular in the mid-nineteenth century. However, it was his bowling which was his stronger suit and in all matches over a period of twelve seasons from 1848 to 1859 he captured the staggering total of 2,707 wickets. In 1851 alone he took 455 wickets in his forty-three matches.

Soon after returning from the tour of North America, he injured himself playing rackets, which put an end to his effectiveness as a bowler, and he resorted to underarm lobs. Seriously affected by rheumatics, his weight increased from 7 to 10 stone which meant that he started to become a liability in the field. His final senior game was at Alnwick in September 1863, when he failed to take a wicket and was dismissed for 0 and 1 in his two innings.

Wisden was always a keen businessman, and as soon as his four-year spell at Harrow was completed in 1855 he entered into partnership with Frederick Lillywhite, establishing a cricket and cigar depot at 2 New Coventry Street, just off Leicester Square in London. At the time, Lillywhite was the publisher of the only cricket annual, which first appeared in 1849. Now freshly retired,

Wisden launched his own rival publication in 1864 from his new premises at 21 Cranbourn Street, a slim, 112-page volume which carried his name and could be purchased for one shilling.

Even though his playing days were over, Wisden continued to be involved on the field, frequently umpiring matches played by the United England Eleven. He also authored a book, entitled *Cricket and How to Play It* and obtained a patent for an early bowling machine, which was 6 feet high, operated by means of a trigger and cost 12 guineas.

He died in 1884 at the age of 57, but he remains one of the best-known of all bowlers, immortalised in his almanack, which lives on to this day and is now well past its 150th edition.

Donald Dinnie (Scotland) 1859–1868

A man who was sometimes renowned as the 'The Nineteenth Century's Greatest Athlete', Donald Dinnie was born on 10 July 1837 in Balnacraig, Aberdeenshire, a small farming community. His father, Robert, was a mason and local strongman and Donald was one of six athletic sons, all of whom grew to six feet. They all followed in their father's footsteps into masonry, except Walter, who became a Scotland Yard detective.

The first sign of the young Donald's athletic prowess came at the age of 10, when he was able to keep up with his school coach over a 2-mile run; he maintained a keen interest in athletics throughout his schooldays.

Although he was a diligent student, Donald left school at the age of 15 and joined his father as an apprentice granite stone mason. During this apprenticeship, he also studied architecture and by the time his training was complete, he was an expert. While working for his father, he received his first lessons from his work colleagues in the traditional Highland sports of hammer throwing, stone putting, leaping, running and wrestling, and he practised keenly every day.

He won his first sporting competition in nearby Kincardine O'Neil at the age of 16 when he defeated local wrestling champion David Forbes – earning £1 in prize money! This ignited an athletic career which spanned over fifty years and saw him win more than 11,000 competitions. Three years later, in 1856, he made his first claim to be the Scottish Highland Champion in the heavy events.

Over the next few years, his fame began to spread and, thanks to his performances on the field, he started to acquire the status of a local hero. He also became aware that he could earn a living from his talent. The honour of having won a competition had always been important but being recognised as a champion also brought significant financial rewards. From 1858, he was able to lay down his mason's tools for several months in the summer to become a professional athlete, and he travelled widely to compete, visiting Edinburgh, Dublin, Newcastle and Birmingham over the course of the next decade. By

1869, he had won sixty-one medals and more than £1,000 in prize money and could justifiably call himself the 'Champion of Great Britain'. That year, he abandoned his family trade and embarked on a career as one of the first truly professional sportsmen.

As life started to become harder for Scots in their homeland during the nineteenth century, many started to look for fresh starts around the world, away from the poor economic conditions of home. There was a continual emigration of Scots to North America, South Africa, Australia and New Zealand, and those who settled in this new Scottish diaspora retained a deep love for not only their roots but also their sporting heritage. It was no coincidence that Dinnie's travels over the next thirty years were to these same countries.

He first visited North America in 1870 by invitation of the Caledonian Club of New York, who paid all his travel expenses. There were similar societies across the US and they were all too happy to invite the Scottish hero to participate in their local sporting activities. This was to prove a lucrative tour as he was able to command appearance fees of up to $125 – a huge sum at the time. He was a great draw at the local events across the North American continent, with as many as 10,000 people attending some of his exhibitions, far more than would have done so in his homeland.

Dinnie returned to America two years later but damaged his left arm while competing in the pole vault at the Buffalo Caledonian Games. Despite that, the tour was another financial success and Dinnie claimed he – and fellow tourist James Fleming – 'left America with more gold in our pockets than we could have found in Britain in three seasons'.

After his second tour, he followed a regular pattern of annual activities, spending the summer months participating in Highland games throughout the country. However, the summer season was short, and so to supplement his income he would arrange challenges, usually at athletics, which the public paid to attend. There were also guest appearances at events organised by others, when he performed feats of strength, or undertook wrestling bouts, sometimes forming part of a music hall programme. He also served as licensee of a succession of hotels in Kincardine O'Neil, Stonehaven and Auchinblae.

However, the hotel business did not prove particularly profitable and Dinnie returned to America in 1882. Whereas his previous tours had been confined to the east coast, this time he was invited to Sacramento, in California, from where he continued to New Zealand the following year. He spent six months touring the country, mainly participating in wrestling matches, before heading to Australia in March 1884.

He was to spend nine years in Australia, where he travelled extensively and met the lady who was to become his wife. However, his health had started to decline, and – recognising that some of his best days were behind him – he would more frequently appear as a referee than as an active participant in wrestling bouts. He was starting to feel the financial pinch too, as he was unable to command his earlier appearance fees.

In 1893, he returned to New Zealand in an attempt to raise some funds by touring with a company of athletes, singers and dancers. This was not a huge success, however, as sparsely populated New Zealand was suffering similar economic woes to those in Australia and in 1898 he planned his return to Great Britain, via South Africa, where he was able to make a few public appearances, before finally arriving home after sixteen years' touring.

When he returned to Great Britain, he performed on the London music hall stage as a strongman until the age of 75. Thanks to a small series of benefits which were held in his honour, he was able to earn enough money to live on a small annuity until he died in 1916, in the middle of the Great War.

Young Tom Morris (Scotland) 1868–1875

Old Tom Morris was born in 1821 and become apprentice to St Andrew's golf club maker Allan Robertson. In 1844, Tom married Agnes Bayne and seven years later they moved to Prestwick, Ayrshire, where Tom earned his living as keeper of the golf links, maker of golf clubs and winner of golfing wagers and prizes. The couple had four children, the oldest of whom would be known as 'Young' Tom Morris, born on 20 April 1851.

Old Tom won the Scottish Open Golf Championship four times and in 1863 he returned to St Andrews, where he became greenkeeper of the Royal and Ancient Golf Club and established his club-making business and shop in the town.

When Old Tom turned up for the Perth Open in 1864, he brought his 12-year-old son on the 90-mile train-ride with him. He was asked 'For why have ye brought your laddie, Tom?' to which he responded, 'You'll see for why soon enough.' Young Tom was not allowed to participate in the proper tournament, but a challenge match was arranged between Tom and a local player of about the same age called William Greig, considered the local rising star of golf. The match received more extensive press coverage than the main tournament, and Young Tom won convincingly.

Whereas many of his friends left school as soon as they reached their teens in order to earn money for their families, Young Tom attended Ayr Academy, possibly with a view to keeping his options open in case a career away from golf became a necessity.

He made his debut in the British Open in 1865 but failed to finish as Andrew Strath won the title and the £8 prize that came with it. Undeterred, he achieved his first major breakthrough in September 1867 on the treacherous course of Carnoustie in a thirty-hole tournament against most of the biggest names of the day. He went round in 140 strokes for the three ten-hole rounds which left him tied for the lead. Young Tom and the two others – Bob Andrews and Willie Park – competed over another round to determine the winner and the youngster left them trailing in his wake with a phenomenal round of 42, to win by 4 strokes.

Strong for his age, he could hit great distances while keeping his ball relatively low, often curving the ball in flight. He took advantage of the loft in his 'rut iron' – a club whose head was very narrow, designed specifically to get into narrow wheel ruts and dig a golf ball out – to enable the ball to fly high and stop quickly on the green. He also created the 'bump and run' stroke and his putting was magnificent, rarely missing a short putt. It was not just his technique that was so impeccable; he was noted for having been incredibly modest, as well as possessing an amiable temperament and incredible determination.

He was fortunate to become a star just as professional golf was becoming popular. However, courses in the 1860s and 1870s were rough and ready affairs, with fairways trimmed by grazing sheep. Greens were sometimes indistinguishable from the fairways and the thick bushes surrounding the greens were unforgiving and almost impossible to recover from.

He made his fourth appearance at The Open in 1868 and took an early lead, shooting 51 in the first round over the twelve-hole course. However, his father then shot 50 in the second round to take the lead by a stroke. Young Tom responded by shooting 49 in the final round to win the title by three shots from his father. At the tender age of just 17, Young Tom became the youngest winner of a Major, a record that still stands to this day.

He successfully defended his title the following year, achieving the tournament's first ever hole-in-one on his way to victory by 11 strokes from Bob Kirk. A third successive victory followed in 1870, by an even wider margin, and – according to the rules of the competition – he was allowed the keep the trophy. At the time, the victor received the 'Championship Belt' made of Moroccan leather with a silver buckle. The tournament was not held in 1871 but by the following year the famous 'Claret Jug' had been commissioned. Alas, it was not quite ready for presentation that year, so when he won the title again, he had to wait until later in the year to receive his trophy. Young Tom's name was the first to be engraved on it.

Young Tom often toured with his father, taking on any challengers who were brave enough, but after Old Tom passed his fiftieth birthday, Young Tom found a new touring partner in Davie Strath, with whom he played exhibition matches throughout Scotland and England. They became the first golfers to insist on payment in advance of the matches, the forerunner of the appearance money commanded by some of the leading players today.

The story of this great golfing pioneer has a tragic ending. In 1875, Morris was playing an exhibition match with his father against Willie and Mungo Park at North Berwick when he received a telegram that his wife had started a difficult labour. There were two holes remaining in the match, and so once they had duly clinched victory, the Morrises made the journey back by ship across the Firth of Forth to St Andrews. Alas they were too late: his wife and child had both died during childbirth.

Young Tom himself never recovered from the shock and he died just a few months later, on Christmas Day at the age of just 24. At the time it was blamed on a broken heart, but his death certificate listed the cause as a pulmonary haemorrhage, possibly caused by a long challenge match he had played in terrible weather a few weeks earlier.

Old Tom designed many golf courses around Britain and brought innovative methods of course management, such as actively managing hazards and top-dressing greens with sand to promote the grass growth. He kept working right to the end of his life, having outlived his son by more than thirty years.

Matthew Webb (England) 1875–1876

Matthew – later universally known as 'Captain' Webb – was born on 18 January 1848 at Dawley in Shropshire, where both his father and grandfather had practised as country doctors. Matthew was one of a family of twelve children, eight of whom were sons.

Matthew learned to swim in the River Severn before he was 8 years old and saved the life of one of his younger brothers who was trying to swim across the river for the first time. As a young man he longed to go to sea, and left his home town at the age of 12 to train on the HMS *Conway*. In 1862, he started a three-year merchant navy apprenticeship with Rathbone Brothers of Liverpool in the East India and China trade. He then served as second mate on seven ships from 1866 to 1875, first hitting the headlines in 1873.

It was while travelling on the Cunard steamship *Russia* on 22 April 1873 that he jumped overboard to attempt to save a fellow seaman who had fallen from the rigging. For that act, he was awarded the first Stanhope Gold Medal by the Royal Humane Society. He also backed himself to stay in the sea for a longer period than a Newfoundland dog, and won his bet after remaining in the water for ninety minutes – by which time the dog was nearly drowned.

In 1873, Webb was captain of the *Emerald* steamship when he read about J. B. Johnson's failed attempt to swim across the English Channel the previous year. Johnson had made his name as a high diver rather than as a swimmer and his attempt ended after just sixty-five minutes. However, the account of Johnson's swim inspired Webb and he resigned as ship's captain in early 1875 to train for his next challenge.

In July 1875, he swam 20 miles along the Thames from Blackwall Pier to Gravesend, and in early August he aroused public interest by announcing that he intended to swim across the English Channel without any artificial aid.

His first attempt on 12 August had to be abandoned after seven hours, due to the fact that he had drifted 9 miles away from his proper course as a consequence of the strong current and the poor weather. Undeterred, twelve days later he dived in from the Admiralty Pier, Dover, a few minutes before one o'clock in the afternoon. On this occasion, the sea conditions were much calmer and he set off at a brisk rate of twenty-six strokes per minute.

He swam through the night, maintaining a steady twenty strokes per minute but as he approached Cape Gris Nez, the wind suddenly grew stronger and the sea became choppy. Between the hours of 8 a.m. and 10 a.m. Webb hardly made any progress and he appeared to be totally exhausted. However, he eventually reached Calais at 10.40 a.m., having spent twenty-one hours and forty-five minutes in the water, swimming a total distance of 39 miles due to the changing tides. He was sustained while treading water by doses of cod-liver oil, beef-tea, brandy, coffee, and strong ale. After completing the crossing, he stated: 'The sensation in my limbs is similar to that after the first day of the cricket season.'

Webb returned to a hero's welcome in England and became a Victorian celebrity. His face was soon to be found adorning everything from pottery to boxes of matches. In May 1879, he won the Swimming Championship of England at Lambeth Baths, by defeating champions from other cities around the country. He was also in demand for lectures and swimming exhibitions and authored a book entitled *The Art of Swimming*. Needless to say, it was not long before promoters recognised his money-making potential.

In September the same year, he defeated American Paul Boyton at Newport, Rhode Island, in a race entitled the 'Swimming Championship of the World'. Although victorious, Webb was accused of cheating and his prize money was withheld. Boyton had successfully crossed the Channel four months before Webb, but with the aid of a specialist suit, so it could not be classed as an 'unaided' crossing.

Over the next few years, he gave exhibitions of swimming and diving around Britain and in the US, and specialised in demonstrating his power of endurance in the water. He once spent 128 hours floating in a water tank at the Boston Horticultural Show, winning £1,000 in the process. He married in early 1880 and had two children, but despite these regular exhibitions, his savings started to dwindle and his health appeared to become more fragile. In an attempt to raise capital, in late 1882 he announced that he would attempt to swim through the rapids and whirlpool at the foot of Niagara Falls.

He arrived in America in June 1883, but he had been unable to attract any sponsorship for the swim – although he had been promised $2,000 if he was successful. On 24 July, he was rowed out in a small ferry and changed into the same red swimming trunks he had worn for his Channel swim. The ferryman made a last-ditch attempt to dissuade him from what most considered a suicidal folly, but Webb jumped off the boat at about 4 p.m. in front of thousands of onlookers brought to the Falls by special trains.

At the start, all seemed to be going well, but he was caught by a sudden, large wave which lifted him up and caused him to cry out and lift up his arms. He was dragged under the water for a distance of about 40 metres, briefly reappearing before being dragged into the whirlpool never to be seen alive again. His body was recovered four days later and an autopsy determined that he had died due to the large weight of water he had encountered, which had paralysed his nerves, preventing him from breathing or using his limbs.

Webb was buried in Oakwood Cemetery, Niagara Falls and in 1909 his elder brother Thomas unveiled a memorial to Dawley's most famous son in his home town. It remains to this day, inscribed with the words 'Nothing great is easy'.

W. G. Grace (England) 1876–1896

W. G. Grace transcended cricket in a way few sportsmen have over their sports in history. Perhaps now best remembered for his huge girth and unparalleled beard, it is easy to forget that he was the dominant cricketer of the last quarter of the nineteenth century with both bat and ball.

He was born in Downend, near Bristol on 18 July 1848 and first played at the age of 9 for West Gloucestershire Cricket Club, which was founded by his father Henry; three years later he scored his first half-century for the club with an unbeaten innings of 51 against Clifton.

His first-class debut came in the summer of 1865 for Gentlemen of the South against Players of the South. He was dismissed without scoring, but took thirteen wickets as his side won by an innings and fifty-eight runs. In the era before Test cricket, the Gentlemen versus Players match was the biggest of its time, and that performance was good enough to earn Grace selection at the age of just 16. He took seven wickets in the match, but far better was to come the following summer.

Less than a month after his eighteenth birthday, he confirmed his potential with an unbeaten innings of 224 for England against Surrey at The Oval. That feat instantly turned him into the biggest name in cricket and the main attraction for spectators. He was also a fine athlete, winning the 440 yards hurdles in the National Olympian Association meeting at Crystal Palace the day after his long innings at The Oval.

In 1868, he became just the second man to score two centuries in the same first-class match and in 1869 he joined the MCC, playing regularly for them, in their red and yellow hooped cap, over the next thirty-five years of his career.

The West Gloucestershire club established by Henry Grace evolved into the full Gloucestershire county side in 1870 and the three Grace brothers – W. G., E. M. and Fred – ensured that it was the strongest county side in the country throughout the first decade of its existence. W. G. himself enjoyed a spectacular season in 1871, scoring a total of 2,739 runs, with the next highest aggregate being Harry Jupp's 1,068.

Of his batting technique, K. S. Ranjitsinhji in his *Jubilee Book of Cricket* wrote that Grace 'revolutionised cricket and developed most of the techniques of modern batting'. Before the advent of Grace, batsmen would specialise in a particular stroke, but he developed a full repertoire of strokes, using whichever one was appropriate to the ball being delivered. Likening W. G.'s use of a cricket bat to a musical instrument, Ranji went on to say that 'he turned the old one-stringed instrument into a many-chorded lyre.'

William Ward's innings of 278 made in 1820 had stood as the highest individual score for fifty-six years before Grace scored cricket's first recorded triple century with an innings of 344 for MCC against Kent at Canterbury in August 1876. Two days later, he made 177 for Gloucestershire against Nottinghamshire at Nottinghamshire's Clifton College, and he rounded off his week's work with an innings of 318 not out against Yorkshire at Cheltenham.

Due to his time spent playing cricket, Grace only completed his medical qualification from the University of Edinburgh in November 1879, the year before he scored England's first Test century – an innings of 152 against Australia. He established his own practice in Easton, a poor area of Bristol, where he became a popular physician. He would frequently visit friends after a hard day in the field to try to lift their spirits and alleviate pain. In 1887, Gloucestershire's Arthur Croome gashed his throat against one of the spiked railings in front of the pavilion at Old Trafford and the cut was deep and potentially fatal. Grace held the edges of the wound together for nearly half an hour as messengers found surgical needles.

He represented England in twenty-two Tests, all of which were against Australia, captaining the side thirteen times, winning eight matches and losing only two. In the early 1890s, he started to suffer increasingly with injuries, his weight started to increase, and he was reduced to no more than an occasional bowler. There was still one more spectacular season left in him, however. In May 1895, he scored his hundredth first-class century for Gloucestershire against Somerset; it was a month in which he scored more than a thousand runs – the first batsman in cricket history to achieve that feat. At the age of 47, he ended the season with a total of 2,346 runs.

Throughout his cricketing career, Grace remained an 'amateur' as it suited him to also work as a doctor. As with his fellow amateurs, he could claim expenses to cover travel and accommodation to and from cricket matches.

However, the Graces appeared to make more money than just their basic expenses and W. G. made more than any professional. The authorities probably knew what he was up to, but they would far rather have had him playing to swell the gate. The signs outside the cricket grounds at the time would say 'Admission 6 pence. If W. G. Grace plays, one shilling.'

Despite playing as an amateur, Grace was keen to win at all costs, and he was among the first sportsmen to employ some kind of gamesmanship in order to gain the upper hand. Australians to this day are still seething about W. G.'s run out of Sammy Jones in the great Ashes Test of 1882 at The Oval. Jones played the ball and then walked up to tap the pitch. W. G. promptly ran in and took the bails off and the umpire had to give Jones run out.

There were other occasions when he was noted to have bent the rules in his favour. When tossing the coin at the start of a match it was suggested he would call 'The Lady' so that he could claim victory whether it landed on Queen Victoria or Britannia. There is also the apocryphal story that he once refused to leave the crease when dismissed bowled, claiming that the crowd had come to watch him bat, not the bowler bowl.

Having ended his international career at the age of 51 in 1899, Grace was invited to form the new London County team, also serving as secretary, manager and captain, for £600 per year. Despite his advancing age and increasing bulk he continued to play minor cricket for several years after retiring from the professional game, top-scoring in his last-ever competitive match for Eltham against Grove Park in July 1914. Reputedly shaking his fists at the Zeppelins flying over his home in south-east London, perhaps fittingly this British icon died during the war which marked the end of Britain's empire.

Bob Fitzsimmons (England) 1896–1903

Bob Fitzsimmons, known throughout his career as 'Ruby Robert', was born in Helston in Cornwall on 26 May 1863. He was the youngest of twelve children of James Fitzsimmons, a policeman, and his wife, Jane Strongman. When Bob was 10 years old, James, Jane and their five youngest children made the ninety-three-day journey to New Zealand, and settled in Timaru, where James established a blacksmith's forge.

Bob was keen to pursue a career at sea, hoping that it would toughen him up for a future boxing career, and he was all set to join the crew of the *Isabella Ridley* at the age of 14 before she was damaged in a storm. That put an end to his quest for adventure on the high seas, and so once he had completed his education, he joined his father and brother Jarrett to learn the blacksmith's trade, specialising in shoeing horses.

This work at the forge enabled him to develop powerful arms and shoulders, which were in stark contrast to his spindly legs. He spent many evenings in the company of Dan Lea, a former regional boxing champion from England, and on occasion he had the opportunity to put his skills to the test. If customers turned up at the forge somewhat the worse for wear, having stopped off in a saloon en route to collect their newly shod animals, Bob would not be shy of demonstrating some of his fighting prowess.

At the time, boxing was moving from a style favouring pure strength to a more refined style in which physical economy was preferred. Fitzsimmons was an innovator in that he was one of the first boxers to incorporate his entire body into his punches and to concentrate a blow's impact into a smaller area.

His introduction to boxing came in 1880 when the former British bare-knuckle fighter Jem Mace visited New Zealand and organised a boxing tournament in Timaru. Fitzsimmons entered and won the tournament, knocking out four opponents in one night. Mace was a keen tactician and favoured defence and coached his pupils to hit from the shoulder. The following year, Bob won the tournament again and decided to turn professional.

After six fights in New Zealand, Fitzsimmons moved across the Tasman Sea to Australia to train at Larry Foley's Iron Pot Gym in Sydney, where he learnt his craft from Foley and Peter Jackson. He spent seven years in Australia, winning most of his forty-seven fights, but notably losing to a tough Irishman called Mick Dooley in four rounds in 1886. However, on 19 January 1889, he defeated his bitter rival Jim Hall at the White Horse Hotel to win the Australian Middleweight title. The following year he fought Hall again, but this time he was knocked out in four rounds to surrender his title.

Pickings in Sydney remained relatively slim and when Fitzsimmons heard that his New Zealand compatriot Billy Murphy had won the World Featherweight Title in San Francisco, he set his sights on a country where there was a thriving economy and boxing was starting to capture the public imagination. The new Marquess of Queensbury Rules had given the sport a new self-respect and there was money to be made if boxers had the necessary talent. He packed his bags and sailed to America in April 1890, where he had four fights before the end of the year, winning three via knockout and having a no-decision with Joe Choynski.

After those victories, he found himself matched with Jack 'Nonpareil' Dempsey for the World Middleweight Championship. Dempsey had held the title since July 1884 and acquired his nickname 'unrivalled' because of his reputation of being unbeatable. The two fighters met on 14 January 1891 at the Olympic Club in New Orleans in front of a crowd of 4,000. In a vicious bout, Dempsey was knocked down thirteen times before finally being knocked out in the thirteenth round. All of a sudden, the underdog Fitzsimmons was a rich man, as he took $11,000 of the $12,000 prize money.

After that victory, Fitzsimmons went on the road, travelling extensively and winning a total of twenty-eight fights over 1892 and 1893. One victory gave him revenge over his old adversary Jim Hall, whom he knocked out in the fourth round in March 1893 in New Orleans. In September the following year, he defended his title against the previously unbeaten Dan Creedon, but he was starting to find it difficult to make the middleweight limit and began fighting as a heavyweight.

Having won a disputed version of the World Heavyweight title against Peter Maher in Texas in February 1896, Fitzsimmons defended his crown that December against Tom Sharkey in San Francisco. With both sides unable to agree on a referee, Sharkey's manager suggested that former Tombstone lawman Wyatt Earp oversee the fight. Fitzsimmons dominated the fight for seven rounds before sending Sharkey to the canvas with a blow to the stomach.

However, Earp – a close friend of Sharkey – declared the punch had been below the belt and disqualified Fitzsimmons. There were rumours that Earp had fixed the fight for a quarter of the total takings, but no one was going to argue after the referee strapped on his Colt pistol.

Fitzsimmons' next bout was to prove the highlight of his career and it took place in Carson City, Nevada, a state in which laws had just been passed to legalise boxing in order for the fight to take place. It was the first time a championship bout had been filmed and there was a prize fund of nearly $40,000 up for grabs. Facing Fitzsimmons was 'Gentleman' Jim Corbett, who had been world champion for more than four years and who was odds-on to win by a knockout.

The champion dominated much of the fight, knocking Fitzsimmons to the floor in the sixth round, but in the fourteenth round, the challenger landed a right to Corbett's ribs followed by a left under his heart. Writhing in agony, he was unable to beat the count from referee George Siler and the world had its lightest-ever heavyweight champion at just 11 stone 11lbs.

Fitzsimmons lost his title on his first defence on 9 June 1899 when James J. Jeffries, to whom he conceded 39lbs and 12 years, knocked him out in eleven rounds at Coney Island. The pair met again three years later in San Francisco when Jeffries was again victorious, knocking Fitzsimmons out in the eighth round despite having suffered a broken nose and cheekbone.

On 25 November 1903, Fitzsimmons won the World Light Heavyweight Championship from George Gardner, winning on points over twenty rounds in San Francisco. He therefore made history by becoming the first boxer to win world titles at three different weights. He lost his crown to Philadelphia Jack O'Brien in 1905 but continued to fight intermittently until the age of 50 in 1914. By the time he died of influenza in Chicago two years later, there was little left of the fortune he had earned over the course of his career.

C. B. Fry (England) 1903–1908

Charles Burgess (C.B.) Fry was born in Croydon on 25 April 1872, the son of a civil servant whose family had deep Sussex roots. That year was a seminal year for sport, as it saw the first FA Cup final, the first football international (a goalless draw between Scotland and England) and the first Varsity rugby match between the universities of Oxford and Cambridge.

Fry's interest in cricket and athletics started at the age of 7, by which time his family had moved to Orpington, where, from the vantage point of his upstairs window, he could watch the local players practise. Soon afterwards he was pressed into action whenever the local team happened to be a player short. At the same time, he started to emulate one of his uncles, a talented jumper, by building his own obstacles and attempting to clear them.

As a boy, Fry enjoyed a variety of other outdoor pursuits, often to the detriment of his school work, and so his mother moved him to Hornbrook House School, where he had his first taste of football and captained the school team, as well as making steady progress with his cricket. At the age of 13, he won a scholarship to Repton School in Derbyshire, where he spent five years, excelling at Latin and Greek as well as representing the school in both football and cricket. Upon leaving the school, he went to Wadham College, Oxford to read Classics.

He starred at university, winning blues in cricket, athletics and football, and would have won a fourth in rugby had he not suffered an injury. Talented though he was on the field, it was at athletics that he really shone, specialising in the 100 yards, long jump and high jump. In 1892 he broke the British long jump record with a leap of 23 feet 5 inches and the following year he equalled the world record of 23 feet 6½ inches, held by American Charles Reber.

Successful though his university career was, Fry was plagued by financial problems, as he found it difficult to live on the £80 a year he received from his scholarship. He therefore spent his holidays supplementing his income from private tutoring and turning his hand to writing articles. Unfortunately, mounting debts caused him to suffer a mental breakdown in his final term at

Oxford and he ended his career with a poor degree that barely reflected his academic talents.

He made his Sussex debut in 1894 and performed well enough early in his career to earn selection to tour South Africa with Lord Hawke's team in 1895/96, which eased his financial situation. He performed well, scoring 43 in his first Test innings, and he became a permanent fixture in the England team in 1899, when W. G. Grace insisted he played in the first Ashes Test. Six times – from 1899 to 1905 – he passed 2,000 runs in a season, peaking with 3,147 in 1901, a year in which he became the first batsman to score six successive first-class centuries. It remains the world record.

His South African tour was to prove his only overseas engagement with England as he forged a successful football career with the amateur side Corinthians during the winter months. However, he yearned for higher honours, and so with an eye on attracting international recognition, he turned professional and joined Southampton of the Southern League, mainly since their home ground of The Dell was close to his home. In his first season with the team, he helped them win the 1900/01 Southern League. He also achieved his aim of playing for England when he was selected at full back to face Ireland at his home ground on 9 March 1901.

The following year, he played in all eight matches as Southampton reached the FA Cup final. However, they lost 2–1 to Sheffield United in a replay and Fry was released by the club soon afterwards due to his lack of availability. A short spell at local rivals Portsmouth ended after just three matches due to injury and that was the end of Fry's competitive football career.

Football's loss was cricket's gain as he turned his attention to scoring runs in huge numbers for Sussex, alongside his best friend Ranji (see p.49). His batting style suffered in comparison with the Indian prince, but he possessed a glorious straight drive and could adjust his style to cope with the varied bowling attacks he faced.

But for all the runs he scored at county level, he frequently struggled when representing England. He only scored five runs in four innings in the 1902 Ashes series, but three years later he scored his maiden Test century when he made 144 at The Oval. This rich vein of form continued when South Africa toured two years later and he scored 129 in the final Test. He headed the English season's batting averages on six occasions, but these would remain the only two centuries in his twenty-six-Test career.

There was time for one last hurrah on the cricket field when in 1912 at the age of 40 he captained England to victory in four of their six matches in the inaugural Triangular Test Series, also featuring Australia and South Africa. The advent of the First World War effectively ended his sporting career, but he was not one to keep out of the headlines for long.

In 1920, Ranji was chosen to be one of India's three representatives in the newly formed 'League of Nations' and he took Fry along to the first meeting in Geneva as his assistant, which rekindled an interest in politics first formed while at Oxford. He tried to enter Parliament three times as a Liberal, standing in the 1922 General Election in Brighton, the 1923 General Election in Banbury and the 1924 by-election in Oxford but lost all three.

He had taken up a teaching post at Charterhouse School soon after he graduated from Oxford, but only spent two years in the role, professing that he could earn far more as a writer. He founded two magazines, neither of which proved particularly successful, but wrote a popular column for the *Evening Standard* later in life and authored a total of nine books. He took up a post as captain superintendent of the Royal Navy's training ship *Mercury* preparing boys for a life at sea and was to hold that post for fifty years.

After he had turned 70, he entered his club and met his friend Denzil Batchelor to whom he said he was proposing to interest himself in horse racing. Batchelor's reply summed Fry up perfectly: 'In what capacity, Charles – trainer, jockey or horse?'

Jack Johnson (USA) 1908–1912, 1913–1915

The first African American to win the World Heavyweight title, Arthur John Johnson was born in Galveston, Texas, on 31 March 1878. His parents were former slaves – his father was a school janitor, and his mother a laundress. Arthur, who later reversed the order of his forenames and took the name 'Jack', was the third of their nine children, five of whom reached adulthood. The couple eventually managed to buy their own home on the eastern end of the island in Galveston's racially mixed Twelfth Ward.

A place in a black high school was available to Johnson, but instead he went to work to help support his family. He worked in a barbershop, as a porter in a gambling house and as a baker's assistant. At one stage, he made his way to Dallas to apprentice for a carriage painter. The owner of that shop – Walter Lewis – was the man who introduced the young man to boxing. Eventually, Johnson returned home and worked odd jobs until he had saved up enough money to buy his first pair of boxing gloves.

Towards the end of the nineteenth century, Johnson was still living at home with his parents and siblings and he soon realised that his prospects in his home town were limited. To try and make it in the boxing world he packed his bags and headed for Springfield, Illinois, where he met former boxer Johnny Connor, the promoter of twice-monthly boxing shows. Connor included Johnson in one of his shows, where he impressed promoter Paddy Carroll enough for Johnson to be invited to fight in Chicago.

His big city debut on 5 May 1899 was not a success, as he was defeated by Klondike Haynes in five rounds. Undeterred, he knocked out Australian Jim Scanlon the following month, but a rematch with Scanlon was cancelled due to the Chief of Police claiming that 'No white boxer should meet a Negro in Memphis.' Johnson returned home to Galveston where he knocked out veteran Joe Choynski, but as the bout ended, the Texas Rangers appeared and both boxers were jailed for twenty-three days for holding an illegal contest.

Eventually he was released on the condition that he left town, so he first headed for Denver and then to California, where he started to clock up the victories. However, his eyes were firmly set on the biggest prize of all – the World Heavyweight title. By the end of 1903, he appeared to be the logical next opponent for the champion Jim Jeffries; Jeffries, however, refused to fight Johnson and retired undefeated in May 1905.

Marvin Hart defeated former Light Heavyweight champion Jack Root to claim the vacant title, but he too refused to fight a boxer of colour. But when Hart himself lost to Canadian Tommy Burns, Burns was more inclusive, stating 'I propose to be the champion of the world, not the white or the Canadian or the American or any other limited degree of champion.' This opened the door for Johnson, who had defeated former champion Bob Fitzsimmons inside two rounds in July 1907.

Burns had been guaranteed $30,000 for the fight, but when the two boxers entered the ring in Sydney, Australia on Boxing Day, 1908, Johnson's physical superiority was immediately apparent. He had a 24lb weight advantage and was 6 inches taller. The champion was sent to the canvas in the opening round and after fourteen one-sided rounds, Johnson was declared the winner and the Heavyweight Champion of the World.

Despite the triumph, he was not universally revered back in America. His victory had heightened the existing racial tensions and Johnson never attempted to conceal his relationships with white women, which was considered a taboo at the time. There was a search for a 'Great White Hope' who could restore respectability to the crown and the first to fight under that banner was Stanley Ketchel. When the two met in October 1909, Ketchel troubled Johnson and knocked him down in the twelfth round. However, Johnson righted himself, and landed a left-right combination which sent the challenger to the canvas, unable to beat the count.

Johnson was a master of defence and was quick around the ring, with an outstanding jab and uppercut. He did tend to fight with his hands held relatively low, but his reflexes were so fast that he was able to intercept an opponent's punches before they had a chance to land.

Former champion Jeffries was working as a farmer, before finally being persuaded to come out of his six-year retirement to 'retrieve the honour of the white race' with a promised six-figure purse, of which 75 per cent would be awarded to the winner. The so-billed 'Fight of the Century' took place in Reno, Nevada on 4 July 1910 in front of a crowd of 20,000 and Johnson dominated from the start. By the end of the fifteenth round, Jeffries had received such a beating that his corner threw in the towel.

The outcome of the bout had implications far beyond the ring itself, as race riots erupted all over the country. Blacks were jubilant at Johnson's victory but whites saw Jeffries' defeat as a personal humiliation, and more than a dozen people were killed. Johnson stayed out of the ring for exactly two years, before returning to defeat Fireman Jim Flynn in New Mexico. However, he was soon making headlines out of the ring.

In late 1912, Johnson was twice arrested for violating the Mann Act against 'transporting women across state lines for immoral purposes'. Johnson was convicted by an all-white jury in June 1913 and was sentenced to a year and a day in prison. Not long afterwards, Johnson jumped bail and made his way to France, where he generally avoided the boxing ring and lived off his wealth.

He defended his title in lacklustre fashion against Jim Johnson in December 1913 in Paris, but the fight ended in a draw – with many spectators demanding their money back. He narrowly beat Frank Moran six months later, but he was starting to become homesick and longed for a return to his family and to the limelight he commanded in America.

That opportunity arose in 1915 when he was approached by Jack Curley, the manager for Jess Willard, and Johnson agreed to fight the challenger in Havana, Cuba. The combination of the hot Cuban sun and Willard's imposing 6 feet 6 inches height took a toll on the ageing champion and he was counted out in the twenty-sixth round.

In 1920, he turned himself in and served his prison sentence and, upon his release, began to campaign for a shot at the new World Heavyweight Champion, Jack Dempsey. Unfortunately, as he was now in his forties, Johnson was unable to secure a fight with any of the major heavyweight contenders and he won just one of his last six contests before retiring in 1931.

Considered by some the single most important athlete in modern sports' history, this icon of the history of racism in the US died in a car accident in June 1946 at the age of 68. His conviction was subsequently overturned by President Donald Trump in 2018 'for what many view as a racially motivated injustice'.

Jim Thorpe (USA) 1912–1913

Few could rival the soaring heights yet tragic lows of James Francis Thorpe, who was born on 28 May 1887 in a one-room cabin near Prague, Oklahoma to Hiram Thorpe, a farmer, and Charlotte Vieux, a Pottawatomie Native American. Young Jim's Native American name was Wa-Tho-Huk, which translates to 'Bright Path' and his athletic abilities showed at a very early age, when he learned to ride a horse and swim at the age of 3. He first attended the Sac-Fox Indian Agency school near Tecumseh, Oklahoma, before being sent to the Haskell Indian School near Lawrence, Kansas, in 1898.

At the age of 16, Thorpe started school at Carlisle Industrial Indian School in Pennsylvania, an establishment offering Native Americans the opportunity to gain practical training in over twenty trades, in addition to off-campus employment at local farms, homes, or industries. His track potential became apparent in 1907, when he cleared the high jump bar at 5 feet 9 inches while dressed in street clothes. That was enough for 'Pop' Warner, the school's sports coach to ask him to join the athletics team.

In 1909, Thorpe left the Carlisle school with two other students to go to North Carolina, where they played baseball at Rocky Mount in the Eastern Carolina Association. Thorpe pitched and played first base for $15 per week. The next year he played for Fayetteville, winning ten games and losing ten games pitching, while batting .236. Little did he know at the time what a major part in his future career these two seasons of paid minor league baseball would have.

He led Carlisle to outstanding football seasons in 1911 and 1912 in which they lost only two matches in total. He led the team to a stunning 1911 victory against Harvard and he was named a first-team All-American in both seasons. Future President Eisenhower played linebacker for the Army against Thorpe's Carlisle with the Native Americans winning, 27–6. In the game, Thorpe dominated Eisenhower, and in the process the general injured his knee and never played again. Years later he recalled 'My memory goes back to Jim

Thorpe. He never practised in his life, and he could do anything better than any other football player I ever saw.'

In his track days, Carlisle was booked to meet the Lafayette team at Easton. A welcoming committee was puzzled when only two Native Americans got off the train.

'Where's your team?' they asked.

'This is the team,' replied Thorpe.

'Only two of you?'

'Only one,' Thorpe said with a smile. 'This fellow's the manager.'

Coach Warner suggested he consider competing at the 1912 Olympic Games in Stockholm. At the US trials in New York, he qualified for the high jump and long jump, and also won a place in the pentathlon and decathlon, alongside the future president of the IOC, Avery Brundage.

At the age of 25, Thorpe sailed with the American Olympic team to Stockholm and once there he dominated the pentathlon, winning four of the five events to triumph by a huge margin. The following day he finished fourth in the high jump and four days later seventh in the long jump, but the best was yet to come. He won four of the decathlon's ten events and triumphed by 700 points, setting a world record which was to stand for fifteen years. King Gustav V presented Thorpe with his gold medals for both accomplishments and grabbed his hand and declared 'Sir, you are the greatest athlete in the world.' Thorpe replied 'Thanks King.'

Shortly after his Olympic victories, his two seasons of low-paid baseball were revealed following an investigation conducted by a journalist from the *Worcester Telegram and Gazette*. The Amateur Athletic Union (AAU) and the American Olympic Committee had strict rules about Olympians receiving financial compensation for participating in professional sports. Thorpe pleaded his case in a letter to the AAU's secretary James Sullivan but it was to no avail. His amateur status was revoked retrospectively and in January 1913 the IOC asked him to return his medals and erased his name from the record books.

Almost immediately, Thorpe signed a large $6,000-per-year, three-year contract with the New York Giants to play baseball. Thorpe was to be mainly used as a gate attraction and he spent six seasons playing Major League Baseball with three teams – the Giants, Cincinnati Reds and the Boston Braves. He ended with a batting average of .252 with seven home runs in 289 games.

He also signed to play professional football in 1915 with the Canton Bulldogs for the 'enormous' sum of $250 a game. Attendance at Canton immediately skyrocketed and Thorpe led the team to the championship over its chief rival, the Massillon Tigers, in 1916, 1917 and 1919. He guided the team into the birth of the modern National Football League of which he was the first president. He continued his playing career through the 1920s and remained the biggest draw in the game until Red Grange debuted in 1925.

A true multi-talented sporting star, he was also a talented basketball player, headlining a forty-five-game tour through Pennsylvania in which Thorpe, then 39, captained a team of Native American all-star basketball players.

After his retirement, life was never dull but Thorpe found things tougher going. He settled in Hawthorne, California, where he was employed as a film extra, appearing in Westerns and in short football features, but he continued to struggle. He toured the country in an all-Native American song and dance show and although past the age for acceptance by the army or navy in the Second World War, he joined the Merchant Marines in 1945 and served on an ammunition ship before the conflict ended. Even the 1951 film of his life, starring Burt Lancaster, earned him just $1,500.

Alas, Thorpe did not live long enough to see his Olympic medals restored. He died in 1953 at the age of 64 but it took until 1983 for IOC President Juan Antonio Samaranch to restore Thorpe's amateur status and award gold medals to his children to replace the ones he was forced to return.

Athletes of today may run faster, jump higher, hit the ball further, and gain more yards on the ground, but it was Thorpe's unique combination of talents that led to him being voted the 'greatest athlete of the first half of the twentieth century'.

Ty Cobb (USA) 1915–1919

Possibly the most competitive, loathed athlete of all time, Tyrus Raymond Cobb was born on 18 December 1886 in The Narrows, Georgia, in the heart of the South. He was the oldest of three children of William Herschel Cobb, a teacher, and his 15-year-old wife Amanda Chitwood Cobb, both of Scottish-Irish descent.

As a youngster, Ty developed a passion for baseball and by the time he was 14 he was playing on the Royston, Georgia town team. Soon he became the team's outstanding player, and started to focus all his energies on baseball rather than on his schoolwork. That did not please his father, who would have preferred his son to follow a path to medical school, a military academy or law school.

In 1904, Cobb contacted teams in the newly formed South Atlantic League and he was invited to Spring Training by the Augusta Tourists, who offered him a contract for $50 per month. His father tried to talk him out of the decision, but finally relented, telling his son, 'You've chosen. So be it, son. Go get it out of your system and let us hear from you.' His stay in Augusta only lasted two games, but he received another offer – this time from a team in Anniston, Alabama. He played well with Anniston, and by the end of August he received a telegram from Augusta asking him to rejoin their team.

Fate smiled upon Cobb in early 1905 when he played two exhibition games against the Detroit Tigers, and the youngster made an instant impression on the team. Later that summer, Augusta's manager George Leidy took Cobb under his wing and taught him the finer points of the game and, shortly afterwards, the Tigers purchased Cobb for $700.

Tragedy struck on 8 August 1905 when Cobb's mother fatally shot his father, claiming she mistook him for an intruder. Understandably, with his mother's trial hanging over him, Cobb found it difficult to settle in the big leagues, and he was treated poorly by his teammates, with his equipment frequently damaged by his fellow players. This treatment changed his personality, and from then on he became more of a loner, waging his own personal war with the world, and playing baseball with a will to win at any cost.

That attitude paid immediate dividends as he morphed into a superstar in the 1907 season, leading the league in hits, runs batted in (RBI), and batting average, as the Tigers won their first American League pennant, a feat they repeated the following two seasons. Cobb's performances on the field continued to dazzle, as he won the home run title in 1909 and led the league in stolen bases in both 1907 and 1909. However, the Tigers lost all three World Series in which they participated – two to the Chicago Cubs and the last to the Pittsburgh Pirates in seven games.

For all his spectacular performances on the field, he soon started to court controversy. In August 1908, he left the team for six days for his wedding and the following year he slid into third base, cutting the arm of Philadelphia Athletics' third baseman Frank Baker. He also got into a fight in Cleveland with an African American hotel night watchman, with a warrant being issued for Cobb's arrest on the charge of attempted murder. The criminal charges were settled after the season, with Cobb pleading guilty to a lesser charge, and the civil suit was settled out of court.

Despite being the biggest star in baseball, he remained unpopular with his teammates and opposing players, and nowhere was this more emphasised than at the end of the 1910 season. Cobb and Cleveland's popular 'Nap' Lajoie were neck and neck for the batting title, which carried the award of a new car and was awarded to the player with the highest batting average at the end of the season. With a small lead, Cobb decided to sit out the season's final two games, but Lajoie still had a double-header against the St Louis Browns to try to catch the Detroit outfielder. The Browns' manager, Jack O'Connor, hated Cobb, and ordered his third baseman to play especially deep, thereby allowing Lajoie to record eight hits over the two games, and claim the title – and with it the car.

Cobb's baseball talent ran deeper than his mere athletic prowess. In his era, there was more emphasis on 'small ball' – important but less glamorous techniques used by players to contribute towards their team's success. Runs were relatively scarce, and Cobb was always trying to remain one step ahead of the opposition, whether it was on the bases or at the plate.

Cobb continued to excel on the field and was the decade's dominant player, developing into one of the greatest players in baseball history. The 1911 season was one of his finest, as he batted .420 and led the league in runs, hits, doubles, triples, RBI, slugging percentage, and stolen bases. He was also a success away from the game, investing early in both Coca-Cola and United Motors (which later merged with General Motors).

Controversy was never far away and in 1912 Cobb attacked a fan who had been heckling him mercilessly throughout a game. He did not realise that the fan in question – Claude Lueker – was disabled due to an industrial accident and the Baseball Commissioner suspended Cobb indefinitely. His teammates were outraged and staged a brief strike, which only ended when Cobb's suspension was reduced to ten days.

In October 1918, Cobb enlisted in the Chemical Corps branch of the army and was assigned to the Allied Expeditionary Forces headquarters in Chaumont, France, spending sixty-seven days there as a captain. Cobb and his fellow soldiers were assigned to the 'Gas and Flame' Division, where they trained soldiers in preparation for chemical attacks by exposing them to gas chambers in a controlled environment.

Despite Cobb's continued excellence, the Tigers generally finished far out of first place after 1909, and eventually Cobb accepted the role as player-manager of the team in 1921. Other than in 1924, the team did not play a major part in the play-off race, and at the end of the 1926 season he announced his resignation and retirement from baseball.

It didn't last long, as he was coaxed back by Philadelphia Athletics' manager Connie Mack, for whom he played two more seasons before hanging up his spikes with ninety Major League Baseball records to his name, some of which last to this day, such as his career batting average of .366. Unrepentant to the end, he was one of the inaugural inductees into Baseball's Hall of Fame in 1936, by which time he had become a hero whom fans hated to love, rather than loved to hate.

Jack Dempsey (USA) 1919–1923

Jack Dempsey – the 'Manassa Mauler' – was the embodiment of the American Dream, and a man who would prove to be the last survivor of America's 'Golden Age' of sport's folk heroes from the 1920s.

William Harrison 'Jack' Dempsey was born on 24 June 1895 in Manassa, Colorado to Hiram Dempsey and Celia Smoot, who were originally from West Virginia and converted to Mormonism in 1880 before moving west. Hiram's ancestors were from County Kildare in Ireland and Celia's mother was half Cherokee. Jack could also trace his ancestry to Jewish pack pedlar Abraham Levy, one of the Virginia pioneers in the eighteenth century.

At the age of 8, Dempsey took his first job picking crops on a farm near Steamboat Springs and over the next few years, worked as a farm hand, miner and cowboy to help support his struggling family. It was this hard manual work that enabled him to build up his muscular body. During this time, Dempsey's older brother, Bernie, earned extra money as a prize-fighter in Rocky Mountain town saloons. It was Bernie who taught young Jack how to fight, instructing him to chew pine tar gum to strengthen his jaw and to soak his face in brine to toughen his skin.

When Dempsey was 12 years old, his family settled in Provo, Utah, but he dropped out of school after the eighth grade to begin working full-time. He shined shoes, picked crops and worked at a sugar refinery, unloading beets for a measly 10 cents per ton. By the age of 17, Dempsey had developed into a skilful boxer, and decided he could make more money fighting than working.

From 1911 to 1916 he drifted from town to town, fighting where he could under the name 'Kid Blackie'. One day in 1914 Bernie fell ill and the younger brother filled in for him. Adopting the name 'Jack' from his brother after the nineteenth-century boxer Jack 'Nonpareil' Dempsey, he won and kept the name for the rest of his fighting career. By the time 1917 dawned, his reputation had grown and he was able to command more prominent and profitable fights on both east and west coasts. Soon afterwards, the US entered the war and Dempsey registered with the US army, but was exempted due to having a dependent wife.

He fought regularly in 1918 and after six successive first-round victories, his chance at the big time came on 4 July 1919 on the shore of Maumee Bay, just outside Toledo, Ohio. His opponent was the 6 feet 6 inches tall, 17-stone champion Jess Willard. Dempsey was 5 inches shorter and weighed just 13 stone 5lbs but looked fit and tanned and up for the fight.

Despite the massive size disadvantage, just three minutes later Willard had been sent to the canvas seven times, and a left hook had broken his cheekbone. After two more one-sided rounds Willard's corner threw in the towel to give Dempsey the World Heavyweight title.

He fought with both hands and carried a powerful punch in both fists. He used combinations well and had an extremely hard left hook. He moved well in the ring, constantly bobbing and weaving. Most of all, he was cool under pressure and used whatever style he thought would enable him to win. He seemed to embody the American dream, in an era when the advent of radio meant that fans could follow sports from their homes.

Following his sensational victory, he didn't fight for fourteen months, spending his time touring the country staging exhibitions and even starring in some low-budget Hollywood films. He finally returned to the ring in September 1920 to knock out Billy Miske in three rounds. Three months later, he was trailing on points to Bill Brennan at Madison Square Garden in New York before recovering to stop Brennan in the twelfth round.

Dempsey's promoter, Tex Rickard, then determined to cash in on his prize client and orchestrated a meeting with Georges Carpentier, who became a hero in the First World War and was awarded two of the highest French military honours: the Croix de Guerre and the Médaille Militaire. Dubbed 'The Fight of the Century' it was staged in front of 91,000 people and generated the first million-dollar gate in boxing history. Despite only really being a light heavyweight, Carpentier troubled Dempsey in the second round, but broke his own thumb soon afterwards, hastening the end of the fight in the fourth round. A Dempsey right to the jaw sent the gallant Frenchman to the canvas before a left hook finished him off.

Dempsey didn't defend his title for another two years until he defeated Tommy Gibbons in July 1923 and then sensationally defeated Argentine Luis Ángel Firpo at New York's Polo Grounds, in one of the greatest fights in history. Dempsey floored Firpo seven times in the first round before Firpo battled back and knocked the champion out of the ring – where he hit his head on a reporter's typewriter. Dempsey had to be helped back into the ring but knocked Firpo out in the second round in front of 86,000 fans.

Dempsey enjoyed another break from boxing after that victory and did not defend his title for three years. He continued to earn money from exhibitions, sponsorship deals and more film appearances. He finally returned to the ring in September 1926 to fight Gene Tunney, a Shakespeare-loving veteran of the Marine Corps. Tunney had only lost one fight in his professional career but was considered the underdog against the champion Dempsey. In front of 120,757 spectators in pouring rain at Philadelphia's Sesquicentennial Stadium, Tunney jabbed and circled Dempsey to record victory in ten rounds. He explained his defeat to his wife by simply saying: 'Honey, I forgot to duck,' a phrase which entered boxing folklore.

A rematch was scheduled for the following year and it would become one of the most controversial in boxing history. In the seventh round, Tunney was knocked down for the first time in his career, but Dempsey failed to retire to a neutral corner until referee Dave Barry had stopped the count and led him there. Returning to the prostrate Tunney, he restarted the count, giving the challenger an estimated thirteen seconds to right himself. Given those extra few seconds, Tunney recovered to floor Dempsey in the eighth round and dominated the final two rounds, retaining his title by a unanimous points decision. To this day the clash is remembered as the 'Long Count' fight.

Dempsey retired from boxing after that defeat but remained in the limelight, opening a popular restaurant in New York City and continuing his acting career. When the Second World War started, he accepted a Coast Guard Reserve commission and found himself on the attack transport USS *Middleton* for the invasion of Okinawa in 1945. He was honourably discharged from the Coast Guard Reserve in 1952 and eventually died in 1983.

Babe Ruth (USA) 1923–1930

A true American icon, Babe Ruth single-handedly dragged baseball out of the 'Black Sox' scandal of 1919 and to this day he remains the benchmark by which all other players are measured. Helped by the booming sports journalism industry and the advent of radio, despite last playing nearly ninety years ago, Ruth is still widely considered the greatest and most revered player in Major League Baseball history.

The man destined to become the biggest name in baseball was born on 6 February 1895 in the home of his grandparents in Baltimore, Maryland. Named George Herman Ruth Jr, he was one of only two of his parents' children to survive infancy and he spent his first seven years on the waterfront streets and docks. He also spent time in the bar owned by his father, drinking the last few drops from beer glasses and developing a taste for chewing tobacco.

That was enough for his parents, who sent him to St Mary's Industrial School for Boys, where they signed over custody of the boy to the Xaverian Brothers, a Catholic Order of Jesuit Missionaries who ran St Mary's. Not only did George Jr learn vocational skills, but he developed a passion and love for the game of baseball, encouraged by Brother Matthias, who took an instant liking to the young man.

Ruth quickly showed his potential and was adept at playing all the positions on the field, but he had a particular talent as a pitcher. The owner of the Baltimore Orioles was invited to come watch young George play and he obviously impressed as he was offered a contract after less than an hour. The other Orioles players referred to him as owner Jack Dunn's 'newest babe', and that was how George Herman Ruth Jr became the 'Babe'. He did not last long with the Orioles though, and just five months later he was sold to the Boston Red Sox. He made his debut as a Major Leaguer in Fenway Park on 11 July 1914 against the Cleveland Indians.

Babe became a permanent fixture for the Red Sox in 1915, and followed up his successful first season by winning twenty-three games the following year, leading the league with an earned run average of just 1.75. In 1917, he won another twenty-four games on the mound and completed thirty-five of his thirty-eight starts. By that time, however, he had also started to display great power when he had the bat in his hand, and it was decided he was too valuable an asset at the plate to be left out of the line-up when he wasn't pitching. Therefore, in 1918 he started to feature more as an everyday player, striking eleven home runs and helping the Red Sox win the World Series.

Little did Boston fans know that would be their last World Series triumph for eighty-six years, and they finished sixth the following year notwithstanding Ruth setting a record of twenty-nine home runs. Despite his on-field heroics, he was proving difficult to manage with his refusal to adhere to the team curfew rules and constant salary demands. It was with those headaches in mind that on 26 December 1919 he was sold to the New York Yankees for $100,000 and the two teams would never be the same again.

Never could there have been a better fit for a team. His prodigious slugging feats and similar appetite suited the Roaring Twenties in New York City to perfection. He moved into the outfield full-time and truly dominated the game, producing numbers that had never been seen before. It was also a time when various ways of scuffing the ball were outlawed and baseball had changed into a game of power and high-scoring games.

In 1920, he beat the home run record he set the previous year by hitting a staggering fifty-four home runs, a season in which only one team hit more than he did individually. He carried on unabated, striking fifty-nine home runs in 1921 to enjoy a popularity never seen before in professional baseball. Inspired by these feats, the Yankees became the dominant team, setting attendance records which necessitated a move to a new stadium across the Harlem River in 1923, appropriately dubbed 'The House that Ruth Built'.

The sportswriters of the day were quick to bestow all manner of nicknames on him. There was the 'Colossus of Clout' or the 'Sultan of Swat', and before long his own name became a nickname given to someone who was the best in his or her field. The adjective 'Ruthian' became defined as 'colossal'. Helped by the legalisation of Sunday baseball and a change in the fan base, Ruth quickly became one of the most famous people in the country. Even people with no interest in baseball would travel for hours just for a glimpse of the Babe.

Records continued to fall to his broad bat. In the twelve seasons between 1920 and 1931, Ruth led the American League in slugging eleven times, home runs ten times, walks nine times, on-base percentage eight times, and runs scored seven times. He also helped the Yankees win seven pennants and four

World Series titles with the fabled 'Murderers' Row' Yankees side still talked about as one of the greatest teams of all time. Their 110 victories set a record which stood until 1954, as did Ruth's sixty home runs – until Roger Maris hit sixty-one in 1961.

Ruth made his final appearance in the World Series in 1932 when he added to his legend. The Yankees defeated the Chicago Cubs 4–0 but it was during the third game that he made headlines which are still talked of to this day. Facing Cubs pitcher, Charlie Root, Babe appeared to point towards the centre-field bleachers, suggesting that was where he would hit the next pitch. Sure enough, with the next swing of his bat, he sent the ball soaring into the seats, laughing as he jogged round the bases.

His final season with the Yankees was in 1934, before he returned to Boston as a member of the Braves for the following season. Sadly, his talents were on the wane by then and he played only twenty-eight games before retiring. He was keen to move into managing, but no Major League team was prepared to give him the opportunity, perhaps worrying that his presence might prove to be a distraction. Nevertheless, he was elected one of the original members of Baseball's Hall of Fame the following season.

Bobby Jones (USA) 1930

Arguments can be made for Bobby Jones being the greatest golfer of all time. However, one thing for sure is that he was the greatest amateur golfer who ever lived. In the Golden Age of American Sport, he dominated golf, winning seven Major professional championships and a further six 'major' amateur championships to become the first global golfing superstar.

Robert Tyre Jones Jr (he was named after his grandfather) was born to well-to-do parents on 17 March 1902 in Atlanta. A sickly child, he was 5 years old before he could eat solid food. In an effort to add some strength to his frail frame, the family bought a summer house next to Atlanta's East Lake Country Club.

The youngster thrived at East Lake. At 6, Jones was swinging sawn-off golf clubs. At 7, he was mimicking the swing of Stewart Maiden, the country club pro. At the age of 11, he shot 80 on the Old Course, which prompted a tear-filled hug from his father.

Just three years later, he won his first major golf event when he claimed the inaugural Georgia Amateur Championship in Brookhaven, at the age of 14. That victory earned Jones an invitation to the US Amateur at Merion near Philadelphia, where he won two matches before bowing out in the quarter-final.

He enrolled in Georgia Tech University to study engineering, but his next seven years on the golf course were plagued by inconsistency and he struggled with his temper. There were successes, such as his second-place finish in the 1919 Canadian Open at Hamilton, Ontario, but there were many disappointments too, most notably in the 1921 British Open at St Andrews. After taking 4 strokes to escape from Hill bunker on the eleventh hole of his third round, Jones picked up his ball and tore up his card, disqualifying himself.

He graduated from university in May 1922 but found a career in engineering unappealing. He was admitted to Harvard to study English Literature, and it was while a student at Harvard that he won his first Major title, the US Open at Inwood Country Club, New York. Jones led by 3 strokes entering the final round, but Bobby Cruickshank caught him up by shooting a final-round 73 to Jones' 76. The pair then played an eighteen-hole play-off which Jones won by 2 strokes 76 to 78 to take home the trophy.

After graduating from Harvard in January 1924, Jones spent two winters in Florida, selling real estate to supplement his income as well as preparing for the US Amateur Championship in September. Deciding to 'match par' in the Match Play set-up of the tournament, he progressed all the way to the final, where he defeated George Von Elm, 9 and 8. With two Major wins – while managing to control his temper – the 'seven lean years' were over.

At the 1925 US Open, Jones moved his ball slightly while setting up for a shot. No one saw it, but Jones was adamant that the ball had moved and assessed himself a 1-stroke penalty, costing him the win, as he went on to lose in a play-off to Willie Macfarlane. Praised for his honesty, his sportsmanship almost eclipsed the winner. Jones stated, 'You might as well praise me for not robbing banks.'

He successfully defended his US Amateur title later that same year before winning the British Open at Royal Lytham and St Anne's in 1926. He was welcomed back to New York City with a grand parade, but remained steadfastly an amateur.

Jones had met golf's first true professional, Walter Hagen, several years earlier while attending the British Open at St Andrews, and the pair met again when Hagen was playing some exhibition games in Florida. Hagen had been trying to convince Jones to turn professional for some time, and proposed a seventy-two-hole exhibition match between the pair, dubbed 'The Match of the Century', in which – naturally – Hagen would earn the $5,000 stake. Played over two courses, Hagen won both matches easily and Jones saw this embarrassing loss as a clear sign that he was not ready, nor did he really want to turn professional and have to rely on golf to pay his bills.

However, Jones proved a terrible salesman and – with a young wife and two children – he decided to turn his hand to his father's profession and enrolled in Atlanta's Emory University Law School. He also concentrated his efforts on golf's Major tournaments, using others purely as warm-up events, and started dreaming of winning all four Majors the next time the US Golf Association subsidised travel to the UK, which would be in 1930.

He finished only eleventh in the 1927 US Open and so decided to try to make amends by entering the British Open at St Andrews. He opened with a 68, then the lowest round ever in an Open at St Andrews and led all the way, completing a 6-stroke triumph. Following that, he won both 1927 and 1928

US Amateur titles and in the 1929 US Open at Winged Foot, he won the title after a thirty-six-hole play-off in which he defeated Al Espinoza by 23 strokes over the West Course.

The stock market crashed in late 1929 but fortunately Jones was relatively unaffected by the time the new year dawned. As a final practice for the British Amateur Championship, Jones won the eighteen-hole Gold Vase at Sunningdale, and then travelled to St Andrews. Conquering the Old Course, which had foxed him in 1921, he swept to victory, defeating Roger Wethered in the final 7 and 6.

Jones opened his account in the British Open at Royal Liverpool with 70 to tie for the lead. He followed with a 72 to take a 1-stroke lead over Fred Robson. However, Archie Compston shot 68 in the third round to give him a one-shot lead over Jones heading to the final round. Compston then collapsed with an 82 and finished sixth. Jones also had his struggles, but a superb bunker shot on the sixteenth helped him card a 75 and a clubhouse lead of 291. With Leo Diegel and Macdonald Smith dropping shots in the last few holes, Jones clung on to take the title.

Jones returned to America a conquering hero and two weeks later travelled to Minneapolis for the US Open at Interlachen, successfully defending his title thanks to his famous shot on the ninth hole when his ball skipped off a lily pad and on to the dry bank. Finally, in the US Amateur at Merion, under enormous pressure, he moved serenely through the draw until he defeated Gene Homans 8 and 7 in the championship match to complete a unique Grand Slam.

Within weeks, he signed a deal with Warner Brothers to make twelve short golf instructional films, and announced his retirement from competitive golf at the age of 28. Using some of his Hollywood income, he co-founded the Augusta National Golf Club with Clifford Roberts. The course opened for play in 1933, and, in 1934, hosted the Augusta National Invitational Tournament, later known as the Masters.

He played lots of friendly golf, but emerged from his retirement only once a year in order to play in the Masters. His last appearance was in 1948, the year he was diagnosed with a rare spinal disease, syringomyelia. Later in life he was confined to a wheelchair until his death in December 1971.

Don Bradman (Australia) 1930–1936, 1936–1939, 1946–1948

Don Bradman's final Test batting average of 99.94 not only looks like a misprint, but it is probably the most famous number in a sport obsessed by numbers.

Donald George Bradman was born in Cootamundra in New South Wales on 27 August 1908, one of five children. The family moved to Bowral when young Don was just 2 years old, but with none of his siblings keen to join him for backyard games of cricket, he had to devise his own methods of practice. This he did by throwing a golf ball against a brick water tank stand and attempting to hit the rebound with a stump.

Growing up, he was talented at other sports, but it was cricket in which he really excelled, making his first century at the age of 11. In 1922, he started work in a local real estate office and his cricket appearances for Bowral became more sporadic, until at 17 he became a regular player. Soon his appetite for big scores became apparent as he struck 234 against Bill O'Reilly's Wingello and bettered that with 300 against Moss Vale which gained him an invitation to a Country Cricket Week competition.

In December 1927, he made his Sheffield Shield debut for New South Wales against South Australia at the Adelaide Oval. Facing the bowling of Test spinner Clarrie Grimmett, he ended the first day unbeaten on 65 and went on to make 118. He followed up with another century against Victoria and soon afterwards moved to Sydney, where he became secretary in a real estate office opened by his Bowral employer.

A century in each innings of a match against Queensland clinched his place in the Test team to face England, but he made just 18 and 1 on a sticky wicket. Australia lost by a record 675 runs and Bradman was demoted to twelfth man for the second Test. Recalled for the third match of the series he made a resolute 79 in the first innings and then 112 in the second, his first Test century. However, England won the match and retained the Ashes.

In January 1930, Bradman faced Queensland in Sydney and in the second innings the records started to flow. By the end of the second day's play, he was unbeaten on 205 and resumed his innings determined to break Victorian Bill Ponsford's world record of 437. By the time captain Alan Kippax declared, Bradman was unbeaten on 452, and when Australia toured England that summer he had become the hottest property in cricket.

His early tour performances confounded his critics who claimed he would struggle in English conditions. He started with an innings of 236 against Worcestershire and less than a month later he stroked an unbeaten 252 against Surrey at The Oval, helping him on the way to completing 1,000 runs before the end of May. He carried on his run of form by making 131 in the first Ashes Test, but his side lost by 93 runs.

England made 425 in the second Test but Bradman countered with what he considered his most perfect innings, making 254 which helped his side amass a mammoth 729 for 6 declared and become the eventual winners. However, even better was to come in the third Test at Leeds. Bradman reached his century before lunch on the first day, and by the time stumps were drawn he was still there, unbeaten on 309.

That match ended drawn as Bradman set a new Test record with 334, as did the following rain-affected encounter at Manchester, but Bradman marked the final Test of the series at The Oval with an innings of 232 which sealed an Australian triumph, and with it the Ashes. He ended the five-match series with a total of 974 runs, a record which still stands.

His run-scoring exploits continued unabated against all-comers. In 1931, he made 223 against the West Indies and later the same year South Africa were treated to scores of 226, 112, 167 and 299 not out in their five-Test series. He celebrated by marrying his long-term partner, Jessie Menzies, in April 1932, and soon afterwards embarked on a tour to America. Over the course of seventy-five days, the Australians travelled 6,000 miles, playing fifty-one matches and Bradman had the opportunity to attend a baseball game at Yankee Stadium in the company of Babe Ruth.

England were determined to stem the flow of runs from Bradman's bat, and so captain Douglas Jardine devised the 'bodyline' tactics for the 1932/33 tour. It worked to a certain extent, as Bradman only averaged 56.57 over the course of the series as England emerged triumphant, but England's tactics lost the respect of the cricket public around the world.

At the end of the first day of the Leeds Test in 1934 he declined an invitation to dinner from writer Neville Cardus, saying that he wanted an early night because the team needed him to make a double century. Cardus pointed out that his previous innings on the ground was 334, and the law of averages was against another such score. Bradman told Cardus, 'I don't believe in the law of averages,' and subsequently scored 304. He made 244 in the final Test of the series to help Australia regain the Ashes.

He captained Australia for the first time in the 1936/37 Ashes series in which his side uniquely came back from losing the first two Tests to win the series 3–2. At Melbourne, he reversed his team's batting order to counter a sticky wicket and scored 270 to assure victory for Australia. Innings of 212 and 169 followed at Adelaide and Melbourne respectively to complete the stunning comeback.

He scored centuries in each of the first three Tests of the 1938 series, with a tight victory at Leeds guaranteeing another Ashes retention. In the final Test of the series, Len Hutton scored 364 of England's record 903 for 7 declared, but Bradman had to be carried from the field with a fractured ankle after he fell while bowling.

Domestic cricket continued in Australia during the Second World War for purposes of morale. However, Bradman joined the Royal Australian Air Force but was seconded to the army where he was made a lieutenant and sent to Victoria to qualify as a physical training instructor bound for the Middle East. A medical examination confirmed that his vision was fading before an All-Services athletics meeting damaged his back. He was hospitalised and effectively incapacitated.

Post-war he was undecided as to whether to continue his cricket career, but he accepted the Australian captaincy against England's 1946/47 touring team and was soon up to his old tricks. He made 187 in the first Test at Brisbane and 234 at Sydney, adding 405 with Sid Barnes. Later in 1947 he marked the first Test series between Australia and India by scoring 715 runs to set up a career finale in England in 1948.

He started with an innings of 138 in the first Test and Australia were set a record 404 runs to win in 354 minutes in the fourth Test at Leeds. Bradman then shared a second-wicket partnership of 301 with Arthur Morris and was still there, unbeaten on 173 when Australia achieved the impossible and won by seven wickets with fifteen minutes to spare.

In what would become his final Test, Bradman walked to the wicket with Australia 117-1 replying to England's paltry first innings total of just 52. He needed just four runs to end his career with an average of 100. He played the first ball from Eric Hollies easily enough, but the second was a googly, which grazed the inside of his bat and clipped the off bail and he was out for a duck. Nevertheless, Australia won the game and the series and completed their tour undefeated.

After retirement, he served Australian cricket in many capacities and probably signed more autographs than any player in history. By the time he died in 2001, he was probably the most famous and revered Australian of them all.

Jesse Owens (USA) 1936

Jesse Owens was one of the most significant figures of the twentieth century, whose achievements went far beyond the sporting field. His feats at Ohio State University and at the 1936 Olympic Games took him to the pinnacle of athletic success. However, his fame continues to rest on how sport relates to the complex world of international politics.

James Cleveland Owens was born in Oakville, Alabama on 12 September 1913. The seventh of ten children and the grandson of a slave, his father was a sharecropper – a cog in a semi-feudal system whereby small tenant farmers paid their rent with a share of the crops they raised. The young boy helped his father by picking up to 40kg of cotton a day despite suffering from bouts of bronchitis and pneumonia.

The family moved to Cleveland in 1922, in search of a better life in the booming steel town. His father and older brothers found employment in the steel mills while James enrolled at Bolton Elementary School, where he accidentally acquired the nickname which was to remain with him throughout his life. His teacher was told 'JC' when she asked his name to enter in her roll book, but she thought he said 'Jesse'. From then onwards he would be known as Jesse Owens.

His first contact with someone who grasped his athletic potential came at Fairmount Junior High School in Cleveland. Charles Riley noticed the 15-year-old running in the playground and encouraged him to train before school. Owens combined his training schedule with earning money from various jobs: delivering groceries, loading freight cars and working in a shoe repair shop. He was soon setting school records in the high jump and leaping more than 23 feet in the long jump.

At the age of 17, he moved to East Cleveland Technical High; Riley followed him as assistant volunteer coach. At the 1933 National High School Championships in Chicago, during his senior year, he ran the 100-yard dash in 9.4 seconds to tie the accepted world record, and set a new high school world record in the 220-yard dash by running the distance in 20.7 seconds.

Owens claimed his philosophy of running was simple: 'I let my feet spend as little time on the ground as possible. From the air, fast down, and from the ground, fast up.'

Thanks to his phenomenal high school pedigree, he was inundated by offers from colleges attempting to recruit him and he chose Ohio State University, even though they were unable to offer a track scholarship at the time. While there, he had to work various jobs to support himself and his young wife. He also acquired a new coach – Larry Snyder – who was one of the few US track and field coaches to allow black athletes to compete in university sports. However, even though he was the first black captain of Ohio State's athletics team, he was forbidden from living on campus, eating at the same restaurants as white teammates when travelling, or staying in white-designated hotels.

The world started to take notice of the 'Buckeye Bullet' at the Big Ten Championships in Ann Arbor, Michigan on 25 May 1935, where he set three world records and tied a fourth, all in forty-five minutes despite suffering from a sore back as a result of falling down a flight of stairs. He ran the 100 yards purely as a fitness test, but ran it in 9.4 seconds, again tying the world record. He carried on, setting new marks in the long jump (8.13 metres), 220 yards (20.3 seconds); and 220-yard hurdles (22.6 seconds).

Owens won a place in the US Olympic squad by winning three qualifying events, but there had already been controversy as the US had threatened to boycott the games over Germany's treatment of the Jews. It was only when Germany promised to withdraw its ban on Jewish participation and remove all anti-Semitic signs that the US agreed to travel and Owens sailed to Europe with the rest of the team.

Hitler believed that the German 'Aryan' race was superior to all others and he hoped that the Olympics would help support his theory. Owens had other plans, and before he had even run a race, he was signed up by Adidas founder, Adi Dassler, to compete in his athletics shoes, the first sponsorship deal for any male African American athlete.

Owens' gold rush started on 3 August when he won the 100 metres in a time of 10.3 seconds, closely defeating his college friend Ralph Metcalfe. The following day, he added the long jump to his list of titles, leaping 8.06 metres after taking advice on his take-off technique from the German silver-medallist Carl Ludwig 'Luz' Long. The two jumpers posed together for photographs after the competition and enjoyed a close friendship which only ended when Long was killed in action seven years later in Sicily.

His haul became three gold medals in three days when he won the 200 metres in a time of 20.7 seconds ahead of teammate Mack Robinson – whose younger brother Jackie would break the colour line in baseball in 1947. Finally, on 9 August he won a fourth gold medal in the 4 x 100-metre relay, setting a new world record in the process and helping to discredit Hitler's master race theory. His tally of four track and field gold medals at a single Olympiad would stand alone until the 1984 Olympic Games in Los Angeles, when Carl Lewis matched his feat.

Despite his success and the fact that he was – for a time – the most famous man in the world, Owens had no guarantees for any future prosperity. He received neither a congratulatory telegram nor an invitation to the White House to meet President Franklin Roosevelt. He took on speaking engagements which led to his amateur status being withdrawn, and with that his sponsorship deals dried up. He had to look for other ways to make money, and raced against motorbikes, trucks, cars and even a thoroughbred horse in Cuba for $2,000. He also returned to the jobs which had supported him throughout his days at Ohio State, such as working in a petrol station and running a dry-cleaning business.

In the 1950s, he started to attract invitations from the corporate world and he became a sought-after motivational speaker, travelling across the country stressing the importance of sportsmanship, health and patriotism. He visited India, the Philippines and Malaysia to lead running clinics and promote US political and economic values and in 1956 he attended the summer Olympics in Melbourne as personal representative of US President Eisenhower.

As he grew older, he was awarded a steady stream of honours, culminating in 1976 with the Presidential Medal of Freedom, the highest US civilian award. He died four years later from lung cancer, revered as possibly the greatest of all Olympic track and field athletes and summed up by President Carter thus: 'Perhaps no athlete better symbolised the human struggle against tyranny, poverty and racial bigotry.'

Joe DiMaggio (USA) 1939–1942

The 1939 English cricket season was almost over when war was declared on Sunday, 3 September and only the last ten scheduled first-class matches needed to be cancelled. England's proposed winter tour to India was also cancelled and the Football Association acted in a similar manner, declaring that all football except that organised by the armed forces was suspended 'until official notice to the contrary'. However, in other countries, sport carried on – at least for a while – and in New York one star burned brighter than any other.

Giuseppe Paolo DiMaggio was born on 25 November 1914 in Martinez, California, 25 miles north-east of San Francisco. His parents had settled there after emigrating from Sicily and Joe was the eighth of their nine children. The next year, his father moved the family to San Francisco because he heard the fishing was better off its waters. DiMaggio's father wanted his five sons to become fishermen like him, but only the two eldest did. Joe and brothers Vince and Dom became Major League Baseball players.

Joe started off playing for several amateur and semi-pro teams in San Francisco, but it was his older brother Vince who helped him break into professional baseball. Vince was then playing for the San Francisco Seals of the Pacific Coast League, who found themselves in need of a shortstop near the end of the 1932 season. Vince convinced the team's manager to give his 17-year-old brother a chance. Joe played in the final three games of the season, and impressed so much that he was signed to a contract in 1933, earning $225 a month.

His arm proved erratic and so he moved to the outfield, but he performed wonders with the bat, hitting safely in a Pacific Coast League record sixty-one successive games. His career was nearly derailed in 1934, however, when he tore ligaments in his left knee, but once he had recovered and passed his physical, he was sold to the New York Yankees for $25,000 and five players on the proviso that he played one more season for the Seals, in which he hit .398 with thirty-four home runs.

Yankee fans were looking for a new hero after the departure of Babe Ruth, and DiMaggio faced high expectations. He didn't let the fans down and halfway through his rookie season his photo appeared on the cover of *Time* magazine as the classic five-tool player – he could hit for average and power, he could run, field and throw. DiMaggio helped the Yankees to totals of 102, 102, 99 and 106 victories his first four seasons, leading to a World Series title each year.

In 1941, he set one of the most enduring records in sports by hitting safely in fifty-six consecutive games. As his hitting streak grew it gradually became a national obsession. Day after day, across the country, the question was: 'Did he get one today?' On 29 June he passed George Sisler's forty-one-game streak set in 1922, commonly referred to as the 'modern record' to distinguish it from Wee Willie Keeler's forty-four-game streak, the 'all-time record' set in 1897. It mattered not, as six days later DiMaggio passed Keeler's mark too.

The streak finally ended in Cleveland, but having been held hitless for a single day, DiMaggio went on to hit safely in his next sixteen games, carrying the Yankees to another pennant and World Series victory. DiMaggio batted .357 for the 1941 season and led the league in runs batted in and total bases and won a second Most Valuable Player award (MVP), ahead of Boston's Ted Williams, who became the last player to bat .400 in a single season.

In the batter's box, DiMaggio was the picture of calm, remaining motionless, hands and head still, feet wide apart. Only at the last moment, when he took his trademark long swing, did he unleash the force that he had kept under control. He was an expert at making the difficult look easy. His contemporaries considered him the best player they had ever seen. Even his rival, Ted Williams, said, 'I have always felt I was a better hitter than Joe, but I have to say that he was the greatest baseball player of our time. He could do it all.'

In no small part due to DiMaggio, baseball had become the most popular sport in the country, but the Japanese attack on Pearl Harbor on 7 December 1941 triggered a discussion as to whether the forthcoming season should be cancelled. Baseball Commissioner Kenesaw Landis wrote to President Franklin Roosevelt, asking his advice about the correct course of action. President Roosevelt was a passionate baseball fan and he replied with what has become known as the famous 'Green Light Letter'. In it, the president wrote, 'I honestly feel that it would be best for the country to keep baseball going.'

DiMaggio had his worst year statistically in seven years in 1942, and on 17 February 1943, he enlisted in the Army Air Force. He never saw combat, instead serving a morale-boosting role on service baseball squads. Embarrassed by the special privileges afforded him, he begged for a combat assignment, but was turned down, and was eventually granted a medical discharge in September 1945 due to suffering from stomach ulcers.

His military service had robbed him of three years in the Major Leagues and his first season back in 1946 was a disappointment. His prognosis was not helped by surgery the following January to remove a 3-inch bone spur from his left heel which necessitated further skin-graft surgery two months later to close the wound. His statistics in 1947 again fell short of his pre-war levels but he was awarded his third MVP award as the Yankees won their first World Series for four years.

DiMaggio had his last truly great season in 1948 at the age of 33. He missed just one game all season and led the league in home runs, runs batted in and total bases. The following year, his lingering heel injury caused him to miss most of the first half of the season, but he returned in heroic fashion to lead the Yankees to another pennant – by just one game over their bitter rivals Boston Red Sox – and yet another World Series title. He played 139 games in 1950, but injury and age limited him to 116 games in 1951, when he hit only twelve home runs. On 11 December, the 37-year-old announced his retirement, saying, 'If I can't do it right, I don't want to play any longer.'

DiMaggio understood his role as a public figure and he did his best to live up to his image as the greatest player in the game and the leader of its best team. His grace and style on the field were matched by his appearance. He was the model of quiet elegance, even if he never felt totally comfortable in his role as an all-American hero.

His legend was enhanced when, in January 1954, he once again made headlines by marrying Marilyn Monroe. But the ill-fated union of two of America's most celebrated personalities lasted only nine months. When Monroe died in 1962, Joe took charge of her funeral and ordered roses to be placed at her crypt twice a week.

His name even entered American culture. Santiago, the indomitable protagonist of Ernest Hemingway's 1952 novella, *The Old Man and the Sea*, says that he must be worthy of his idol, the great DiMaggio. Paul Simon's 1968 song, *Mrs. Robinson*, expressed nostalgia for a simpler, more innocent time by asking, 'Where have you gone, Joe DiMaggio, a nation turns its lonely eyes to you.' Fiercely protective of his privacy, he remained one of the most admired men in America, even when his career was long over.

Joe Louis (USA) 1942–1946

Joe Louis – the 'Brown Bomber' – is considered by many people to be the greatest of all World Heavyweight boxing champions. Holding the crown for eleven years, he made a record twenty-five successful title defences.

Joseph Louis Barrow was born on 13 May 1914, 6 miles from LaFayette, Alabama, the seventh of eight children to Munroe and Lillie Barrow. Both his parents were children of former slaves – his father was African American with European ancestry and his mother was half Cherokee. However, when Joseph was just 2 years old his father was committed to an asylum. His mother eventually remarried and followed the path of many Southern black families, moving to Detroit, where factory work was plentiful. The family lived in the Black Bottom area and Joe attended the Bronson Vocational School where he learned the craft of cabinet-making.

The young Joe was shy and quiet, but a friend took him to Brewster's East Side Gymnasium and introduced him to boxing. He instantly fell in love with the sport and shortened his name to Joe Louis so that his mother would not discover what he was up to. In his first amateur bout, at the age of 17, he was knocked down seven times by Johnny Miller, but he was a quick learner and rapidly improved, capturing the 1934 National Amateur Athletic Union Light Heavyweight Crown. With fifty wins in fifty-four amateur fights, he decided to turn professional.

Despite attracting the attention of a number of promoters, Louis signed with black Detroit bookmaker John Roxborough, who became his lifelong manager. Roxborough brought in a promoter, Julian Black, and a trainer, Jack Blackburn, and Louis made his professional debut on 4 July 1934, knocking out Jack Kracken in the first round. He won all twelve of his fights that year, ten by way of knockout.

He was victorious in all thirteen of his fights in 1935, including beating two former champions: Primo Carnera in four rounds and Max Baer in six. However, white America had no appetite for another black champion considering the previous reign of Jack Johnson. Johnson had refused to adhere to the prevailing opinions of the day of the proper role and manner of black people, not attempting to hide his romantic relationships with white women, a huge taboo at that time. It would need a great deal of work for Louis to have a shot at the champion James J. Braddock.

Former heavyweight champion Max Schmeling of Germany was also keen for a shot at Braddock to try to reclaim his title. The Schmeling and Louis camps agreed to a fight in 1936, with a contract providing that they would not schedule any other fights for six months beforehand. In the interim, Louis took up golf, having won his first twenty-seven professional bouts – twenty-three by knockout.

Louis was the hot favourite going into the fight at Yankee Stadium, but in the fourth round Schmeling landed a right hand which sent Louis to the canvas for the first time in his professional career. By the time the fight reached the twelfth of the fifteen scheduled rounds, the German was well ahead on points and he applied the *coup de grâce* with another right to the jaw which sent Louis crashing to the floor to be counted out.

Hurt by his first professional defeat, Louis returned to training with a renewed purpose – to defeat Schmeling. The German had hoped for a title shot at Braddock, but the champion's manager feared that if Schmeling defeated Braddock, there was a good chance that the Nazi government might forbid Schmeling from giving Louis a title shot. After Louis knocked out former champion Jack Sharkey in the third round, the scene was set for a showdown with Braddock at Comiskey Park, Chicago on 22 June 1937.

Braddock struck first, surprising the younger challenger with a first-round knockdown but Louis responded strongly and wore the champion down, finally knocking Braddock out in the eighth round to the acclaim of Black people all over the country. A tough first defence against Tommy Farr followed before easier victories over Nathan Mann and Harry Thomas, but he was desperate for a rematch with Schmeling.

After his victory over Louis, Schmeling had become a national hero in Germany and he was feted by Nazi government officials as an example of Aryan superiority. The US press inaccurately portrayed Schmeling as a Nazi and Louis as a defender of American ideals. President Roosevelt told the champion 'We need muscles like yours to beat Germany.'

The rematch was staged at Yankee Stadium in front of more than 70,000 people and Louis was on the attack right from the opening bell. He landed punch after punch, totally incapacitating Schmeling, who was only able to land two punches of his own the entire fight. After the third knockdown in the first round, the referee stopped the fight after just 124 seconds.

From January 1939 to May 1941, Louis defended his title thirteen times against fighters who some derided as the 'Bum of the Month Club'. However, despite that moniker, most of his defeated opponents were top-ranked fighters. On 18 June 1941, Louis took on Billy Conn in front of a crowd of 54,487 fans at the Polo Grounds in New York. Conn was the lightweight champion and weighed in at around 174lbs, much lighter than Louis' 200lb fighting weight. Conn used a 'hit and run' strategy and it worked, as he dominated the fight over the first twelve rounds. Only needing to stay out of trouble to gain the win, Conn decided to go for the knockout. This move allowed Louis to turn the tables and Conn was knocked out in the thirteenth round.

Louis enlisted as a private in the US army at Camp Upton, Long Island, serving in the Special Services Division as an inspiration for the troops and often taking part in boxing exhibitions. However, his service was plagued by racism and he was once ordered to move to the back of a military bus in which he was travelling. Despite that, he was promoted to the rank of sergeant and ultimately awarded the Legion of Merit before his release from military service on 1 October 1945.

He returned to the ring, knocking out Conn in a rematch before facing Jersey Joe Walcott, who knocked him to the canvas twice in the fourth round and appeared to have done enough to win the fight. Yet in a controversial split decision which drew loud boos from the crowd, Louis was named the victor. The champion was determined to go out with a victory despite his diminishing skills and met Walcott again on 25 June 1948. The fight followed a similar pattern as Louis was knocked down in the third round, but this time he came back and knocked Walcott out in the eleventh round.

He announced his retirement on 1 March 1949, but it was discovered that he owed more than half a million dollars in tax to the government. The only way he could find to earn the money was to come out of retirement and give all his earnings directly to the government. It didn't start well as he fought the new champion, Ezzard Charles. His absence from the ring for over two years showed; not only did he lose thoroughly but his smaller share of the purse meant that he needed to continue boxing.

After eight smaller fights – all victories – in ten months, the International Boxing Club guaranteed Louis $300,000 to fight the young and talented Rocky Marciano. The match was not even close as the former champion took a savage beating, eventually knocked out in the eighth round. Afterwards, a distraught

Marciano tried to comfort Louis, his childhood idol, who responded by telling Marciano that the better man had won. He then promptly retired again – this time for good.

He invested in a number of businesses, but all eventually failed and in retirement he was forced to do almost anything to make money. He worked as a professional wrestler and as a greeter at Caesar's Palace in Las Vegas until the government finally agreed not to collect on the back taxes. When he died in 1981, President Reagan allowed him to be buried at Arlington National Cemetery.

James Figg.
Wellcome Collection: James Figg, a pugilist. Line engraving by R. Graves, after J. Ellys.

Young Tom Morris. *Public domain*

Eclipse. *Public domain*

Captain Matthew Webb. *Public domain*

Don Bradman.
Public domain

Ty Cobb.
Public domain

Roger Bannister. *Alamy*

Pele. *Alamy*

Muhammad Ali. *Alamy*

Mike Tyson. *Alamy*

Ayrton Senna. *Alamy*

Steffi Graf. *Alamy*

Michael Jordan. *Alamy*

Tiger Woods. *Public domain*

Michael Schumacher. *Public domain*

Roger Federer. *Alamy*

Usain Bolt. *Alamy*

Lionel Messi.
Public domain

Serena Williams.
Alamy

Fanny Blankers-Koen (Netherlands) 1948

Many people told Fanny Blankers-Koen that she was too old to be competing in the 1948 London Olympics and would have been better served at home looking after her two young children. But compete she did, becoming the first woman to win four athletics gold medals at the same games.

She was born Francina Elsje Koen, near Baarn in the Netherlands, on 26 April 1918 into an athletic family, and she excelled in every sport she tried: gymnastics, swimming, tennis and athletics. When it became clear that she could not pursue all of them, she took advice from the local swimming pool supervisor in Hoofddorp, where the family lived at the time.

> Let her start an athletic career. Next year the Berlin Olympics will be organised and although your daughter is an excellent swimmer, the competition in that sport is such that it will be a miracle if she would qualify in that sport for the Games. In athletics the competition is much less and consequently her chances for qualifying are much better.

Following his advice, she joined an all-female athletics club in Amsterdam – the Amsterdam Dames Athletics Club – and cycled from her home in Hoofddorp to Amsterdam twice a week for training sessions with the country's best athletes. Soon it became clear that the Netherlands had a new star in high jumping, even if she struggled with her sprinting.

Her first competitive race was in the 1935 Dutch Championships at Groningen, when she finished last in the 200 metres. However, within a month she had defeated the reigning Dutch champion in the 800 metres. At that same meeting, she met coach – and former Olympic triple jumper – Jan Blankers, who recognised her potential as a sprinter and jumper. On his insistence, she was invited to join the Dutch team for the 1936 Berlin

Olympics, where she finished in a tie for sixth place in the high jump and fifth place as a member of the Dutch 4 x 100-metre relay squad.

Soon after the Olympics, she started working full-time with Blankers and her career continued to blossom. She excelled not only in the 100-metre and 200-metre sprints, but also in the high jump and the pentathlon.

In 1938 and 1939 she continued to improve and started to focus her training on the 1940 Olympic Games in Helsinki, specialising in the high jump and the 100-metre sprint. Unfortunately, the start of the Second World War swiftly put an end to those dreams.

Fanny married Jan Blankers on 29 August 1940 and despite Germany having invaded the Netherlands, she still participated in a few races. The following August, Jan Blankers Junior was born, curtailing her athletics for that year, but she resumed indoor training just three months after giving birth, and went from strength to strength. Domestic competition in the Netherlands continued despite the German occupation and she set six world records between 1942 and 1944 in the 80-metre hurdles, high jump, 100 metres and long jump.

At the time of the war's end in May 1945, initially she had no plans to recommence her athletic career, and in February 1946 she gave birth to a second child – this time a daughter. However, with the European Athletics Championships due to be held in Oslo that year, she resumed light training in April. She won five titles at the Dutch National Championships, but the Oslo competition did not go quite to plan since the high jump and the semi-finals of the 100 metres were scheduled for the same time. As a result, she fell and failed to make the sprint final and needed two hours of treatment to be in a fit state to contest the 80-metre hurdles final the following day.

She was victorious in the hurdles, but her teammate Gerda Koudijs won the long jump – which convinced Blankers-Koen that she needed to rethink her strategy for major competitions. She trained hard that following winter and had a successful 1947 season, winning six out of eight events at the Dutch Championships. At the end of that season, she discussed her possibilities for the London Olympics in 1948; it was concluded that her greatest chances for success would be in the 100-metre and 200-metre sprints, the 80-metre hurdles and the sprint relay. Considering the high jump and long jump too much of an injury risk, Blankers-Koen concentrated her winter training on running alone.

She started the 1948 season in great form, firstly breaking the Dutch record in the 200-metre sprint. This was followed by equalling the 100-metre world record with a run of 11.5 seconds and then setting a new record in the 80-metre hurdles of 11.0 seconds, three-tenths of a second better than the previous mark. With those achievements under her belt, she headed for London with high hopes, although she was the recipient of some criticism from home for neglecting her family duties.

The final of the 100 metres was a rainy, muddy affair, but she overcame the poor conditions to cross the line first in 11.9 seconds, easily beating her opponents Dorothy Manley and Shirley Strickland, who took second and third places respectively. It was the first athletics Olympic title for a Dutch athlete, but she had no time to rest on her laurels, as her next event was the 80-metre hurdles, in which her main opponent was Maureen Gardner, also coached by Blankers-Koen's husband. The two runners finished almost simultaneously, and it was not until the photo finish had been examined that Blankers-Koen was discovered to have won the race. The final of the 200 metres was – like the shorter sprint final four days earlier – held in torrential rain. Blankers-Koen won convincingly in 24.4 seconds, a full seven-tenths of a second ahead of Audrey Williamson of Great Britain.

After winning her third gold medal, she broke down and wanted to return to her children, who were staying with her parents. Reminding her that the other relay team members were totally dependent on her presence on the track, her husband convinced her to stay. She was the final runner in her team, and when she received the baton, she had a 6-metre deficit to make up on the leading teams, Australia and Canada. She made up the gap with ease, crossing the finish line first in 47.5 seconds, just ahead of Australia in 47.6 and Canada in 47.8 seconds.

She returned home as a household name throughout the world with four gold medals, repeating the performance of Jesse Owens twelve years earlier, and being the first woman to win four gold medals in one Olympiad. Inundated with sponsorship deals after her triumphs, the strict amateur rules at the time meant that she had to turn most of them down, although she did accept the modest gift of a bicycle from the people of Amsterdam.

By then nicknamed 'the flying housewife' she duplicated her Olympic victories in the 100 metres, 200 metres and 80-metre hurdles at the 1950 European Championships in Brussels, finishing second in the sprint relay, which was won by the British team. Having missed out on the originally scheduled Helsinki Olympics, which had been cancelled due to the war, she travelled to Finland for the 1952 games. Despite arriving in good physical condition, she was troubled by a skin boil and failed to win a medal in what would be her last major competition. She retired from competitive athletics in 1955 at the age of 37 with a total of fifty-eight Dutch national track and field titles to her name.

In 1989, she received the Olympic Order from IOC President Juan Antonio Samaranch and in 1999 she was crowned 'Female Athlete of the Twentieth Century' by the International Amateur Athletic Federation (IAAF).

Sugar Ray Robinson (USA) 1948–1951

The man born Walker Smith Jr set the standard by which all other modern boxers are judged. Many boxers have laid claim to have been the best 'pound for pound fighter' over the years, but the term was invented for Sugar Ray Robinson.

He was born on 3 May 1921, although the location of his birth remains a source of debate. Robinson's birth certificate lists his place of birth as Ailey, Georgia, while the boxer stated in his autobiography that he was born in Detroit, Michigan. Whatever the location, he was named Walker Smith, after his father, a farmer who had moved north from Georgia when the cotton grew infested with pests and Ku Klux Klan membership started to grow.

Buoyed by Henry Ford's announcement that workers could earn $5 a day in his automobile plants, the population of Detroit increased from 5,000 to 120,000 in the twenty years between 1910 and 1930. The Smiths settled in Canfield, just north of Black Bottom, an area full of recent migrants from the South, where the older Walker would spend plenty of time in the many clubs alive with blues and jazz. Eventually, his drinking grew too much for his wife Leila, who packed up the 5-year-old Walker Junior together with his siblings and returned to her mother's farm in Georgia.

After leaving the children with her mother, Leila travelled back to Detroit and to a new job as a seamstress at General Line, where she worked long enough to enable her children to join her. Back in the city, the young Walker started attending the Brewster Centre, Detroit's first community centre specifically for Black people. Another youngster who frequented the gym at the centre was the man who would become Joe Louis, and the young Walker was delighted when the future champion allowed him to carry his bags. The Great Depression hit at the start of the 1930s and when a friend of Leila's wrote to her suggesting that opportunities would be greater in New York City, she gathered up her children and boarded a bus eastward.

The family moved several times, eventually settling in Harlem, where young Walker's fighting career started almost by accident. One day he was provoked by one of the local bullies by the name of Samuel Royals – nicknamed 'Shake'. After challenging Walker to a race and losing, he threw a punch at him, whereupon Walker responded with a punch of his own which sent his aggressor flying. A couple of days later he was invited to fight an amateur bout at the Police Athletic League. He was hooked, and his enthusiasm intensified when a school classmate convinced him to visit the Salem Crescent gym, located in the basement of the Salem Methodist Church, where he came under the wing of trainer George Gainford.

Gainford's original advice was for the young boxer to add a few pounds and drink more milk. Eventually, he begged his trainer to give him a chance in the ring. The only issue was that he didn't possess the necessary Amateur Athletic Union card, which certified his amateur status. Gainford solved that problem by giving the promoter a card belonging to a former fighter of his, named Ray Robinson. The nickname 'Sugar' came from Gainford, who had described the young boxer as 'sweet as sugar'; reporters soon began using the moniker. 'Sugar Ray Robinson had a nice ring to it,' Robinson later said. 'Sugar Walker Smith wouldn't have been the same.'

His skills were improving at such speed that he was fighting experienced amateurs within a few weeks and he quickly moved up through the ranks. He won his first New York Golden Gloves title for amateur boxers at featherweight in 1939, and then repeated the accomplishment in 1940 at lightweight, before turning professional later that year.

His first professional bout was against Joe Echevarria at Madison Square Garden on 4 October 1940 and Robinson knocked him out with a left hook in the second round to earn $150, the equivalent of three months' rent. He went on to fight twenty bouts in 1941, winning them all – including notable victories over Sammy Angott, Marty Servo and Fritzie Zivic, all of whom had been world champions at some stage of their careers.

By the end of 1942, his professional record stood at forty wins and no defeats and he was named 'Fighter of the Year'. Robinson had already defeated Jake LaMotta in October 1942, but he was to suffer his first professional defeat four months later in their rematch when he was worn down through LaMotta's repeated body shots. Their rivalry was to become legendary over the coming years, with LaMotta claiming that he fought Sugar so many times he almost got diabetes.

In the meantime, there was a huge appetite for a third fight, which duly came just three weeks later. Robinson made no mistake this time, winning by a unanimous decision. However, he only had a few hours to savour his victory as he was inducted into the US army the following day where was known as 'Private Walker Smith'.

He discovered that he was in far better physical shape than his fellow soldiers and he found his training camp boring. After basic training, he was assigned to the Army Air Corps at Mitchell Field in Hempstead, Long Island, about 15 miles east of New York City, close enough to the city for him to visit dancer Edna Mae Holly, who was to become his second wife.

He never saw active service during the war, as the military authorities used him – along with Joe Louis – to form a touring boxing troupe to entertain the army and air force as a morale booster before they embarked on their tour to Europe. The pair were to entertain more than a million servicemen at 110 camps across America in the six months from August 1943. However, Robinson's military career was soon to end in an inglorious manner. According to his account, he tripped and hit his head in the barracks and blacked out. The following week, he was in hospital, where the report stated he had suffered a bad case of amnesia. There was some speculation that he might have faked it all to avoid going overseas and on 3 June 1944 he was honourably discharged, three days before the launch of the invasion of Normandy.

By the start of 1946, having moved up the divisions, had defeated all the leading welterweights, but had been denied a chance of a world title fight on account of his refusal to cooperate with the Mafia. His chance eventually came against Tommy Bell on 20 December and he took it, recovering from having been knocked down to win a close decision and claim the World Welterweight title. His first title defence ended in tragic circumstances as his opponent Jimmy Doyle died from injuries sustained from being knocked out in the eighth round.

Robinson held the welterweight title for five years, successfully defending his crown against Chuck Taylor, Bernard Docusen, Kid Gavilan, and Charlie Fusari, but he was finding it increasingly difficult to make the 67kg welterweight limit. This prompted a move up to middleweight, a weight division which also promised some large paydays against some of the other biggest names in boxing at the time.

In 1951, he challenged LaMotta for the middleweight title and dominated his opponent with a combination of speed and power, finally stopping him in the thirteenth round. However, later that same year he was upset by British champion Randolph Turpin before making amends in the rematch two months later with a tenth-round knockout in front of 60,000 fans in New York. He followed with successful defences against Rocky Graziano and Bobo Olson before challenging light heavyweight king Joey Maxim in the summer of 1952.

On that occasion, it was the heat that overcame him. Despite leading on all three judges' scorecards, he remained on his stool when the bell sounded to begin the fourteenth round and announced his retirement. A tap-dancing career occupied the next two years before he decided to return to the ring, and he would win and lose the middleweight title three more times in a series of bouts with Olson, Gene Fullmer and Carmen Basillio. He finally relinquished his belt for the last time in defeat to Paul Pender in January 1960.

By 1965, an over-the-hill Robinson was bankrupt and was forced to fight regularly to raise some money before finally retiring for good after his 201st professional bout. He resumed his showbusiness career and moved to southern California with his third wife, Millie. To this day, whenever lists are compiled of the greatest pound for pound fighters in boxing history, Sugar Ray Robinson's name is invariably near the top.

Emil Zatopek (Czechoslovakia) 1951–1953

Emil Zatopek remains the most beloved Czech athlete of all time, a man whose rugged training regime was rewarded with unprecedented success on the track. To this day he is the only runner to win the 5,000 metres, the 10,000 metres and the marathon at the same Olympic Games.

Emil Zatopek was born on 19 October 1922, in Koprinivince, Czechoslovakia, the seventh of eight children of a carpenter. Emil started working as an apprentice at the local Bata shoe factory at the age of 14 and his running career started several years later. In 1941, Bata sponsored the annual race through the streets of the town of Zlin and the strict factory sports coach pointed at four of the boys and ordered them to run. Emil protested that he was too weak to participate, but a physical examination passed him fit to race and he finished in second place out of 100 runners.

At the end of the war, he joined the Czech army which gave him increased freedom to create his own training regime. He stated: 'Running is easily understandable: you must be fast enough and you must have enough endurance,' and so he perfected a system now known as 'interval training' to develop both aspects. He would run a short distance very quickly, then rest while running more slowly, then run the distance again, rest again, run again, and so on. Unlike running long distances at a steady pace, this technique built speed as well as endurance. Having perfected his method, he applied it in ever-increasing volumes. He would run in his army boots during his guard duty, training every day regardless of the weather, and using a torch to run in the dark if necessary.

Efficient though it might have been, Zatopek's running style, with his face constantly contorted, as if in pain, with his head rolling around wildly was anything but graceful. Newspapers called him 'The Beast of Prague', 'The Czech Express', and 'The Human Locomotive' and each step he took appeared to be torturous.

A typical day might consist of five 200-metre sprints, twenty 400-metre runs, then five more 200-metre sprints. The harder he trained, the faster he became, and so he pushed it up to fifty 400 metre runs, often totalling more than 25 miles per day and he started to aim for the 5,000 metres in the 1948 Olympic Games in London.

Two months before the Games, he discovered that he was also proficient at 10,000 metres, and he took his place at the start line on the opening day of the Games for the event. Zatopek's aim was to cover each lap in seventy-one seconds, with his coach in the stands holding up coloured shirts to show him whether he was up with – or behind – the pace. Only once was a red shirt held aloft and Zatopek ended up winning by forty-eight seconds.

A few days later, the 5,000-metres final took place in pouring rain, which turned the dirt track to mud. and for once it appeared that Zatopek's famous endurance had deserted him. At one stage he was 100 metres behind the leader, Gaston Reiff of Belgium, but he started to claw back the difference over the final lap. However, he had left himself too much work to do and he ended up having to settle for second place, a mere 0.2 seconds from gold.

Also on the 1948 Olympic team was javelin thrower Dana Ingrova, who coincidentally was born on the same day as Zatopek. Their relationship blossomed while they were together in London, and they were married two months later. Zatopek refused to let his disappointment in the London 5,000 metres get the better of him as he competed in sixty-nine long-distance races from 1949 to 1951, winning every single one of them. He won gold at both 5,000 and 10,000 metres in the 1950 European Athletics Championships at Brussels and also set world records in the 10,000 metres, one-hour run, 20,000 metres and 30,000 metres. However, in the build-up to the 1952 Olympics he injured himself by skiing into a tree, and was plagued by illness.

The Helsinki Olympic Games were the first in which athletes from the Soviet Union and its former satellites would participate and tension between the Communist governments and the US was running high. However, once at the Olympics, athletes from behind the Iron Curtain and those from the West coexisted peacefully both on the track and socially.

The day after the Games opened, Zatopek claimed victory in the 10,000 metres, successfully defending his title. He took the lead right at the start and surged ahead of the other runners, with only Alain Mimoun of France able to keep up with him. By the twenty-first lap, Mimoun was nearly half a lap behind as Zatopek sped to the finish line. His winning time of twenty-nine minutes, seventeen seconds broke the Olympic record he had set in London in 1948 by more than forty seconds.

Having missed out four years earlier, the 5,000-metre title was the one that Zatopek particularly coveted in Helsinki. The day before the final, it was confirmed that the women's javelin would begin shortly after the 5,000 metres. He reasoned that as he and Dana trained together, they may as well compete for gold medals together. It was a strong field for the final and many doubted Zatopek's powers of recovery after having won the 10,000 metres.

The German Herbert Schade was considered the favourite, with Reiff, the fastest man in the world that year, defending his crown. The British challenge came from Chris Chataway and Gordon Pirie, and 10,000-metre silver-medallist Mimoun was also in the picture. Schade was determined to run from the front despite the heat, but he was eventually caught by the other medal hopefuls. Zatopek led at the bell but was almost immediately passed by Chataway, Mimoun and Schade. With 200 metres to go, Zatopek gained a second wind, putting the pressure on leader Chataway who fell on the last bend. Zatopek crossed the line in 14 minutes 6.6 seconds, a second Olympic record.

After he won his second gold, Zatopek lent the medal to his wife just before she began competing in the javelin throw. She put it in her bag for good luck, and with her first throw, set a new Olympic record of 50.47 metres and won the event.

Zatopek had never competed in a marathon before but, buoyed by his two wins, announced that he would compete in the Olympic marathon, just three days after the 5,000-metre race. Jim Peters of Great Britain was expected to win so Zatopek decided that his best course of action was to stay close to Peters throughout the race.

Peters was soon in the lead, closely followed by Zatopek. Halfway through the race and unsure of what pace a marathon should be run, he asked Peters if he thought the pace was too fast. Peters replied 'pace too slow', attempting to put off his Czech rival. However, Zatopek took Peters at his word and continued at a fast pace which proved too much for Peters, who began to slow and eventually dropped out. Zatopek moved ahead of Swede Gustaf Jansson and entered the stadium to a crowd chanting his name. By the time second-placed Reinaldo Gorno crossed the finish line, Zatopek had already changed his clothes and greeted his wife.

He retained his European 10,000-metres title in Bern in 1954 but decided to concentrate solely on the marathon at the 1956 Olympics in Melbourne. He took his training to extremes, often running with his wife on his shoulders, which ironically had the adverse effect of giving him a hernia. After surgery, he was advised not to compete, but he entered nonetheless.

He finished only sixth and retired soon afterwards. But his life after athletics was not easy. The crackdown after the 1968 'Prague Spring' forced him into life as a labourer a long way from the capital and he scarcely saw his wife. He eventually returned to Prague in 1975 working for the Ministry of Sport but – despite his revered status around the world – it took the fall of Communism in his native Czechoslovakia in 1989 for his status as a national hero to be recognised.

Ben Hogan (USA) 1953–1954

If not the greatest golfer of all time, Ben Hogan is often considered the most influential golfer of all time. Remembered for his 'golf swing theory' and his ball-striking skills, his *Five Lessons: The Modern Fundamentals of Golf* is still read extensively by aspiring golfers to this day.

The son of a blacksmith, William Ben Hogan was born on 13 August 1912 in Dublin, Texas. When he was 8 years old the family moved to Fort Worth, but they struggled financially. This culminated in his father, Chester, committing suicide, a reason often cited as the younger Hogan's introverted personality later in life.

Ben and his older brother, Royal, started working odd jobs and at the age of 11, Ben started to caddy at Glen Garden Country Club, where his interest in golf was first kindled and he switched from his natural left-handed stance to striking the ball right-handed. One of his fellow caddies at the time was Byron Nelson, a future rival on the golf tour, and the pair finished in the top two positions in the 1927 annual Christmas Caddy tournament, when both were just 15 years old.

Glen Garden did not allow caddies who were older than 16 so when Nelson was offered the only junior membership for 1928, Hogan had to look elsewhere to play and took himself to three local courses instead.

He dropped out of Central High School at the age of 17 and decided to focus all his energies on playing golf professionally, making his debut in the 1930 Texas Open in San Antonio, despite being plagued by a terrible hook. He started his career with rounds of 78 and 75 and withdrew from the competition. He joined the PGA as a member in 1931 and joined the tour the following year, making his debut in the Los Angeles Open, where he made the cut and took home $50 for finishing in a tie for seventeenth place.

He played in his first Major championship in 1934 – the US Open – but he shot 75 and 79 at Baltusrol and missed the cut, which was symptomatic of his early career. Hogan frequently arrived at a tournament with little money to speak of and with the pressure of supporting his new wife, Valerie. At one tournament, Hogan leapt over the fence and stripped an orange tree of its fruit, returned and played on without allowing his group to fall too far behind. He and his wife lived on oranges for two weeks. Times were tough and many professionals gave up the tour and found alternative employment. Twice Hogan returned to Fort Worth and took on a job as a croupier in a casino.

His breakthrough finally came in 1938. After coming close to winning the Miami International Four-Ball in March with Willie Goggin, he teamed with Vic Ghezzi at the Hershey Four-Ball in Pennsylvania in September, defeating the pair of Paul Runyan and Sam Snead, for his first professional title. It was worth $550 to each player and enabled Hogan to end the season in thirteenth place on the money list. Despite his promising season, he accepted a job at Century Country Club in Purchase, New York as an assistant pro and later became a head pro.

He continued to play well in 1939; although he failed to win a title, he had three runner-up positions among his sixteen top-ten performances. He also played in his first PGA Championship, at Pomonok Country Club in Flushing, NY, where he won his first and second-round matches before losing his quarter-final to Paul Runyan 5 and 4. His season's performances were good enough to earn him a place in the US Ryder Cup squad, but the competition was cancelled due to the outbreak of war.

The year 1940 was to prove a seminal one for Hogan as he finished top of the money list and took home the Vardon Trophy for the lowest stroke average for the first time. He also won his first individual title, at the North & South Open Championship at Pinehurst, where he shot a course record, 11-under par 277 over his four rounds. He won three more titles before the end of the year and finished runner-up in a total of five other tournaments, establishing himself as one of the tour's premier players.

He played in twenty-eight tournaments in 1941 and didn't miss a single cut, finishing in the top ten of all except one. He took home five titles and finished second on a further eleven occasions. Six more victories followed in 1942 before he was drafted into the US Army Air Corps in March 1943 and assigned to Fort Worth Army Air Field, where he helped teach exercise and physical education to other draftees. He was promoted to captain in the Army Air Corps and finally resumed full-time sport in 1946.

That year was to prove the most prolific of his career as he had thirteen wins on the tour, including his coveted first win in a Major – the PGA Championship, having not competed in the event since 1942. He dominated the contest, defeating Ed Oliver in the final 6 and 4. That final match pitted the lightest player in the field (Hogan at 135lb) playing against the heaviest, Oliver, at 220lb.

He was named Playing Captain of the 1947 US Ryder Cup team and led the team to a convincing 11–1 victory over Great Britain, and won a second PGA title in the gruelling five-day schedule of thirty-six holes a day in late May 1948. The very next month, he picked up his first US Open title at Riviera Country Club, California; this began a streak of six successive tournament wins, which only came to an end with a ninth-place finish in the Utah Open. He earned the inaugural PGA Player of the Year Award after completing a ten-win season.

On 2 February 1949, Hogan was travelling with his wife, Valerie, on the way home from his second-place finish at the Phoenix Open. On a country road near Van Horn, Texas, a Greyhound bus struck the couple's car head on. The impact drove the engine into the driver's seat, and the steering wheel into the back seat. While Valerie's injuries were minor, Ben suffered a broken collarbone, a smashed rib, a double fracture of the pelvis and a broken ankle. His doctors said he might never walk again, let alone play golf competitively. He finally left hospital fifty-nine days after the accident, but he would suffer circulation problems and other physical limitations for the rest of his life.

That summer, he travelled to England to captain the victorious Ryder Cup team again, this time as a non-playing captain as he was too weak to swing a club or walk far. He worked on his fitness by walking extensively, and in January 1950, he returned to tournament play, tying Sam Snead for first place in the Los Angeles Open, but losing the play-off.

From then onwards, he decided to play just seven PGA Tour events each single year, picking his tournaments carefully and concentrating on the Major events. Just sixteen months after his near-fatal accident, Hogan won the 1950 US Open at Merion in Pennsylvania. He defended his title the following year when his score of 32 on the back nine in the final round enabled him to win by 2 strokes at demanding Oakland Hills in Michigan. He also won his first Masters, shooting a then-record 274 to win by 2 strokes from Skee Riegel.

Hogan was even better in 1953 at the age of 41, when he produced one of the greatest golfing years in history. That year, he revealed that he had discovered a 'secret' to aid his swing which involved cupping the left wrist at the top of the backswing and using a weaker left-hand grip to prevent himself hooking the ball off the tee. It worked, as he won five tournaments, including all three Majors he entered: the Masters Tournament by five shots, the US Open by six shots, and the British Open Championship at Carnoustie by four shots. He arrived in Scotland two weeks before the tournament to acclimatise to the smaller British golf ball, and he was amazed at the extra distance he gained. He returned home to a ticker tape welcome and the same year he started his own golf equipment company.

After retiring with sixty-four tournament victories and nine career professional Major championships he concentrated on managing the company which carries his name to this day.

Roger Bannister (England) 1954

On a blustery spring evening in Oxford in 1954, Roger Bannister established himself as the most celebrated British sportsman of the period following the Second World War. Despite never winning an Olympic gold medal and setting only one world record, he ran a mile in under four minutes, breaking through what had been previously considered an impenetrable track and field barrier.

His father Ralph had been born in Colne, Lancashire – one of eleven children – his family having lived in the same village for four centuries. However, Ralph passed the Civil Service examinations which took him to London, where he lived in the north-west London suburb of Harrow, and it was there that Roger was born on 23 March 1929.

The family was evacuated to Bath during the Second World War, where the young boy attended City of Bath Boys' School and won the junior cross-country cup three years running. The family moved back to London in 1944 where Roger attended University College School in Hampstead and he continued his dominance on the track. He also developed an enthusiasm for medicine, and he was awarded a scholarship to begin medical studies at Exeter College, Oxford, in 1946.

While he was still a teenager, he was elected president of the University Athletics Club and re-instituted the athletics matches between joint teams from Oxford and Cambridge and America's Ivy League universities. He was also a driving force in converting Oxford's running track from an uneven, three laps to the mile clockwise run, to a new flat, six-lane quarter-mile anticlockwise cinder track.

He was named as an Olympic 'possible' for the 1948 London Games, but he declined the invitation as he felt at the age of 19 that he was not yet ready to compete at that level. By the time the track was opened in 1950, Bannister had established himself as the best mile and 1,500m runner in Britain, with several important American and European scalps to his name. He also won a bronze medal in the 1950 European Championships in Brussels.

He was among the favourites for the 1952 Olympic title at 1,500 metres at Helsinki. However, he was having to combine his training with his medical studies at St Mary's Hospital. Therefore, he was seldom able to train for more than half an hour a day at lunchtime, which he thought would be enough to sustain him over a heat, a rest day and a final. He was disappointed to discover that not only would there be additional semi-finals in the Helsinki schedule, but the three rounds would be run on successive days. As a result, Bannister finished out of the medals, in fourth place, but was motivated to continue his athletic career towards the Empire and European Championships in 1954.

The leading runners around the world had steadily improved their mile times as the world record assumed an ever-increasing importance. In the US, Wes Santee clocked 4 minutes 2.4 seconds, but failed in a much-publicised attempt at a four-minute mile. Australian John Landy ran four separate races around 4 minutes 2 seconds and Bannister himself, with the help of Chris Chataway, broke the British record in Oxford with 4 minutes 3.6 seconds.

The four-minute mark remained elusive and the world record remained at 4 minutes 1.4 seconds set by the Swede Gunder Hägg in Malmö in 1945. Early in 1954, Landy announced that he would spend the early part of the summer training – and racing – in Finland. With expectations of a four-minute mile at fever pitch, Bannister knew he had to respond quickly. He was blessed with two friends who could provide an elite pace-making squad and together with Chataway and Chris Brasher, Bannister devised an even-paced three-and-a-quarter-lap schedule that would leave him to capitalise on his speed and strength in the final 350 or so yards.

The scene was set on 6 May 1954 in a meeting between the British Amateur Athletics Association and Oxford University at the Iffley Road Track in Oxford. There had been strong winds before the event, which had put Bannister off, and he threatened to withdraw before the winds dropped shortly before the start. The race started at 6 p.m. and Brasher and Bannister took an early lead. Brasher led them through the first lap in 58 seconds and the second in 1 minute 58 seconds before Chataway took over and the runners reached the bell in 3 minutes 1 second. Bannister kicked for home 275 yards out and ran the last lap in just under 59 seconds to cross the line in 3 minutes 59.4 seconds.

Once other runners saw the barrier could be broken, they did so too. Forty-six days later, Landy not only broke the barrier again but set a new mark with a time of 3 minutes 58 seconds at a meeting in Turku, Finland. The stage was set for the two record-setters to meet for the first time in what was billed as the 'Miracle Mile' at the British Empire and Commonwealth Games in Vancouver in July. The race would produce one of the greatest contests in track history due to the different tactics employed by the two runners. Landy was happy to lead races from the gun, setting a fast pace that normally drained his rivals of energy and finishing speed. Bannister, on the other hand, had the ability to sprint hard at the end of races and sweep past his opponents.

Landy led from the start and built up a lead of 15 yards as the first two laps progressed. However, mid-way through the third lap, Landy began to slow and Bannister's even stride started to close the gap. By the time both runners reached the bell, Bannister was just behind Landy. At the end of the final bend Landy glanced inwards over his left shoulder, only for Bannister to pass him on the opposite side. The Australian didn't have anything left in the tank, and Bannister won with both men having run under four minutes.

Bannister trained on for one final triumph at the end of August, a comfortable victory in the European 1,500 metres in Bern, before retiring from athletics at the age of 25 to concentrate on his work as a junior doctor.

He had passed his exams for his basic medical qualification just a month after the victory over Landy in Vancouver and from 1955 to 1957 he carried out his house physician and house surgeon jobs. He spent his National Service working at the army hospital in Millbank, London and then volunteered to travel to Aden to investigate deaths among young soldiers.

Leaving the army in 1959, he started his training in neurology and was awarded a Radcliffe Travelling Fellowship from Oxford University to Harvard University. On his return, he was appointed consultant neurologist at the Western Eye Hospital and St Mary's Hospital in London, where he remained until 1985. He acquired a reputation for his ability to organise resources and was a popular choice to run medical committees. He was knighted in 1975 and, upon leaving his London hospital posts, he returned to Oxford as master of Pembroke College, where he served until his retirement in 1993.

Juan Manuel Fangio (Argentina) 1954–1958

Arguably the greatest racing driver to set foot in a Formula One car, one of his chief rivals for that crown – Michael Schumacher – claimed that he considered Fangio the finest of all time.

Juan Manuel Fangio was born on 24 June 1911 in the potato-growing town of Balcarce, 180 miles from Buenos Aires. He was the fourth of six children to Loreto and Herminia Fangio, Italian immigrants who had come from the Chieti province of east-central Italy. Loreto worked as a stonemason and painter and Herminia as a housekeeper and the family lived on a farm.

The young Juan Manuel began his schooling at the age of 5 but he soon decided that he did not want to follow in his father's footsteps in the building industry. When he was just 11 years old, he became an apprentice in a local workshop, fetching tools for the mechanics and here he had the chance to drive his first car – a Panhard & Levassor with chain transmission. That started a lifelong fascination with automotive mechanics.

At the age of 13, he found employment at the local Studebaker dealership as a trainee mechanic, where he discovered to his delight that they also prepared race cars, thus enabling him to learn about the internal combustion engine. Responsible for delivering customers' cars from Buenos Aires to Balcarce, Fangio often had to drive along Argentina's dirt roads, which were particularly dangerous in the rain. Thus, he honed his driving skills and learned the art of driving in slippery conditions. Opting to forgo a salary, at the end of his first year he was rewarded with his first car – a four-cylinder Overland.

He was called up for military service in 1931 and he was sent to the 6th Cavalry Regiment of Campo de Mayo where his driving skills contributed to his assignment as a driver for the commanding officer. Fangio was discharged in 1933 and returned to Balcarce, where, with his brother, he established a garage, repairing customers' cars during the day and working on their own at night.

His racing debut came on 25 October 1936 at the wheel of a modified 1929 taxi on the dirt track of the Benito Juarez circuit. Argentina's dirt-road tracks had become known as the 'killing fields' due to the number of fatalities caused by the dust which restricted visibility for the drivers. He was in third place before a broken drive shaft ended his race, but he was already hooked on the sport.

His favourite events became South America's infamous long-distance races, which took place over many days. He first came to prominence when he finished seventh at the 1938 Gran Premio Argentino de Carretera, a 4,590-mile race. Pleased with the result, the citizens of Balcarce contributed funds towards a new car for Fangio: a six-cylinder Chevrolet with which he won the 5,800-mile Gran Premio Internacional del Norte road race in 1940. Another victory came in 1942 in the 'Sea and Sierras' before the Second World War intervened and stalled his promising career.

His garage was kept busy during the war; Fangio bought and sold trucks and used tyres, items in high demand and scarce supply. Racing finally resumed in 1947 but tragedy struck the following year, when he crashed during the 6,000-mile Gran Premio de la America del Sur, killing his friend and co-driver Daniel Urrutia. However, any thoughts Fangio might have had to give up were quickly put aside when the Argentinian government purchased two Maseratis and decided to launch a full-fledged race effort for the 1949 season.

Competing in Europe for the first time, Fangio won five of his races, triumphing at San Remo, Pau, Perpignan, Marseille and Albi. He returned to Argentina a national hero and soon afterwards he signed up for the Alfa Romeo team for the inaugural FIA World Championship in 1950, alongside Nino Farina and Luigi Fagioli.

Fangio finished as runner-up that season, despite winning each of the three races in which he finished: at Monaco (when he managed to avoid a multi-car shunt), Spa, and Reims. However, Farina was able to take advantage of Fangio's mechanical failures and claim the title. Undaunted, Fangio returned in 1951 driving an Alfa Romeo Tipo 159 and won the Swiss, French and Spanish Grand Prix to claim his first world title at the age of 40.

The 1952 Championship was run to Formula Two specifications and Alfa Romeo – unable to fund a new car – withdrew from the competition leaving Fangio without a car to drive. Instead, he opted to drive for the British Racing Motors team in non-championship races at Albi in France and Dundrod in Northern Ireland. However, after running in the Irish race on 7 June he had to travel to Monza in Italy for a race the following day in a Maserati. Having missed his connecting flight in Paris, he was forced to drive all night through the Alps, arriving just before the start of the race. He had no time for a practice run and lost control soon after the start. His car became airborne and Fangio was thrown from the car and knocked unconscious with a broken neck. He finally left hospital after four months and spent the rest of the 1952 season recuperating.

Ferrari dominated the 1953 season with Fangio's more fragile Maserati only finishing four of the nine races, enabling Alberto Ascari to win the title. The following year, although officially driving for Mercedes, he was assigned to the Maserati team again while development of Mercedes' new cars was completed. In the eight Grand Prix races he entered that year that counted towards the drivers' title, he won six to win his second championship. In 1955, he joined Stirling Moss in driving full-time for Mercedes and the pair dominated proceedings, with Fangio winning four races to successfully defend his crown.

Mercedes withdrew from the sport after the 1955 season and Fangio joined Ferrari's strong team, racing alongside Eugenio Castellotti, Luigi Musso and Peter Collins. Plagued by mechanical failures, Fangio asked Ferrari if he could have a mechanic exclusively to work on his car. That seemed to do the trick, as he won in Argentina, Britain and Germany. Going into the final race of the season at Monza, Fangio led the championship by eight points from Collins and Maserati's Jean Behra. The only way he could be overtaken was for Collins to win the race and set the fastest lap. Fangio retired from the race, paving the way for Collins to win his first world title, but the British driver elected to hand his car over to Fangio to allow the Argentine to finish second in the race and complete a hat-trick of world titles.

Fangio's fifth, and last, championship came back with Maserati in 1957, a move which proved a master stroke as Ferrari failed to win a race that year. He won four of the eight races, with his performance in the German Grand Prix on the Nürburgring particularly notable. He started in pole position, but a slow mid-race pit stop put him a minute behind Collins and Musso in the two Ferraris. However, Fangio gave chase, setting ten lap records in the process and passed Collins and then Mike Hawthorn on the final lap to claim his fifth Drivers' Championship at the age of 46.

His final season in the cockpit was in 1958, one of the most tragic in Formula One history, with four drivers dying in races during the season. Fangio's year started in bizarre fashion as he was kidnapped by Fidel Castro's revolutionary movement in Havana in an attempt to have the non-Formula One Cuban Grand Prix cancelled. The ploy didn't work and Fangio was handed back to the Argentinian embassy. The season didn't pan out as he would have liked and after failing to win any of the first five races, Fangio finished fourth in the French Grand Prix at Reims. Out of respect, the winner Mike Hawthorn allowed Fangio to cross the finish line ahead of him without being lapped. After the race, Fangio turned to his mechanic and said simply 'it is finished' and promptly retired from racing.

He raced in fifty-one Formula One Grands Prix, starting from the front row forty-eight times, including twenty-nine pole positions. He finished on the podium thirty-five times, twenty-four of them victories. His record total of five world championships stood until Michael Schumacher passed it, and he is still revered in Argentina as one of the country's greatest sporting sons.

Pelé (Brazil) 1958–1962, 1967–1970

By popular consensus the greatest footballer of all time, Pelé was a perfect mix of strength, courage, speed, technique, and ability.

He was born Edson Arantes do Nascimento on 23 October 1940, the first of three children to João Ramos and his wife Dona Celeste. His father played football for the local side Minas Gerais where he was spotted by a scout for Atlético Mineiro in Belo Horizonte, the state capital. However, in his first match for his new team, he tore ligaments in his right knee and was released from the squad. He returned home to Minas Gerais and continued to play as it was the only way he knew to make money for his family.

The young boy known as 'Dico' moved with his family to Bauru in the state of São Paulo at the age of 4, but they were plagued by poverty as the promised job for his father at the football club in the town fell through. It didn't bother Dico as he played football with all the other local children using anything they could lay their hands on – a sock filled with newspapers took the place of the football they could not afford.

He was not a keen student and neglected his homework in favour of earning money shining shoes at the local Aero Club where, as he polished the pilots' shoes, he dreamed of one day flying his own plane. When his father finally obtained a job as an assistant in a health clinic, Dico helped and became inspired by his father's stories of his football career, especially when he became increasingly aware of the dangers in flying.

He became known as Pelé around the age of 10, when he was part of his local neighbourhood team – who still lacked a proper ball, boots and kit. Eventually, they were invited to participate in the Mayor of Bauru's football tournament and had their first outing on grass. The team reached the final, where 12-year-old Pelé – the youngest member of the side – scored in their victory.

The local Bauru Athletic Club formed a youth team, which Pelé quickly joined and was first coached by Waldemar de Brito – a veteran of Brazil's 1934 World Cup team. De Brito was stunned by the youngster's natural ability and helped him develop many of his skills that were to serve him so well in the future. However, de Brito eventually returned to São Paulo and Pelé finally completed his schooling, taking six years instead of the usual four.

The following year, de Brito reappeared in Bauru with an interest in taking the 15-year-old boy to Santos, a team whose president was keen to break the stranglehold on the Brazilian championships held by Corinthians, São Paulo FC and Palmeiras. Despite initial reservations, once they had spoken to the club's president, his parents gave their blessing and Pelé boarded a train for Santos, just south of São Paulo.

He made his senior team debut on 7 September 1956 at the age of 15 against Corinthians Santo Andre and scored a goal in Santos' 7–1 victory. He scored fifteen goals in his first eleven games and soon afterwards signed his first senior contract for the equivalent of $10 a month. An international debut soon followed in the Roca Cup – a two-legged tie against Argentina, and he scored in both legs to help Brazil to a 3–2 aggregate victory.

There was ongoing debate in Brazil as to whether the youngster should be selected for the 1958 World Cup squad or held back four years when he would have matured. In the end, he won selection for the tournament in Sweden as Brazil were keen to win the World Cup for the first time. They had picked a strong squad, featuring Didi, Garrincha, Vavá and Zagalo and neither Pelé nor Garrincha played in the opening 3–0 victory over Austria. They were again missing in the second game against England which ended goalless.

Pelé finally appeared in Brazil's third group match against the Soviet Union in Gothenburg, in which he set up a goal for Vavá in the 2–0 win. His first goal in the tournament came in the quarter-final against Wales – the only goal Brazil scored in a 1–0 win which catapulted him to stardom. However, it was in the semi-final against France at Solna that Pelé truly came into his own. With both semi-finals kicking off at the same time, many of the crowd at the Rasunda Stadium were listening to the Sweden v. West Germany game on their radios. However, Pelé put on a show of brilliance against the second-best team in the tournament scoring three goals in a 5–2 victory. Pelé and Vavá scored two goals each in the final against Sweden as the world welcomed a new footballing superstar who was just 17 years of age.

With Pelé in the team, the titles started to flow for Santos. He carried the team to ten São Paulo championships and six national championships. They became the first Brazilian team to win the South American Copa Libertadores, which led to victories in the Intercontinental Cup against the champions of Europe. Pelé's heroics soon attracted attention from some of Europe's biggest clubs, but Brazilian President Jânio Quadros countered by declaring the striker a 'National Treasure' which prohibited any foreign team from exporting Pelé to play.

Many of the victorious 1958 squad returned four years later for the tournament in Chile, but Pelé felt a twinge in his groin in Brazil's first warm-up match against Portugal. Nevertheless, he played in all four of the warm-up games and he was fit enough to score a goal in Brazil's opening 2–1 victory in the tournament proper. However, his groin gave way in the next game against Czechoslovakia and he was forced to watch the rest of the competition from the sidelines. Even without their talismanic striker, Brazil were still too good for the rest, as they successfully defended their world crown with a 3–1 victory over the Czechs in the final.

By the time the 1966 competition in England started, teams had devised tactics to deal with Pelé's threat, and man-marking was commonplace in what was to become a brutal tournament. He scored in Brazil's opening 2–0 win over Bulgaria, but Dobromir Zhechev's aggressive play left him with an injured leg. He was unavailable for the next game – a 3–1 defeat to Hungary – and Portugal's João Morais was inexplicably allowed to remain on the pitch after committing one of the worst fouls in World Cup history in the following game, which resulted in a 3–1 victory for the Portuguese at Goodison Park. Battered and bruised, Pelé vowed never to play in another World Cup.

The goals continued to flow for Santos, but it was two years before Pelé donned the gold shirt of Brazil again. With the 1970 World Cup scheduled to be played in Mexico, a shorter distance from home and with a similar climate, Pelé was convinced to change his mind after an overhaul of the Brazilian coaching management. He scored six goals as Brazil won all six of their qualification games by a combined score of 23–2 and the appointment of his former teammate Mário Zagalo as manager for the tournament served to inspire him further.

The Brazilian 1970 World Cup team is frequently described as the greatest team in football history, featuring Pelé alongside Rivelino, Jairzinho, Gérson, Carlos Alberto Torres, Tostão and Clodoaldo. In their opening match, Pelé attempted to lob the Czech goalkeeper from the half-way line, only narrowly missing the target, but Brazil still won 4–1. He forced Gordon Banks to make the 'save of the century' and set up the only goal in the 1–0 win against England. Two goals followed in the 3–2 victory over Romania as Brazil made their inevitable run to the final.

Pelé scored the opening goal in the final against Italy in Mexico City, before contributing assists for Brazil's third goal – scored by Jairzinho – and the fourth, which was Carlos Alberto's epic strike, often considered the greatest World Cup goal of all. The 4–1 victory was capped with Pelé named as the Player of the Tournament.

Having retired from Brazilian club football in 1974, he signed with the New York Cosmos of the North American Soccer League eighteen months later. Even though he was past his prime, he significantly boosted interest in the sport in the US. He inspired other foreign players to try their luck there and over the next few years Franz Beckenbauer, Johan Cruyff, Eusebio, Bobby Moore, George Best and Gordon Banks all appeared.

After leading the Cosmos to the league championship in 1977, Pelé retired and moved into a new role as a global ambassador for soccer, even becoming Brazil's Minister of Sport in 1994. Still adored throughout the world, when a reporter asked if his fame compared to that of Jesus Christ's, Pelé replied, 'There are parts of the world where Jesus Christ is not so well known.'

Rod Laver (Australia) 1962–1963

The only male or female player in tennis history to win two calendar Grand Slams in singles, Rod Laver won a record 200 tournaments, and probably would have won more Grand Slams had he not been barred from competing in the Majors for six years having turned professional.

Born on 9 August 1938 in Rockhampton, Queensland into a tennis-loving family, his parents built their own court on their cattle ranch. The young Rod started playing at the age of 6, with his two older brothers keen opponents. Soon afterwards he met Charlie Hollis – a friend of his father – who was to become his first coach and a huge influence on the young Laver. He also met Australian Davis Cup Coach Harry Hopman, who ironically nicknamed the scrawny youngster 'Rocket'. His game began to strengthen, and his left forearm became far more muscular and defined. His body filled out proportionately from his days as a tiny youth but his slim 5 feet 9 inches frame would pale in comparison with today's players. His left wrist eventually measured 7 inches around, an inch more than his right wrist. His left forearm was 12 inches around, an inch and a half more than his right forearm.

In 1953, Laver quit school and moved to Brisbane and started work at the Dunlop Sporting Goods Company, where he could also concentrate on his tennis. The hard work paid off as, after a year in the Australian army, he became Australian and US Junior Champion in 1957.

His breakthrough came in 1959 when he reached all three finals at Wimbledon, winning the mixed doubles with Darlene Hard, but losing the singles final to Alex Olmedo, following an eighty-seven-game semi-final victory over Barry MacKay in the days before tie-breaks. However, he didn't have long to wait until he won his first Grand Slam title, saving a match point and coming back from two sets down to defeat Neale Fraser in the final of the 1960 Australian Championships.

Fraser gained his revenge in the finals of both Wimbledon and the US Open that year, and Roy Emerson beat Laver in the final of the 1961 Australian and US Open finals. However, Laver did produce a spectacular performance to defeat Chuck McKinley in the Wimbledon final of 1961 in just fifty-three minutes. He rounded off his year by winning the New South Wales Championships just before Christmas and set himself the target of trying to win all four Grand Slam titles the following year, a feat only previously achieved in the men's game by Don Budge in 1938.

He started well, winning the Australian Open final in four sets against Roy Emerson, but he found the clay of Roland Garros in the French Open more tricky. Marty Mulligan came within a point of defeating him in the quarter-final, Fraser served for the match at 5–4 up in the decisive fifth set in the semi-final, and Emerson let a two-set lead slip in the final. However, Laver came through all those challenges to win his first French Open title.

He went on to lose only one set at Wimbledon, where his booming serve-and-volley game overcame Mulligan in the final by a score of 6–2, 6–2, 6–1 in just fifty-two minutes, a minute less than the previous year. Graciously, Don Budge practised with Laver in advance of the US Championships at Forest Hills and predicted that his 1938 record would be equalled. He was to be proved correct as Laver breezed through the field, defeating Emerson in four sets in the final, to complete the Grand Slam. It was not just the four Major titles that Laver won that year; he won an additional seventeen titles, including clay-court titles in Germany and Italy.

Laver helped Australia win the Davis Cup for the fourth year in succession in December 1962 and then signed a reported $100,000 contract with tennis-star-turned-promoter Jack Kramer to turn professional. Having been awarded a £15 voucher for winning Wimbledon the previous year, he now had the chance to play some of the best professionals in the world, such as Ken Rosewall, Lew Hoad, Pancho Gonzales and Barry MacKay and earn far more money than had he stayed as an amateur.

He found the Pro tour more gruelling than expected, at one stage playing in 150 different cities over 250 days. The competition proved tougher too, as he lost nineteen matches out of the first twenty-one he played against Rosewall and Hoad. Fortunately, he started to improve, and won seventeen titles in 1965, beating Rosewall thirteen times in eighteen matches and defeating Gonzales in all eight finals they contested. He won sixteen events in 1966, including the US Pro Championship, and nineteen further titles in 1967, including the Wimbledon Pro. In total, he won sixty-nine tournaments as a pro, compiling an 83 per cent winning record.

Tennis's Open Era started in 1968 with the professional players invited to compete alongside their amateur compatriots. Those who doubted that the ageing pros would be able to compete were shocked when 34-year-old Rosewall won the first French Open and Laver won his third Wimbledon crown, defeating Tony Roche in straight sets. At the end of the year, he set himself another target – this time to achieve the first 'Open' Grand Slam.

He started at the Australian Open where he battled Tony Roche in searing heat in a match lasting a total of ninety games which Laver finally won 7–5, 22–20, 9–11, 1–6, 6–3 before defeating Andrés Gimeno in the final. Laver then overcame a two-set deficit against Dick Crealy in the second round at Paris, before coming through to win, and then beat Ken Rosewall in straight sets in the final. History repeated itself at Wimbledon, as India's Premjit Lall took the first two sets in their second-round match before Laver prevailed in the fifth. He defeated John Newcombe in a memorable four-set final to complete the third leg of a possible Grand Slam.

The US Open final against Tony Roche was delayed for a day due to rain, and when play commenced conditions were slippery – despite the best efforts of a helicopter hovering above the court in a bid to dry it. Laver found himself sliding all over the grass court, and so he asked Match Referee Bill Talbert whether he could change his shoes into spikes. Permission was granted, but Roche took the first set 9–7 helped by five double-faults from Laver. Once into the second set, Laver discovered that his spikes allowed him to make effective lobs whereas Roche was hampered by traditional tennis shoes that offered him little stability on the slippery grass and in the mud. The end result was a 7–9, 6–1, 6–2, 6–2 victory to clinch a second Grand Slam.

After 1969, Laver concentrated on playing World Championship Tennis and never won another Grand Slam championship. The trophies continued to pile up, however, and in 1970 he won fifteen titles and became the first player to win more than $200,000 in prize money. Professionals were allowed to play in the Davis Cup for the first time in 1973 and he promptly won a fifth championship – one of his seventy-seven tournament wins in his Open Era career from 1968 to 1976.

In 1976, he semi-retired from the main tour but played for the San Diego team in the World Team Tennis League for three seasons before retiring for good in 1978. The ultimate honour came in 2000 when the Centre Court at the Melbourne home of the Australian Open was renamed the Rod Laver Arena.

Jim Clark (Scotland) 1963–1964

In the eyes of some, the greatest driver of all time, Jim Clark was born on 4 March 1936 in Kilmany in Fife. At the age of 6, his parents moved the family – Jim together with his four older sisters – to a farm just outside the rural hillside village of Chirnside, Berwickshire in the Scottish Borders.

His first job was at the age of 10, driving a tractor at harvest time, and at any opportunity he found himself behind the wheel of a car. Aged 16, his education was cut short due to being called back to help on the family farm, following the sad loss of both his grandfather and uncle. His first passion was shepherding, but at the time he had no intention whatsoever of becoming a racing driver.

He joined the local Young Farmers' Club and became friends with Ian Scott-Watson who introduced him to motorsport. After passing his driving test in 1953 he was taken to Berwick & District Motor Club. His parents did not believe that motorsport was a suitable career path as it was dangerous and expensive and so Clark began to compete during the mid-1950s without telling them.

He started to enjoy some regional success towards the end of 1957 when he competed in three races and won the final one – the BMRC Trophy. As a result, he joined the newly re-formed Border Reivers Racing team for the following season and won twelve of the twenty races he started, becoming the first driver to average over 100mph in a British sports car race in a Jaguar D-Type.

He switched from Jaguar D-Type to Lister-Jaguar for the 1959 season when he made his debut at Le Mans, sharing the tenth-placed Lotus Elite with Sir John Whitmore. His performance was so impressive that he signed with Aston Martin for 1960 but a race-worthy car was never produced. Instead, he signed for Lotus, for whom he participated in four Grand Prix, and achieved his first ever podium finish with third place in Portugal. He also finished third in that year's Le Mans 24 Hours when sharing a Border Reivers Aston Martin DBR1/300 with Roy Salvadori.

Ferrari dominated Formula One in 1961 – the first season in which the naturally aspirated engines had to be of a maximum displacement of 1.5 litres to reduce the speeds of the cars. Clark won the non-championship Pau Grand Prix and finished third in Holland and France. Tragedy struck in the opening laps of the Italian Grand Prix when his car touched the Ferrari of championship leader Wolfgang von Trips. The Ferrari flew into the crowd killing the driver and fourteen spectators.

In 1962, Lotus introduced the Lotus 25 with its revolutionary fully stressed monocoque chassis. As the undisputed team leader, Clark won the Belgian, British and US Grand Prix as he challenged Graham Hill for the World Championship. The title decider was the South African race at East London and the rivals qualified together on the front row of the grid. Clark steadily pulled away at the front of the field and was set to clinch a first world title before suffering an oil leak with twenty laps to go.

Clark began his third full Formula One season as one of the favourites to take the title. He was leading at Monaco before having to retire, but later that week travelled to America to race in the Indianapolis 500 for the first time. Clark started America's richest race from the middle of the front row and finished in an impressive second place. In the same year, he went on to win the Milwaukee 200 to become a driving superstar on both sides of the Atlantic. Back in Formula One, he won seven of the remaining nine races to clinch the title with three races to spare.

In 1964, poor reliability hampered his chances of defending his title after he won three of the first five races of the season. He qualified on pole position for the Indianapolis 500 but was forced to retire when his suspension failed while in the lead. Three racers started the final Formula One race of the year in with a chance of the title: Clark, Graham Hill and John Surtees. Clark started in pole and built up a lead before his engine gave up on the final lap, handing Surtees the title.

However much of a disappointment 1964 was, the following year was a triumph. He decided to miss the Monaco Grand Prix in order to compete at Indianapolis and clinched a famous win after leading for 190 of the 200 laps. He then returned to Europe and won the next four races to again win the world championship with three races to go. Furthermore, he won the first of his three Tasman Series championships and the Formula Two Championship.

The Formula One specifications were changed again for 1966, to a 1500cc engine with a compressor or a 3000cc naturally aspirated engine. Clark struggled through the season with just a single victory to his name: the

US Grand Prix. Competing again in the Indianapolis 500, he qualified in second position and held that place to the chequered flag finishing only behind Graham Hill's Lola. He also raced in the RAC Rally, where he won three stages before eventually rolling his Lotus Cortina on Stage 45 and therefore did not finish.

Perennial adversary Graham Hill joined Clark at Lotus for the 1967 season and the new Lotus 49-Ford was unveiled at the Dutch Grand Prix, in which Hill qualified on pole and Clark won after Hill retired. Further victories followed in the British, US and Mexican Grands Prix, confirming his place as Formula One's finest driver, but five retirements cost him dearly. A typical example came at Monza where he managed to make up a complete lap lost in a pit stop only to run out of fuel at the last corner.

Now living as a tax exile in Paris, Clark started 1968 full of confidence as he won his third Tasman Series Championship and converted pole position into a victory in the South African Grand Prix. However, that was to prove to be his final Formula One race. During qualifying for the Formula Two Deutschland Trophy at Hockenheim on 7 April, Clark was in eighth place after four laps on a wet track when his Lotus 48-Cosworth somersaulted and collided with a tree at 150mph, killing Clark instantly.

Lotus boss Colin Chapman and Graham Hill were joined by the rest of the world in total shock at his death. Clark was always considered to be one of the safest and most skilful drivers and no one could believe that driver error could have caused the crash, with a deflated rear type widely blamed. A visibly shaken Hill would win the 1968 title, which he dedicated to his friend's memory, and fellow racing driver Chris Amon summed it up thus: 'If it could happen to him, what chance do the rest of us have? I think we all felt that. It seemed like we'd lost our leader.'

Clark's death signalled the beginning of the end of Formula One's 'amateur' era. Although many more drivers would die for want of even basic safety measures, under the leadership of Clark's great friend and rival Jackie Stewart, the push for change started. Run-off areas, guard rails and gravel traps would start to flank circuits, not trees, ditches and banks of earth.

Muhammad Ali (USA) 1964–1967, 1970–1972, 1974–1978

A three-time heavyweight champion, and nicknamed 'The Greatest', Muhammad Ali is widely considered one of the finest boxers of all time. It was more than that though, as he is now remembered as much for his showmanship as anything he achieved in the ring.

Cassius Marcellus Clay Jr was born on 17 January 1942 in Louisville, Kentucky to Cassius Marcellus Clay Sr and Odessa Grady Clay. His boxing career started at the age of 12 when his bike was stolen. Clay told police officer Joe Martin that he wanted to beat up the thief. Martin also happened to train boxers and – taking Clay at his word – persuaded the youngster to work out at the local gym. His boxing career was underway, and Clay had his first amateur fight in 1954, winning by a split decision.

He left school at the age of 16 and devoted himself to boxing, winning six Kentucky Golden Gloves championships, two National Golden Gloves tournaments and two National Amateur Athletic Union titles by the time he was 18 years old. He was a natural choice for the US team for the 1960 Olympic Games in Rome, but he was so afraid of flying that it needed Joe Martin to calm him down and convince him that a boat was not a practical option to travel to Italy to have a chance of winning a gold medal.

Once in Rome, he became one of the most popular athletes in the Olympic village, stopping to introduce himself to all-comers. He also won his first three contests in the light heavyweight division, via two unanimous decisions and a second-round knockout. In the final, he faced Zbigniew Pietryzkowski from Poland, who had won the bronze medal in Melbourne four years earlier. After a slow start in which he struggled to cope with his opponent's southpaw style, Clay finally found top form in the final round, which resulted in a points victory and the gold medal. He was later to throw the medal into the Ohio River after having been refused service in a whites-only restaurant.

His professional debut came on 29 October 1960, in a six-round victory over Tunney Hunsaker in his home town of Louisville and he proceeded to dominate all-comers over the first years of his professional career. He was so sure of his own ability that he was able to predict in which round he would finish off his opponent. There was the occasional nervy moment, none more so than when he travelled to London to fight Henry Cooper in June 1963. Clay was sent to the canvas by a left hook at the end of the fourth round and only saved by the bell before recovering to win in the fifth.

That victory earned Clay a chance at the World Heavyweight champion Sonny Liston with the two stepping into the ring on 25 February 1964 in Miami Beach. Clay was a heavy underdog, but he stunned the boxing world when Liston failed to answer the bell for the seventh round. After the fight, Clay celebrated by dancing around the ring, yelling 'I'm the greatest.' It was a description which stuck.

The day after the fight, Clay changed his name to Cassius X after joining the Nation of Islam and eventually settled on the name of Muhammad Ali. Ali and Liston would fight again a year later in a rematch but the former champion didn't make it past the first round. He also had little trouble with another former champion Floyd Patterson, winning in the twelfth round. The victories continued to pile up and on 22 March 1967 Ali defeated Zora Folley at Madison Square Garden for his ninth successful defence of the title, but it would turn out to be his last fight for more than three years.

In 1964, Ali had failed the qualifying test for the US draft due to his subpar writing and spelling skills. However, in 1966 he was reclassified, making him eligible for induction into the US army. Ali was outspoken about serving in the war and publicly said he would not go to Vietnam if he was drafted. He said that the war went against the teachings in the Qur'an and famously said, 'I ain't got no quarrel with them Viet Cong.'

At Ali's scheduled induction he refused to step forward and after a warning, he was arrested for committing a felony that was punishable by five years in prison and a fine of $10,000. As a result of his arrest and induction refusal, Ali was stripped of the heavyweight title and had his boxing licence suspended by the New York State Athletic Commission. Other boxing commissions followed suit and did the same.

His case went to trial in June 1967 and Ali was convicted of draft evasion, sentenced to five years in prison, fined $10,000 and banned from boxing for three years. A court of appeal upheld Ali's conviction, and the case went to the US Supreme Court. However, while he waited to be heard, opposition to the war was gathering pace in the US and Ali spent a great deal of time visiting colleges around the country preaching his anti-war message.

He returned to the ring on 26 October 1970 while waiting for the Supreme Court ruling, fighting in Georgia, which didn't have a boxing commission. There was no sign of ring rustiness as he needed just three rounds to defeat Jerry Quarry. Soon afterwards, he won his case against the New York State Athletic Commission, who were forced to grant Ali a licence and that set up a showdown with the reigning champion Joe Frazier in what was dubbed 'The Fight of the Century' between two undefeated fighters.

Ali started off the stronger when the pair met on 8 March 1971 at Madison Square Garden. Frazier was able to keep things close before taking the advantage in the eleventh round. Ali managed to avoid serious trouble until Round 15, when Frazier knocked him down for just the third time in his career. A shaken Ali got up and finished the final round, but the damage had been done. Ali had suffered his first professional loss as Frazier won by unanimous decision, retaining his heavyweight championship.

Ali rebounded with six victories in 1972, including wins over Floyd Patterson and Jerry Quarry. He then defended the North American Boxing Federation (NABF) heavyweight title against Ken Norton on 31 March 1973. Norton managed to break Ali's jaw in the fight and won by split decision. Ali gained some measure of revenge against Norton by winning back his NABF championship and he also won a second fight with Frazier which set the scene for a challenge to George Foreman for the heavyweight title. Foreman had won the crown after knocking down Frazier six times in a span of two rounds.

Promoter Don King accepted an offer from Zaire president Mobutu Sese Seko to host the fight in Kinshasa and it was dubbed 'The Rumble in the Jungle'. Originally scheduled for September, the fight was pushed back until 30 October after Foreman was injured during training. Foreman was a heavy favourite, but he had not counted on Ali's new 'rope-a-dope' strategy in which he leaned on the ropes while covering up his body as Foreman threw punches that were deflected and didn't land squarely.

After several rounds of this strategy, Foreman started to tire in the ring while Ali's trademark taunting was in full effect. In the eighth round, Ali knocked Foreman down after a series of combinations. Foreman just made it up before the standing 10 count, but referee Zack Clayton stopped the fight. Ali had handed Foreman his first loss and regained his championship.

Ali and Frazier met for the third and final time on 1 October 1975 in the Philippines. The two men slugged it out in what would go down as one of the greatest fights of the twentieth century, justly titled the 'Thrilla in Manila'.

Muhammad Ali (USA) 1964–1967, 1970–1972, 1974–1978

With Frazier's eye closing, Ali took advantage in Round 14 and Frazier's trainer threw in the towel before the start of the fifteenth and final round.

Ali successfully defended his title four times in 1976 and twice more in 1977, but he entered his fight with Leon Spinks in Las Vegas in February 1978 badly out of shape. It showed, as Olympic champion Spinks won a split decision. Embarrassed by his defeat and determined not to make the same mistake again, Ali trained properly and defeated Spinks in a rematch seven months later to become the first three-time World Heavyweight champion.

Following the victory, Ali retired, but his retirement was short-lived. He returned to the ring on 2 October 1980 against Larry Holmes in an attempt to win the heavyweight championship for the fourth time. Holmes proved too much for the 38-year-old Ali, and the fight was stopped before the eleventh round. Ali's final fight was a unanimous decision loss to Trevor Berbick in 1981. Retiring for good, Ali finished his career with a 56-5 professional record.

Seldom out of the limelight after his retirement, he was given the honour of lighting the Olympic cauldron at the start of the 1996 Atlanta Olympics, where he was also given a replacement for his lost gold medal. A final accolade came in 1999 when the BBC voted him Sports Personality of the Century.

Mark Spitz (USA) 1972

The 1972 Munich Olympics remain etched in people's minds for two contrasting reasons. The first was for the massacre of Israeli athletes by Black September terrorists. The other was for the swimming of Mark Spitz.

Spitz was born on 10 February 1950, in Modesto, California, to Arnold and Lenore Spitz. When Mark was 2 years old, the family relocated to Hawaii where his father taught him to swim. After four years in Hawaii, the family returned to California, settling in Sacramento. At the Sacramento YMCA, Spitz began to train in competitive swimming for the first time. Sensing that Spitz had surpassed the training available at the YMCA, Arnold Spitz took his son to the Arden Hills Swim Club, where he began to train under Sherm Chavoor, a well-known swimming instructor. Chavoor was to remain a mentor to Spitz throughout his career.

Spitz's father was a driving force behind Spitz's swimming, drilling into his son the mantra 'Swimming isn't everything: winning is.' Spitz took his father's advice to heart; by the time he was 10 years old, he held seventeen national swimming records for his age group and one world record. He also earned the title of the world's top swimmer in the 10-and-under age group.

When Spitz was 14 years old, his father moved the family to Santa Clara so that Spitz could train under a new coach, George Haines, who was based at the famous Santa Clara Swim Club. This move increased Spitz's father's commute to work to 80 miles each way, but he was determined that his son became the best swimmer he could. The move paid off. When Spitz was 16 years old, he won the 100-metre butterfly title at the National Amateur Athletic Union (AAU) Championships. It was the first of twenty-four AAU titles he would win during his career.

In 1967, he won five gold medals at the Pan-American Games, held in Winnipeg. These were for the 100-metre butterfly, the 200-metre butterfly, the 400-metre freestyle relay, the 800-metre freestyle relay, and the 400-metre medley relay. With those achievements behind him, he predicted that he would win six golds at the 1968 Mexico City Olympics. However, he fell some way short of those lofty aims, winning two gold medals in team events – for the 4 x 100 and 4 x 200-metre freestyle relays, a silver in the 100-metre butterfly and a bronze in the 100-metre freestyle.

Following the 1968 Olympics, Spitz started college at Indiana University studying a pre-dental programme while continuing to swim competitively under the famous swimming coach Doc Counsilman. Disappointed in his showing at the Olympics, he vowed to work on his mental preparation. He began to develop a new attitude of relaxed concentration that was in contrast to his earlier boastful air.

In 1969 – his freshman year at university – he won the 200-metre and the 500-metre freestyle, as well as the 100-metre butterfly at the NCAA swimming championships. He also won the 100-metre butterfly at the NCAA championships the following year. The year after that, 1971, he again won the NCAA championship in the 100-metre butterfly, as well as the 200-metre butterfly. His achievements earned him the Sullivan Award in 1971 for being the best amateur athlete in the US and he was also named 'World Swimmer of the Year' in 1969, 1971, and 1972.

Spitz graduated from Indiana University in 1972, just in time for the Munich Olympics. This time, he vowed to take home no less than seven gold medals. He started by winning the 200-metre butterfly, and then the 200-metre freestyle, followed by the 100-metre butterfly. His final gold-medal-winning performance in individual competition was for the 100-metre freestyle. In addition to his four individual gold medals, Spitz also won three gold medals in the relays. With each winning performance, Spitz set a new world record, claiming his seven gold medals over a period of just eight days. No other athlete had ever taken home that many gold medals at a single Olympic Games.

However, within twenty-four hours of his final victory, his performance was marred by tragedy. In the early hours of 5 September, members of the Palestinian 'Black September' terrorist organisation invaded the dormitory where the Olympic athletes were sleeping. They killed two Israelis and kidnapped nine others while Spitz was asleep nearby. Spitz immediately left Germany for London, without waiting to attend the Olympics' closing ceremony. Meanwhile, the nine hostages were all killed during a botched rescue attempt.

Despite the tragedy overshadowing Spitz's unprecedented achievements at the Olympics, he returned home to the US a major celebrity. He became the second most-recognised person in the US, after then-president Richard Nixon. Spitz cancelled his plans to become a dentist and looked forward to making a career as a corporate spokesperson.

Soon after his return to the US, Spitz landed several lucrative endorsement contracts and established himself in his new career. Companies and organisations for which he endorsed products included the Schick Company, the California Milk Advisory Board, Adidas, Speedo, and many more. A photograph of Spitz wearing a pair of trunks with his seven gold medals around his neck quickly became a best-seller.

Spitz's bid to become a Hollywood star was less successful. Many potential film roles were sent his way and one of the projects he was offered was a film adaptation of a horror novel by a young and upcoming director called Steven Spielberg. Spitz was screen tested for the part of Chief Hooper in the movie *Jaws*, the part which ultimately went to Richard Dreyfuss.

He managed to maintain a presence as a sports commentator for a few years including a period with ABC Sports, helping to cover both the 1976 and 1984 Summer Olympics. As the 1980s drew to a close, Spitz decided to come out of retirement and become an Olympic swimmer for the first time since 1972. In 1989, now 39 years old, Spitz began to train for the 1992 Olympic Trials. In 1991, he raced against Tom Jager and Matt Biondi, both Olympic swimmers, in two separate 50-metre butterfly races. Unfortunately, Spitz lost both races and fell just over two seconds short of the qualifying time he needed to rejoin the US Olympic swimming team.

At Beijing in 2008, Michael Phelps broke Spitz's record by winning eight gold medals at one Olympic Games and Spitz was present in Rio de Janeiro when Phelps became the most-decorated Olympian of all time. However, it was Phelps who paid tribute to Spitz by mimicking the pose with his own haul of Olympic medals.

Johan Cruyff (Netherlands) 1972–1974

Very few players have earned the right to be mentioned in the same breath as Pelé and Diego Maradona. Although he never won an international title with his country and played in only one FIFA World Cup, Johan Cruyff is one of them. Such was his natural talent, he still enjoys an undisputed reputation as one of the game's all-time greats.

Born Hendrik Johannes Cruyff on 25 April 1947, he was the second son of Hermanus and Petronella (Nel) Cruyff from a working-class background in east Amsterdam. Encouraged by his influential football-loving father and his incredibly close proximity to Ajax's stadium, the young boy played football with his schoolmates and older brother, Henny, whenever he could; by the age of 10 he was on the books of the Ajax Academy.

He also helped out in the family greengrocer, but everything changed when he was 12 years old and his father died from a heart attack. Unable to carry on at the shop without her husband, Nel began working at Ajax as a cleaner, and the following year Johan left school to become a part-time clerk, which he combined with his morning training.

Cruyff continued to impress in the youth team and, as part of his growing reputation, was appointed as a ball boy at the Olympisch Stadion in Amsterdam when Benfica beat Real Madrid 5–3 in the 1962 European Cup final. Inspired by Real Madrid's playmaker, Alfredo Di Stéfano, he signed his first professional contract on the day he turned 16 years of age.

Cruyff made his first-team debut at the age of 17, scoring Ajax's only goal in a 3–1 defeat to GVAV-Rapiditas, but after a thirteenth-place finish in the league, Ajax's worst finish in their nine-year professional era, they sacked their English manager Vic Buckingham and replaced him with Rinus Michels. Michels implemented an attacking style of play, and Ajax won the 1965/66 Eredivisie and a domestic double in 1966/67

Cruyff was named Dutch Footballer of the Year in both 1967 and 1968, and in 1969 Ajax became the first Dutch side to ever reach a European Cup final, although they lost out 4–1 to AC Milan in the final at the Bernabeu Stadium in Madrid. The following year, their bitter rivals Feyenoord lifted the title – which inspired Ajax to match and then even better their fiercest competitors.

Cruyff missed the start of the 1970/71 season through injury and – with Gerrie Mühren wearing the number 9 shirt, Cruyff was forced to pick number 14 out of a basket of shirts when he returned to the team. It was a number that he stuck with for the remainder of his career, and within a month of returning from injury, he scored six goals against Alkmaar in the league.

Ajax looked supreme as they moved effortlessly into the 1970/71 European Cup final against Panathinaikos, scoring fifteen goals against their first four opponents: KF Tirana, Basel, Celtic and Atlético Madrid. Determined to make amends for their 1969 defeat, a header from Dick van Dijk and a deflected shot from Arie Haan set up by Cruyff gave Ajax a 2–0 victory to win their first European Cup. Having achieved his aim, Michels left to take charge of Barcelona. Despite rumours that he was also to follow the manager out of the door, Cruyff signed a seven-year contract extension and celebrated by winning his first European Player of the Year award in 1971.

Michels was replaced by Romanian Ştefan Kovács for the 1971/72 season, but the team carried on from where they had left off the previous year and reached another European Cup final, this time in Rotterdam against an Inter Milan side who were playing in their fourth European Cup final in eight seasons. Cruyff scored two goals to lead Ajax to a 2–0 win and finish as the tournament's top scorer with nine goals.

Cruyff's following season was hampered by an ongoing groin problem, but Ajax still won the Eredivisie and their third straight European Cup, finishing unbeaten in the competition, defeating Bayern Munich and Real Madrid before a 1–0 final victory over Juventus. That was to prove to be Kovács' final match, as he was replaced by George Knobel, but not before Cruyff had won another European Footballer of the Year trophy.

Despite the successes on the field, Cruyff's popularity with his teammates was on the wane and after he was defeated in an election to select the captain for the 1973/74 season, he was transferred to Barcelona in the autumn of 1973, becoming the world's most expensive player at $2 million, and rekindling his relationship with Michels.

Barcelona had been in the shadow of their bitter rivals Real Madrid since their foundation in 1902 and Cruyff was seen as their saviour. It started well as the team were unbeaten in the league for five months after his debut, which included a 5–0 victory over Real Madrid. Attention then turned towards the 1974 World Cup in West Germany – the Netherlands' first appearance in the competition since 1938. The fact that the Netherlands had not qualified for the previous four World Cups and three European Championships was a huge source of national embarrassment.

With Michels at the helm and with Ajax proving themselves as one of the greatest sides of all-time, confidence was high. The tournament began well for the Netherlands, winning two out of three of their group games against Uruguay and Bulgaria, scoring 6 and conceding just 1, and drawing the other group fixture 0–0 with Sweden. That goalless draw produced one of the greatest moments in World Cup history: the 'Cruyff Turn' when he swivelled and dragged the ball at a 90-degree angle past Swedish fullback Jan Olsson.

The Netherlands swept aside their opponents in the second round, beating Argentina 4–0, East Germany 2–0, and reigning champions Brazil 2–0. Their opponents in the final would be West Germany, who, with the likes of Franz Beckenbauer, Berti Vogts, Paul Breitner and Gerd Müller in their team, had triumphed in the 1972 European Championships.

The final started in sensational fashion with a minute-long weaving passage of play from the Dutch culminating in Cruyff being fouled for a penalty. The spot kick was suitably dispatched by Johan Neeskens and the first time the Germans found themselves touching the ball was to pick it out of their own goal. However, after twenty-five minutes they were level through a penalty of their own and two minutes before half-time, the prolific Müller scored his most crucial goal for his national team. The Dutch threw whatever they could at the Germans during the second half, but to no avail, and the final score ended 2–1.

Cruyff was unable to repeat his earlier European successes with Barcelona, losing in the 1974/75 semi-final to Leeds and failing to qualify for the tournament in his final three years at the club. Barcelona did win the Copa del Rey in 1978, but Cruyff was never as good as he had been in his first season with the Catalan giants. In 1979, at the age of 32, he decided to follow other stars such as Pelé, George Best and Franz Beckenbauer and headed to the US to join the Los Angeles Aztecs.

He played one season with the Aztecs and spent a season with the Washington Diplomats, but seeking the competitiveness of Europe again, Cruyff made a shock move to Levante in Spain in March 1980. It was a disappointing time, however, and resulted in just two goals in ten games, before he returned home to a faltering Ajax side as a technical adviser to manager Leo Beenhaker in November 1980.

Never having officially retired from playing, he helped Ajax win the Eredivisie in both the 1981/82 and 1982/83 seasons, but the club refused to offer Cruyff a new contract; in return, he signed for arch-rivals Feyenoord and helped them win their first Eredivisie title for ten years. Having been voted as the Dutch Footballer of the Year again, he finally retired in May 1984.

Although Cruyff had no formal coaching qualifications, he took over as technical director at Ajax at the beginning of the 1985/86 season and led them to the UEFA Cup Winners' Cup in 1987. The following year, history repeated itself as he left for Barcelona where he put together another superb team, which won the 1992 European Cup and four domestic championships in a row.

A heavy smoker his entire life, Cruyff suffered a heart attack during his reign in charge of Barcelona, and left after eight years at the helm. He died in 2016, but not before his legacy as one of the most influential footballers in the game's history was secure.

Björn Borg (Sweden) 1978–1980

Björn Borg's massive appeal was based not only on his extraordinary tennis ability but on his good looks and shy manner. It made him tennis's first teen idol. Everything he did was the epitome of cool – the way he walked on to the court, the way he wore his hair, and the way he played – it all added up to an irresistible mix.

Born on 6 June 1956, Borg was brought up in Södertälje, an industrial town of 100,000 people 20 miles south-west of Stockholm, the only child of Rune and Margaretha. His father had won a table tennis tournament when Björn was 8 years old, and the youngster asked his father to choose a tennis racquet for his prize. The very next day he was playing tennis with his friends and was to spend hours pounding the ball against a garage door.

He was not always such a cool, calm customer. At the age of 12, he was banned from tournaments for six months by the Swedish Tennis Association for throwing his racquets. The punishment did the trick, and three years later he met his long-time coach and mentor Lennart Bergelin, who selected the raw teenager to play on Sweden's Davis Cup team the following year.

In 1972, a notable year for Borg, he played his first Davis Cup singles match, beat Buster Mottram to win Junior Wimbledon, and won the prestigious Orange Bowl tournament in Miami, defeating Vitas Gerulaitis in the boys' under-18 final.

Borg turned professional for the 1973 season and made his Wimbledon debut as the number six seed, losing in a five-set quarter-final to Roger Taylor. The following year, just short of his eighteenth birthday, Borg claimed his first career title with victory at the Italian Open. Then, only a few weeks later, he added his second singles title, and his first ever Grand Slam victory, when winning on the French clay at Roland Garros. He came from two sets down in the final to defeat Spain's Manuel Orantes 2–6, 6–7, 6–0, 6–1, 6–1.

Borg's western grip, which he used on both sides produced great topspin. The grip may have limited his volleying, but it dramatically enhanced his baseline game. The slight 15-year-old had filled out over the previous three years, and he had great stamina which made five-set matches less of a struggle for him than many other players.

Borg retained his French Open crown in 1975, defeating Guillermo Vilas in the final in straight sets. He lost in the quarter-finals at Wimbledon to the eventual champion Arthur Ashe, while in the US event he advanced through to the semis before losing to the reigning champion Jimmy Connors. However, in Borg's eyes, the highlight of the year was being instrumental in helping Sweden secure their first ever Davis Cup triumph.

Facing Czechoslovakia in the final, Borg gave Sweden an early advantage when he defeated Jiří Hřebec 6–1, 6–3, 6–0 but Jan Kodeš then levelled the tie. In the crucial doubles, Ove Bengtson and Borg combined to win in straight sets 6–4, 6–4, 6–4. With the opportunity to win the Davis Cup for Sweden, Borg duly defeated Kodeš 6–4, 6–2, 6–2 to clinch not only a first victory for the Swedes, but a record nineteenth successive singles win, breaking Bill Tilden's previous record set in the 1920s.

Borg arrived in Paris in 1976 as the red-hot favourite to complete a hat-trick of titles, but in the quarter-finals he lost in four sets to the eventual champion, Adriano Panatta. Disappointed, he travelled to London and practised his grass court game relentlessly, which paid off as he reached his first Wimbledon final without losing a set. It was the hottest summer of the century and the final with Ilie Năstase was played at 41°C, but the scorched turf helped the young baseliner as he won in straight sets to win his first Wimbledon crown. In the year's final Grand Slam, Borg reached the US Open final, but lost in four sets to Jimmy Connors.

World Team Tennis duty denied him the opportunity in 1977 to add to his two French Open titles, but he was in no mood to relinquish his grip on the Wimbledon trophy. In his match against the Australian Mark Edmondson, it appeared as though a massive upset was on the cards when Borg lost the opening two sets, but he battled back valiantly to win through in five hard-fought sets.

Three straight sets victories followed to set up a semi-final clash with Vitas Gerulaitis, in which Borg again proved his resilience, winning in five sets to set up a final clash with Connors. In a memorable final, Borg won the deciding set to retain his trophy with a 3–6, 6–2, 6–1, 5–7, 6–4 victory. His success in the tournament's centenary year enabled him to topple Connors from the top of the world rankings in August 1977. Unfortunately, his Grand Slam year ended when he was forced to retire from his fourth-round clash in the US Open against Dick Stockton with the match level at a set apiece.

Björn Borg (Sweden) 1978–1980

Borg started 1978 in great form and defeated Guillermo Vilas in the French Open final, but in the opening round at Wimbledon he lost two of the first three sets to unfancied American, Victor Amaya. However, Borg was able to extricate himself from that sticky situation and eventually reached another final, again facing Connors. Unlike the epic, five-setter from the previous year, this final was a more one-sided affair with the Swede winning in straight sets. Connors would have his revenge in the US Open final later in the year, when he inflicted his own straight-sets defeat on Borg.

At the 1979 French Open, Borg defeated big-serving Victor Pecci in a four-set final, and in that year's Wimbledon final he came up against the even bigger-serving Roscoe Tanner, with his tight mop of blond hair. Borg led 5–4 in the fifth set, 40–0 up on his own serve, but for the first visible time, he faltered. He netted a nervous volley and was then passed as Tanner came back to deuce. But Tanner could not capitalise and Borg eked out the two more points required for victory – his fourth title in a row. Tanner gained some small measure of compensation in the US Open later in the year when he defeated Borg in a four-set, floodlit quarter-final, but Borg won the season-ending Masters tournament in January 1980 to finish the year top of the world rankings.

Borg started 1980 by winning a fifth French Open, again without dropping a set, and moved effortlessly into yet another Wimbledon final where he would play John McEnroe – the 'enfant terrible' of the tennis world – the complete antithesis to the ice-cool Borg. It was a final for the ages, and is still considered one of – if not – the finest ever played. Having lost the opening set 6–1, Borg took the next two 7–5, 6–3 and had two championship points at 5–4 in the fourth. However, McEnroe saved them and five more in the memorable, twenty-minute tie-breaker which came at the end of the fourth set to level the match. Borg regrouped, and won nineteen successive points on his own serve in the deciding set to win it 8–6 after three hours fifty-three minutes of drama.

The two players met again in the US Open final and it was McEnroe who prevailed in five sets, with Borg unable yet again to win the concluding Grand Slam of the season. He made amends by winning the season-ending Masters title, and started to focus his attention on the 1981 French Open. He didn't let his fans down, as he defeated Ivan Lendl in five sets in the final, despite rumours of a lingering shoulder injury. He then headed to London to try to equal Willie Renshaw's record of six straight Wimbledon titles.

He met McEnroe again in the final, but this time the result was reversed. Possibly burned out from too many flights, matches and injuries, it was to prove the last day of his reign. Borg took the first set 6–4, but the American roared back and took the second set tie-break by 7 points to 1. The third set also went to a tie-break and again McEnroe won it before closing out the match 6–4 to end Borg's 41-match unbeaten run at Wimbledon.

Tennis fans were delighted when the two gladiators met again in the US Open final, with Borg desperate to win his first title at Flushing Meadows at the tenth attempt. It started well for him as he took the opening set but he was unable to get out of sight of his left-handed opponent. McEnroe's high-kicking serve caused problems for the Swede and he soon levelled the match and went on to win 4–6, 6–2, 6–4, 6–3. At the conclusion of the match, Borg picked up his bag and walked off court before the awards ceremony, hopped into a waiting car, which drove him straight to the airport still in his tennis gear.

Despite eleven Grand Slam titles, the magic had gone. He only played one tournament in 1982 and on 23 January 1983 he announced his retirement at the age of 26. He came back in 1991, with his old wooden racquet, but was out-gunned by the graphite-wielding Jordi Arrese. Similar attempts over the following two years also failed, but those did not diminish his earlier achievements, and he remains an all-time great.

Martina Navratilova (USA) 1980–1984

Martina Navratilova took women's tennis to a new level in the 1980s, revolutionising the sport with a combination of speed, power and strength. To this day, she is considered by many the greatest women's player – if not athlete – of all time.

She was born Martina Subertova in Prague on 18 October 1956 to Miroslav and Jana Subert, but her parents divorced when she was just 3 years old. Her mother married Mirek Navratil, a tennis instructor from Řevnice, and it is this name that the young Martina took on for the rest of her life.

She received her first tennis racquet from her grandmother, a former tennis player, who once ranked number two in Czechoslovakia, and she learned a valuable lesson from her sports-mad mother, who was also a ski instructor. It was that sports are good for young women and that sports could be combined with having a family and a job. With that in mind, she started having lessons from her stepfather at the age of 6, and was soon at home on the red clay.

At the age of 8 she reached the semi-finals of the local Under-12 tournament, and the following year received some lessons from George Parma, the Czech Tennis Federation coach, who encouraged her serve-and-volley technique. But just two years later, the USSR invaded Czechoslovakia and Parma defected to the West.

Despite the unrest around her, she continued to improve and she won the National Under-14s Girls' Title and the following year won the national women's title, paving the way for a trip to the US in 1973 to participate in the eight-week USLTA tournament circuit. At Akron, Ohio, she lost to Chris Evert in the first round, marking the start of a fifteen-year rivalry with the American. Her time in America left an indelible mark on the young Navratilova and she returned the following year and won her first professional title in Orlando in September. Two further victories – over Margaret Court in the Australian Open – and over Evert in Washington – catapulted her into the top echelons of female tennis.

A pivotal year for the young Navratilova was 1975. She finished runner-up in the first two Grand Slams of the year – in Australia to Evonne Goolagong and in France to Chris Evert and she led Czechoslovakia to its first Federation Cup triumph in May. After losing to Evert in the semi-final of the US Open in September, she travelled to the offices of the Immigration and Naturalisation Service and informed them that she wished to defect in order to escape the clutches of Czechoslovakia's repressive Communist Party and pursue her tennis career – and a Western lifestyle.

After a difficult period of adjustment in which her weight ballooned and her game suffered, she finally made her breakthrough in 1978 by beating world No. 1 Chris Evert for the title at Wimbledon. It was to be the start of a love affair with the grass courts of Wimbledon which would eventually bring her a record nine singles titles.

She successfully defended her Wimbledon crown in 1979, but a turning point was to come in 1981 when Evert defeated her 6–0, 6–0 in the final of the Amelia Island Championship. Navratilova began to run and lift weights to improve her physical fitness and transformed herself into a superb specimen of lean athleticism. She also played basketball with star Nancy Lieberman, learned game tactics with Renée Richards and perfected the technical aspects of her game with Mike Estep. She also forced all her rivals to shape up – literally – as they were all left trailing in her wake.

All her efforts paid off, as she produced a decade of excellence almost unrivalled in any professional sport. In 1982, she lost only three of her ninety-three singles matches and in 1983 she lost just a single match (to Kathy Horvath in the fourth round of the French Open) out of the eighty-seven matches she played. Her fitness helped her reverse the tide in her rivalry with Evert and make it one of the greatest duels between individuals in sports history. The duo would face each other eighty times with their contrasting styles – Evert's baselining and Navratilova's serve-and-volleying – with Navratilova ending with a narrow 43–37 advantage.

When she won the 1984 French Open, she held all four Major singles titles simultaneously and her accomplishment was feted as a 'Grand Slam' by Philippe Chatrier, president of the International Tennis Federation, even though the titles had not been won in a single calendar year. It mattered not to Navratilova, who, following victories at Wimbledon and the US Open, extended her Major singles tournament winning streak to six. By the time she entered the Australian Open she had the opportunity to win all four titles in the same year, but Helena Suková ended Navratilova's record seventy-four-match-winning streak in the semi-finals.

Towards the end of the 1980s her fiercest rival became Steffi Graf, to whom she lost in four Major finals: the 1987 French Open, 1988 Wimbledon, and 1989 Wimbledon and US Open. However, despite the age gap of more than twelve years between the two, the overall head-to-head score between them ended at nine wins apiece.

Her serve-and-volley technique enabled her to excel at doubles, and she and Pam Shriver formed one of the greatest doubles partnerships in tennis history. The pair won 109 matches in a row between April 1983 and July 1985, and a total of eighteen Grand Slam ladies' doubles titles. She was still competitive in 2006 when she won the mixed doubles championship at the US Open with Bob Bryan, becoming the oldest player in history (at just a month away from her fiftieth birthday) to win a Major title.

Navratilova won eighteen Major singles titles, thirty-one in ladies' doubles and another ten in mixed doubles. Her fifty-nine Major championships rank second all-time, only behind Margaret Court's total of sixty-two. Since the Open Era started in 1968, no male or female player has won more singles tournaments (167), doubles tournaments (177) or matches (2,189). She spent nineteen years ranked in the world's top ten singles players, including 332 weeks in the No. 1 spot.

Awarded American citizenship in 1981, she reacquired her Czech citizenship in 2008 and became a respected commentator on the sport. Perhaps the final word should go to one of her former rivals – Billie Jean King – who described her quite simply as 'the greatest singles, doubles, and mixed doubles player who ever lived.'

Carl Lewis (USA) 1984–1986

Named 'Sportsman of the Century' by the International Olympic Committee in 1999, Carl Lewis was a supreme sprinter and long jumper who possessed grace on the track, yet was seemingly underappreciated by his own countrymen at the time.

Frederick Carlton Lewis was born on 1 July 1961 in Birmingham, Alabama to William and Evelyn Lewis, who had been talented athletes when they attended the Tuskegee Institute. William ran and played football, while Evelyn was a world-class hurdler who represented the US at the 1951 Pan-American Games, only missing out on Olympic selection due to injury. Both parents later became schoolteachers and civil rights activists, marching with Martin Luther King Jr.

In the mid-1960s, they moved Carl, his two older brothers and his younger sister to Willingboro, New Jersey, where, in 1969, they started the Willingboro Track Club to encourage local youngsters to become interested in athletics. The club made a huge impact on Carl and, at the age of 13, he began competing in the long jump. Little Carl dreamed about becoming the next Jesse Owens or Bob Beamon. He marked out 29 feet, 2½ inches in his front yard – the world record distance Beamon had jumped at the 1968 Olympics – and tried even then to match it.

He took his talents to Willingboro High School a couple of years later, where by the age of 16 he was jumping nearly 8 metres and running the 100-yard dash in 9.3 seconds. With his talents highly evident, Lewis had a plethora of colleges to choose from as a young man; however, he set his sights on the University of Houston, due to the reputation of their track and field coach Tom Tellez.

Tellez taught Lewis a more scientific way of performing and Lewis qualified for the 1980 Olympics both in the long jump and as a member of the 4 x 100-metre relay team. With the US boycotting the Olympics, Lewis instead competed in the Liberty Bell Classic, where he won bronze in the long jump and gold in the relay.

In early 1981, the 19-year-old stunned the track and field world with a 27 feet, 10¼-inches jump at the Southwest Conference Indoor Championships in Fort Worth – the fourth-best long jump in history. He then entered the 60-yard dash and won it in 6.06 seconds, coming within two-hundredths of a second of tying the world record. Although he remained in Houston to work with Tellez, he stopped attending university after only two years so that he could travel on the international circuit and start accepting endorsements. He was given $65,000 a year in base pay just for wearing Nike shoes.

Lewis made huge strides on the track in 1981, and became the fastest 100-metre sprinter in the world. He ran 10.00 seconds at the Southwest Conference Championships in Dallas in May and won national titles at both 100 metres and the long jump. He rounded off the year by winning the James E. Sullivan Award as the top amateur athlete in the US. In 1982, he jumped at least 28 feet on seven occasions but fell short of Beamon's long-standing record. The same year, he left Houston to compete under the auspices of the Santa Monica Track Club in California. Coach Tellez followed him west and continued to work closely with him.

The IAAF organised the first World Championships in 1983 to be held in Helsinki. Lewis won the long jump and 100 metres with relative ease and ran the anchor leg in the 4 x 100 metres relay, crossing the line in 37.86 seconds, the first world record of his career. Away from the championship, he became the first person to run a sub-10 second 100 metres at low-altitude and he also set a new low-altitude record in the long jump of 8.79 metres. During the early months of 1984 he set an indoor world record by long jumping 8.79 metres again and it seemed a certainty that he would return from his home Olympics draped in gold medals.

Lewis arrived at the 1984 Olympics under intense media scrutiny, but he fulfilled his pre-competition predictions. He won the gold in the 100 metres with a time of 9.99 seconds. His performance in his second event, the long jump, drew jeers from the crowd when he decided to let his first leap of 8.54 metres stand and passed on his last four attempts to conserve his strength for the later sprinting events. No one came close, and he took a second gold medal. For his third, Lewis set an Olympic record with a 19.80-second run in the 200 metres. Lastly, he anchored the 4 x 100-metre relay team to a new world record of 37.83 seconds.

Although his performances on the track were astounding – he had duplicated Jesse Owens' 1936 haul of four gold medals – America was not convinced. Perhaps not helped by his manager telling the media 'We think

Carl will be bigger than Michael Jackson', the public saw Lewis as someone who was using his athletic career to land big-money endorsements and draw Hollywood's attention. That was a view not shared by his European and Japanese fans, who knew him as 'King Carl' and showered commercial endorsements on him. He continued to participate in important indoor and outdoor track meetings, consistently winning the 100 metres and the long jump. Even one of the albums he recorded sold more than half a million copies in Sweden alone!

A new rival appeared on Lewis's horizon in 1985 in the muscular shape of Canadian sprinter Ben Johnson, who not only began to beat Lewis consistently over 100 metres but took gold in the 1987 World Championship at Rome in a scarcely believable time of 9.83 seconds. Lewis entered the 1988 Olympic Games in Seoul as the underdog in the 100 metres and initially he came second to Johnson, who finished in another new world record. Johnson, however, had been so consumed with beating Lewis that he had taken large doses of illegal steroids and after he tested positive in Seoul, he was stripped of his gold medal and it was given to Lewis, who also earned a second gold for his signature event, the long jump.

At the 1991 World Championships, Lewis, then 30 years old, ancient for a sprinter, set a world record in the 100 metres with a time of 9.86 seconds, and in the long jump he leapt 8.87 metres – the best jump of his life under legal wind conditions. Unfortunately, he lost to Mike Powell, who broke Beamon's world record to end Lewis's undefeated run in the long jump; it had lasted for a decade over sixty-five successive competitions.

At the 1992 Olympic trials, he failed to make the cut for both the 100-metre and 200-metre sprints. He did qualify for the long jump and the 4 x 100-metre relay, and in Barcelona he beat Powell to earn his seventh gold medal, and then anchored the relay squad for an eighth. In August 1993, he won only one medal at the World Track and Field Championships – a bronze in the 200 metres – and many wondered if that was the end of his glittering career.

By 1996, Lewis was the grand old man of track and field – but he kept training, hoping for one more shot at the Olympics. He started weight-lifting, fine-tuned his vegetarian diet, and went to several little-known Texas meets, far from the network television cameras, to work on his sprints. He only just made the Olympic team, but at the Atlanta Games, he uncorked an 8.50 metre jump in the third round to win the gold. Twelve years on from his initial triumphs, he was treated to the kind of roar from the crowd he deserved.

Never too far from controversy, in 2003 came the revelation he had tested positive for small traces of stimulants before the 1988 Olympics. He was cleared at the time, but the news took some of the shine off his squeaky-clean image. Despite that, he remains one of the greatest athletes of all time, even if he was seen to not carry himself with the same grace Americans might have expected of him. They could not complain with his results on the track.

Diego Maradona (Argentina) 1986

Diego Maradona was more than a football hero – he was a symbol of hope to millions and became an idol thanks to his feats on the pitch. Diego Maradona was born in Lanús, Buenos Aires on 30 October 1960 and grew up in the shanty town of Villa Fiorito, which had the reputation of being the most dangerous area in the city. His father, Diego Sr, a low-paid worker in a bone-meal factory, was from Guaraní Indian stock; his mother, Dalma, known as Tota, was the descendant of poor immigrants from southern Italy. As her first son after three daughters, the young Diego was doted on by Tota and she emphasised his responsibilities as the eldest son. Put to work early, he sold small items of scrap and discarded tinfoil from cigarette packets, but it was the leather football given to him for his third birthday by his uncle Cirilo that provided his route out of poverty.

Aged 8, Maradona's prodigious skills brought him a trial with the youth team of the first division side Argentinos Juniors. When the coaches saw what he could do with the ball, they asked Maradona to give them his identification card; they simply could not believe that the boy was really that young. Once it became clear that Maradona was telling the truth, they took him on and in 1974 the side won the youth championship in Córdoba.

He made his professional debut for Argentinos Juniors in 1976, ten days before his sixteenth birthday and scored his first goal twenty-five days later to become a teenage sensation. Just a few months later, he made his debut for the Argentina national team, in a friendly against Hungary. With the World Cup due to be held in Argentina in 1978 there was high expectation that he would be included in the national squad, but the coach, César Luis Menotti, excluded him, considering him too young. Diego was devastated.

He made up for that disappointment by leading Argentina to victory in the 1979 FIFA World Youth Championship in Japan and emerged as the star of the tournament, scoring six goals in six appearances. In 1981, his time with Argentinos Juniors came to an end, after 116 goals in 166 appearances. Although River Plate offered the most money, Maradona wanted to play for

Boca Juniors, the team he supported from his childhood. His twenty-eight goals in forty appearances helped him fulfil a childhood dream as the club won the Argentina Primera División title in his first season.

At the end of that season, he took part in his first World Cup but it was not a great tournament for him. Due to internal tensions within the team and the opposing players fouling him at every opportunity, Maradona could not assert his dominance. After losing to Brazil (when Maradona received a red card after kicking a Brazilian player in the midriff) and Italy, Argentina failed to qualify for the semi-finals. However, the Spanish World Cup had proved a successful shop window and Maradona was transferred to FC Barcelona for a world record fee of £5 million.

Despite the fact that he was only 21, he failed to make the impact in La Liga many had expected. It was not entirely his fault, as on the field he was constantly fouled and his ankle was broken after a horrific tackle by Andoni Goikoetxea of Athletic Bilbao. Off the field, there were numerous disputes with club president, Josep Lluís Núñez, and after he instigated a mass brawl in front of King Juan Carlos of Spain in the 1984 Copa del Rey final after Barcelona lost to Athletic Bilbao, that was the last straw and he was promptly transferred to Napoli for another world record fee of £6.9 million.

Upon his arrival in Naples, a local newspaper noted that the city lacked schools, buses, houses, employment, and sanitation, but none of that mattered as they had Maradona. Once he saw the 75,000 Neapolitans at his presentation, Maradona decided that he would repay their love by giving it all on the pitch. In his second season, Napoli came third in Serie A and by the time the 1986 World Cup in Mexico rolled around, there was no doubt about who the world's best football player was.

This time, there was no stopping him – violent fouls or otherwise – as he was simply too fast and too powerful for everyone else. With the referees stamping down on the foul play that had been an effective method for the opponents four years earlier, he used his low centre of gravity to exert his influence against every team he faced at the tournament.

After defeating Uruguay, Argentina faced England in the quarter-finals in a match where he would cement his legend – and not necessarily for the right reasons. Six minutes into the second half, Maradona cut inside from the left and played a diagonal low pass to the edge of the area to teammate Jorge Valdano and continued his run in the hope of a one-two movement. England's Steve Hodge tried to hook the ball clear but the ball looped off his foot towards Maradona, who had continued his run. England goalkeeper

Peter Shilton came out of his goal to punch the ball clear. Maradona, despite conceding 8 inches in height, reached the ball first with his left hand. The ball bounced into the goal with referee Ali Bin Nasser of Tunisia unsighted despite England's protests. Maradona's claim after the game that the goal was 'a little with the head of Maradona and a little with the hand of God' did him no favours in the English press.

Maradona was not done. Just four minutes later he received the ball in his team's own half and then ran past five English players before slotting the ball past Shilton. He took eleven touches in a ten-second run covering 60 metres.

He followed up by scoring a brace against Belgium in the semi-finals, setting up a final against West Germany. Although the Germans managed to contain him by constantly placing two defenders on him, Maradona still decided the match by threading the ball through to Jorge Burruchaga for the winning goal. After leading his country to the title, Maradona was unanimously voted Player of the Tournament.

Following the triumphant end to the World Cup, Maradona returned to club football. In his first season back, he led Napoli to the Serie A title, as well as the Coppa Italia. That occasion marked the first time that a mainland team from the south of the country had won the league title and the following season he was Serie A's leading scorer. In 1989, Napoli won their first European trophy, the UEFA Cup, and a second league title followed in 1990.

Despite his success on the field, Maradona's personal life was beginning to get the better of him. He seemed to have connections with the Camorra crime syndicate and he had had a cocaine addiction since the mid-1980s. He also fathered a son, the result of an extramarital affair, whom he refused to acknowledge for many years.

In the Italian World Cup in 1990, troubled by an ankle injury, he was not the dominant force of four years previously, although he captained Argentina to the final. West Germany were too tough an obstacle to overcome this time. His time at Napoli came to an end in 1991 following a failed drug test for cocaine which resulted in a fifteen-month suspension until he finally accepted a detox programme and began to train again.

After the suspension, he joined Sevilla, coached by the former Argentine national coach Carlos Bilardo. Maradona would play only twenty-six matches for his new Spanish club and he was far from the success that he had been in Napoli. After a row with the coach after being substituted in a game against Burgos in June 1993, he was shown the door and returned to Argentina where he was given a lifeline by Newell's Old Boys.

At the age of 33, he made his final two international appearances in the 1994 World Cup in the US. His impressive comeback on the field was overshadowed by a positive drug test for ephedrine which saw him sent home from the tournament in disgrace. He played on for a couple of years for Boca Juniors before calling it quits in 1997.

His cocaine addiction lasted until 2004, when he also finally gave up drinking. In 2008, he was appointed coach of the Argentinian national team and kept that position until the 2010 World Cup, when he was sacked following a 4–0 defeat to Germany. Plagued by health problems later in life, he suffered a heart attack and passed away in 2020 at the age of 60. Despite his many controversies, at his peak he was undeniably one of the footballing greats.

Mike Tyson (USA) 1986–1987, 1988–1990

The youngest World Heavyweight champion in history, Mike Tyson electrified the division with a succession of sensational performances early in his career. Unfortunately, his career and life were plagued with controversy, both in and out of the ring, and he left the division as a flawed, defeated champion.

Michael Gerard Tyson was born on 30 June 1966, in Brooklyn, New York, to Lorna Tyson and Jimmy Kirkpatrick. Kirkpatrick left the family when Mike was just 2 years old, and the family struggled financially before eventually moving to Brownsville, Brooklyn, a high-crime area of the city.

Tyson was bullied as a child, and to protect himself he joined a gang called the 'Jolly Stompers', for whom he robbed shops while other gang members held the staff at gunpoint. By his thirteenth birthday, Tyson had been arrested more than thirty times for his criminal activities and he was sent to the Tryon School for Boys, where he met Bobby Stewart, a former amateur boxing champion. In exchange for Tyson's promise of good behaviour, Stewart agreed to teach the boy to box. His schoolwork improved and he excelled at the sport.

In 1979, Stewart introduced Tyson to Cus D'Amato, Floyd Patterson's former coach, who owned a gym in Catskill, New York. Tyson and D'Amato became extremely close as he coached the young boxer and, after Tyson left Tryon in 1980, D'Amato became his legal guardian. Tyson lived with D'Amato and worked on his boxing while attending Catskill High School, but two years later he was expelled from the school for disciplinary reasons; his mother died of cancer in the same year.

He continued his school studies with private tutors while he kept working on his boxing, hoping to qualify for the 1984 Olympic trials. He competed in the 1981 and 1982 Junior Olympic Games, winning the gold medal twice – and winning every bout by a knockout. Although Tyson failed to make the 1984 Olympic team, D'Amato decided that it was time for him to turn professional, despite only being 18 years old.

He made his professional debut on 6 March 1985, in a fight against Hector Mercedes in Albany, and he won by a first-round technical knockout. That

November, though, Tyson's world was rocked by the death of D'Amato, who died of pneumonia at the age of 77. Kevin Rooney, D'Amato's assistant, took over Tyson's training, and he fought less than two weeks after D'Amato's death.

By the time he was 20, Tyson had a 22–0 record, twenty-one of those fights won by knockout. A year after his mentor died, in 1986, Tyson was given the chance they both had worked for: his first championship fight, against Trevor Berbick. In just the second round of their fight at the Las Vegas Hilton on 22 November, Tyson knocked out Berbick and won the World Boxing Council heavyweight championship at just 20 years and 4 months, becoming the youngest heavyweight champion in history.

Four months later, he defended his title against James 'Bonecrusher' Smith, adding the World Boxing Association title to his resumé, and on 1 August 1987 he defeated Tony Tucker to win the International Boxing Federation heavyweight title, thereby unifying the three titles.

He successfully defended his titles three times in 1988 – against Larry Holmes, Tony Tubbs and a sensational ninety-first-second knockout of Michael Spinks. However, despite remaining undefeated, he fired his trainer Kevin Rooney and signed on with promoter Don King. He also started to make headlines out of the ring, breaking a bone in his hand after a brawl in Harlem and knocking himself unconscious after driving his BMW into a tree.

Amid this personal turmoil, he fought only two professional bouts in 1989 – defeating Britain's Frank Bruno in five rounds before knocking out Carl Williams in the first round. His winning streak came to a shocking end on 11 February 1990 in Tokyo, however, when he faced Buster Douglas. Tyson, undefeated in thirty-seven fights, was a clear favourite, and he knocked Douglas to the canvas in the eighth round. But thirty-five seconds into the tenth round, Douglas unleashed a brutal uppercut which he followed with a four-punch combination which sent Tyson to the floor for the first time in his professional career. He was counted out by referee Octavio Meyran to complete one of the most shocking upsets in all sporting history. Tyson redeemed himself with first-round wins against Henry Tillman and Alex Stewart later that year and fought two more bouts, both against Donovan 'Razor' Ruddock, before his life changed.

In 1992, Tyson was found guilty of rape and sent to prison for a six-year sentence. He served three years at the Indiana Youth Centre before his release in March 1995. His first comeback fight against Peter McNeeley grossed nearly $100 million worldwide on pay-per-view and Tyson triumphed in just eighty-nine seconds. Another straightforward victory followed against Buster

Mathis Jr before he regained his WBC title from Frank Bruno at the MGM Grand in Las Vegas in March 1996.

He reclaimed the WBA title with a first-round victory over Bruce Seldon six months later, but his first real challenge since leaving prison came later that year. In November, he faced Evander Holyfield, one of the only boxers who could claim as much fame as Tyson, for the WBA belt. Holyfield, having recently returned from retirement, was not given much of a chance in the fight, but he surprised many by defeating Tyson by knockout in the eleventh round.

Tyson accused Holyfield of numerous headbutts during the bout, which helped set the scene for a rematch six months later in a bout which set numerous records for viewers and money. Tyson received $30 million and Holyfield $35 million for the fight, the largest purse ever, and a record 1.99 million households purchased the pay-per-view showing of the fight.

The ensuing fight would become one of the most controversial events in sporting history. Tyson bit Holyfield on the ear in the third round, causing the referee to deduct him two points. When the fight resumed, Tyson repeated the act – this time severely enough to remove a piece of Holyfield's right ear. Tyson was disqualified immediately, and Holyfield was awarded the fight. The Nevada State Athletic Commission withheld $3 million from Tyson's purse and rescinded his boxing licence for more than a year.

Eighteen months later, Tyson was back in the ring, knocking out Frans Botha in the fifth round, but then came more trouble. He was convicted of punching a 62-year-old man and kicking another in the groin after a traffic accident in suburban Washington DC. He received a one-year sentence after pleading no-contest, but served only three and a half months in jail.

After his release, he won two of three of his bouts in 2000, both by knockout, before finishing with a no-contest with Andrew Golota. Despite an initial win in that bout, the result was changed after Tyson tested positive for marijuana in a post-fight urine test. Although he'd only fought once in 2001, Tyson was given the chance to fight Lennox Lewis for the World Heavyweight title in 2002. After a brawl at the press conference to publicise the fight, the Nevada State Athletic Commission refused to grant Tyson a licence and the fighters eventually met in Memphis. Lewis dominated the fight and knocked out Tyson with a right hand in the eighth round.

He would win only one more fight in his career before retiring in late 2005. He may have ended a pale shadow of the 20-year-old who burst on the scene, but his early-career combination of power and intimidation made him the sport's most bankable box-office draw.

Ben Johnson (Canada) 1987–1988

A photograph taken just after the start of the 100-metre final at Seoul shows Carl Lewis glancing across at his rival Ben Johnson clearly wondering how the Canadian had managed to storm out of the blocks quite so quickly. Soon, the rest of the world would know the answer. After sprinting to victory in 9.79 seconds, Johnson was asked which he valued more, the world record or the gold medal. 'The gold medal,' he replied, 'that's something no one can take away from you.' But take it away from him they did, along with most of his other accomplishments.

Johnson was born on 30 December 1961 in Falmouth, a port town on Jamaica's north coast. His father worked for the Jamaica Telephone Company while young Ben enjoyed an outdoor childhood which featured swimming in the sea and racing his friends barefoot. When Ben was 11, his mother travelled to visit her sister in Canada and returned to Jamaica suggesting that the family move there. It took four years for the plan to fully materialise, but in April 1976 Ben joined his mother, although they left his father – who was not a fan of the cold – behind.

In 1976, the Olympics came to Canada and the young Ben was suitably inspired by the Jamaican Don Quarrie, who won silver in the 100 metres and gold in the 200. That same year, he joined the Scarborough Optimists Track & Field Club, where he first met the man who would change his life: the coach Charlie Francis.

Francis had himself been a champion sprinter and reached the second round of the 100 metres at the 1972 Olympics in Munich. While Francis was acknowledged to be a technically brilliant coach, his detractors said he became involved with every aspect of the lives of the athletes he coached, demanding complete dependency and adherence to his word. It was in a quiet meeting in Toronto in September 1981 that Francis first brought up the subject of steroids.

He informed Johnson that steroids represented 1 per cent of performance, or the equivalent of 1 metre in the 100 metres, and he suggested that it was time to put Johnson in touch with his doctor. Johnson was aware how far ahead the drugs were of the testers and despite improving his career-best to an impressive 10.25 seconds in 1981, he informed Francis that he wanted that extra metre.

Johnson won his first major medal at the 1982 Commonwealth Games in Brisbane, a silver in the 100 metres, having led until 2 metres from the line before losing out to reigning Olympic champion Allan Wells. However, in the follow year's inaugural World Athletic Championships in Helsinki, he only just managed to qualify from his first-round heat, and finished sixth in his semi-final.

Francis' training techniques started to have an effect and in just a couple of years. Johnson's appearance altered from a scrawny teenager to an imposing, muscle-bound athlete who could bench-press 180kg. His performances on the track also started to improve, and he won his heat on the way to the 1984 Olympic final in Los Angeles. After false-starting at the first attempt, he made another blistering start at the second time of asking and was vying for the lead at the half-way mark, before Carl Lewis turned on the afterburners and roared past the rest of the field to leave Johnson in the bronze medal position. He added another bronze in the sprint relay which helped to convince his coach that even better returns lay ahead.

Johnson's work on and off the track – with the help of another Caribbean expat, Dr Jamie Astaphan – was bearing fruit. Having moved from human growth hormone on to injectable anabolic steroids, Johnson began to challenge Lewis for supremacy and finally defeated his rival – at the ninth time of asking – at the 1985 Weltklasse meeting in Zurich. However, the biggest news for Johnson came at the end of the season, when Astaphan informed him that he had discovered a new, undetectable steroid.

Johnson's 1986 season started superbly with a new 60-metre indoor world record, and he set the inaugural Goodwill Games alight in Moscow with a winning time of 9.95 seconds, the fastest ever recorded at sea-level. He went on to triumph at the Commonwealth Games in Edinburgh and defeated Lewis again in Zurich to end the American's five-year grip on the top-ranked position in *Track & Field News*' world rankings for the 100 metres.

The scene was set for the rivalry to increase at the World Athletics Championships at Rome in 1987 and media scrutiny was intense. Johnson had lowered his 60-metre world record to 6.41 seconds earlier in the year and arrived in Italy as undeniably the world's fastest man. They lined up next to each other in the final on 30 August and flash bulbs lit up the night sky as the gun sounded. And as the gun sounded, Johnson already seemed to be ahead of the field. His reaction time of 0.129 seconds enabled him to be a metre ahead after just 20 metres and he led all the way from gun to tape as he crossed the line in 9.83 seconds, a new world record by a tenth of a second.

The world was stunned, as was Carl Lewis, who three days after the final stated that he could not believe that certain performances would be possible without the use of performance-enhancing drugs. Most people dismissed the comments as sour grapes and the pair spent most of the rest of the season avoiding each other both on the track and off it.

The Rome victory elevated Johnson into the stratosphere in terms of earning potential. He bought himself a new Ferrari and started building a new home, but his 1988 season started with a spate of injuries, culminating in a torn hamstring just four months before the Seoul Olympics. There was also a much-publicised falling-out with Charlie Francis before Johnson headed off to the Caribbean to treat his injury under the care of Dr Astaphan.

The pair had put their differences behind them by the time the Canadian trials took place in early August, and Johnson qualified easily, reassuring the world's media that the rematch with Lewis in Korea was back on track. Despite losing to Lewis in Zurich, he still clocked 10.00 seconds and passed his nineteenth drugs test in two years. Even so, Dr Astaphan gave Johnson an additional injection in an attempt to remove the drugs from his body shortly before he arrived in Seoul.

A media frenzy surrounded the rivals once they reached the South Korean capital, with Lewis the clear favourite. He appeared to be an even hotter favourite as Johnson slowed up in the first quarter-final to finish third and miss out on automatic qualification. He suffered an anxious wait for the remaining five races to finish before his place in the semi-finals was confirmed. He made no such mistake in his semi, winning in 10.03 seconds to progress to his second straight Olympic final.

At nearly 1.30 p.m. on Saturday, 24 September 1988 the scene was set for the greatest 100-metre race in history. The starter's gun exploded, and Ben Johnson burst out of the blocks. His reaction time was remarkably similar to the previous year in Rome, and after just 20 metres, Lewis took his first, incredulous glance to his right. Having seemingly not learned his lesson from the quarter-final, Johnson slowed up in the final 20 metres, lifting his finger skywards as he crossed the line in 9.79 seconds. Lewis also recorded a personal best of 9.92 seconds, but he finished trailing in Johnson's wake. After the subsequent medal presentation, Johnson headed to the doping control centre before facing the awaiting media. In the meantime, his urine samples were sent to the laboratory for analysis.

In the laboratory, one of the samples tested showed significant amounts of the anabolic steroid Stanozolol, but it was only when the code on the bottle was matched to the master list that the sample was discovered to have been Johnson's. Johnson denied everything, but when the 'B' sample also tested positive 'the writing was on the wall' and the press smelled a huge story about to erupt. At 9 a.m. on 27 September, Michèle Verdier read the IOC's official statement which confirmed the positive test and the reallocation of the gold medal to Carl Lewis; by that time Ben Johnson was already on his way out of Seoul to face embarrassment from his home country – just days after adulation.

Eventually, Johnson came clean in front of the Canadian 1989 Dubin Inquiry into drug use in sport. Later that year, the IAAF voted to decertify an athlete's records, titles and results if he or she later is shown to have used a banned substance before those performances. All of Johnson's results between 1983 and 1989 were removed, stripping him of his world records of 9.83 in the 100 metres and 6.41 in the indoor 60 metres.

He completed his two-year ban and even competed at the 1992 Barcelona Olympics, but his comeback stalled after he failed a second drugs test in 1993 and was banned for life. He worked as a personal trainer in Libya for Colonel Gaddafi's son Saadi; he even had a brief acting career and continues to coach to this day. He may now be best remembered for having been caught up in the biggest Olympics drugs scandal of all time, but for twelve months Ben Johnson was not just the fastest man on earth, but the fastest man there had ever been.

Steffi Graf (Germany) 1988

With twenty-two Grand Slam singles titles and the only player to win the 'Golden Grand Slam', capturing all four Majors and an Olympic gold medal in the same year, Steffi Graf was one of the greatest women's tennis players in history. Furthermore, she is the only player – male or female – to have won each of the Grand Slam tournaments at least four times.

Stefanie Maria Graf was born on 14 June 1969 in Mannheim, West Germany. Her father Peter, a car and insurance salesman, was an aspiring tennis coach who began teaching her to swing a racquet in the family's living room. She graduated to playing on proper courts at the age of 5 and won a junior event at Munich when she was 6.

Two years later, the family moved to Brühl, where Peter opened the Graf Tennis Club and began to coach his daughter on a full-time basis. It soon paid off, as she won the German age-group championship every year until she was 12 years old. In 1981, she won both the German Under-14 and Under-18 titles, and with no one else to prove herself against in her age range, she turned professional at the age of 13 years 5 months in November 1982.

She had a tough time during her first two years on tour, but Peter Graf closely controlled her schedule, limiting her play so that she would not burn out like many other youngsters. In 1984, she travelled to Los Angeles where tennis was a demonstration sport at the Olympic Games. At 15 she was the youngest of the thirty-two competitors, but it mattered not as she defeated Sabrina Goleš of Yugoslavia to take home an honorary gold medal.

She started to make her presence felt in 1985, entering ten tournaments and ending the year ranked sixth in the world. In April 1986, she defeated Chris Evert in South Carolina to win her first title, and the floodgates soon opened, ending the year with seven more crowns and third place in the world rankings.

Her game was based on superb footwork backed up with a rigorous training schedule that made her strong, fast and quick. She had impeccable timing and her mental toughness gave her a crucial competitive edge. Her forehand, often played running around her backhand side remains perhaps the greatest shot in women's tennis history and gave birth to the nickname 'Fraulein Forehand'.

She captured her first Grand Slam title at the 1987 French Open, when she defeated Martina Navratilova in three sets. Navratilova returned the favour in both the Wimbledon and US Open finals, but they were to be Graf's only two defeats in a year in which she won eleven of the thirteen tournaments she entered. But however good 1987 had been, the following year was to prove even better.

She started by beating Chris Evert 6–1, 7–6 in the Australian Open final. In Paris, she took just thirty-two minutes to embarrass Natalia Zvereva in the French Open final 6–0, 6–0. Next up was the grass at Wimbledon, where Graf had struggled in her earlier years and where Navratilova had won six straight titles. This time, Graf came through 5–7, 6–2, 6–1 with her opponent admitting she had lost to the better player. Graf completed the Slam by beating Gabriela Sabatini 6–3, 3–6, 6–1 in the US Open final. A month later she travelled to Seoul and defeated Sabatini again to win the gold medal and complete a unique 'Golden Slam'.

Graf successfully defended three of her four Grand Slam titles in 1989 and only an upset loss in the final of the French Open to Arantxa Sánchez Vicario – a match in which she led 5–3 in the final set – prevented her from completing back-to-back Grand Slams. At the Australian Open she beat Helena Suková, won a second successive Wimbledon final against Navratilova and also beat Navratilova in the US Open final.

In 1990, she won a total of ten tournaments, including repeating as Australian Open champion. She was the beaten finalist in the French and US Opens and reached the Wimbledon semi-final, where she was surprisingly beaten by Zina Garrison. She made amends the following year, winning a third title on the grass and soon afterwards became the youngest female player to complete 500 victories.

In the early 1990s, she started to suffer from injuries, requiring surgeries to her foot and knee, and also had back issues which caused her to miss three Australian Opens early in the season. There was also the rise of Monica Seles, who established herself as the new dominant force in women's tennis and finally displaced Graf as the top-ranked player after a record 186-week reign.

Graf's second period of dominance started in 1993 but not in the way she would have liked. During a quarter-final match between Seles and Magdalena Maleeva in Hamburg on 30 April, Seles was stabbed between the shoulder blades by a mentally ill German fan of Graf. He claimed that he committed the attack to help Graf reclaim the world No. 1 ranking. It would be more than two years before Seles competed again, and Graf won the remaining three Grand Slam events of the year.

After winning the 1994 Australian Open, Graf struggled through the rest of the year, losing to Mary Pierce in the French Open semi-finals before a stunning first-round defeat to Lori McNeil at Wimbledon. A bone spur in her back hampered her US Open, but she still made the final before losing to Sánchez Vicario.

She won all three of the Majors in which she competed in both 1995 and 1996, missing the Australian Open both years with a strained right calf and bone splinters in her left foot respectively. Those would prove to be her last great years as she injured her knee in Tokyo and twice had surgery. The year 1997 was the first since 1986 in which she failed to win a Grand Slam title and another rising star – this time Martina Hingis – took her place as the number one ranked player in the world.

Her playing career also included seven years on the German Federation Cup team, in which she won twenty of her twenty-two matches and led the team to the championship in 1987 and 1992. Although doubles was far from her speciality, she teamed up with Sabatini to win the 1988 Wimbledon Ladies' Doubles title.

There was time for one more glorious last hurrah. Having battled through her injuries, she closed out her career in 1999 by winning the French Open at the age of 30, beating Hingis in three sets. Her final appearance in a Major tournament came at Wimbledon the same year, where she lost to Lindsay Davenport in the final. She retired soon afterwards, claiming that she had won everything she wanted to in tennis.

In 1991, she founded The Steffi Graf Youth Tennis Centre in Leipzig, Germany and she is also the founder and active chairperson of 'Children for Tomorrow', a non-profit foundation with the goal of implementing and developing projects to support children who have been traumatised by war or other crises. In 2001 she married fellow Grand Slam winner Andre Agassi, and both are now members of the International Tennis Hall of Fame.

Ayrton Senna (Brazil) 1990–1991

Over the course of a career which was brought to a tragically early end, Ayrton Senna was idolised like no previous racing driver. Others may have won more world titles, won more races and appeared on pole position more times, but few could match the control he had over his car, especially in the wet, and he is remembered as one of the greatest of all racing drivers.

Ayrton Senna da Silva was born on 21 March 1960 in Santana, a neighbourhood of São Paulo, the middle child of factory owner Milton da Silva and his wife Neide Senna da Silva. As a young boy, Senna was athletic, and he had developed a keen interest in cars by the time he received a go-kart with a lawnmower engine for his fourth birthday. Within three years he had learned to drive a jeep around his family's farm.

It would be another nine years, however, before he was able to take part in a professional kart race at his local Interlagos circuit, due to the minimum age restriction of 13 years. However, he soon made up for lost time, winning the South American Kart Championship in 1977. For the next five years he competed for the World Karting Championship, where he stood out from the crowd, driving in black overalls with a bright yellow helmet with a blue and green stripe – his adaptation of the Brazilian flag. He finished in second place behind Peter Koene and Peter de Bruijn in 1979 and 1980 respectively, but it was his teammate Terry Fullerton whom he later identified as the greatest rival of his racing career.

Although his father remained unconvinced by his son's racing abilities, he backed him financially and the young Ayrton moved to England where he won twelve races to claim the 1981 Formula Ford 1600 Championships for the Van Diemen team. Senna then returned to Brazil to see his family rather than race in the Formula Ford Festival, despite being the overwhelming favourite for the end-of-season event at Brands Hatch.

His parents wanted him to give up racing and work in the family business, but Senna had already been offered the chance to race in Formula Ford 2000 in the 1982 season for £10,000. He went on to dominate both the EFDA Euroseries and Pace British championships from the opening weekends – winning twenty-two times to clinch both titles with time to spare. He also had time to make his Formula Three debut in the end-of-season non-championship race at Thruxton – qualifying West Surrey Racing's Ralt RT3-Toyota on pole position and leading all the way in front of the BBC television cameras.

He remained with West Surrey Racing for the 1983 British Formula Three Championship and began the season by winning the first nine races. However, Senna proved himself fallible as Martin Brundle grew increasingly competitive and at Silverstone Senna crashed while chasing the Englishman's leading car. They crashed together at Snetterton and Oulton Park as Senna's points lead evaporated. A couple of retirements handed Brundle a slim championship lead, but Senna won the final race at Thruxton to secure a deserved title, which really put him on the map.

Senna's first taste of Formula One would be at the wheel of a Williams, and it happened by accident. Senna sat next to Frank Williams on a flight to Zandvoort to attend a 1982 Formula Ford 2000 race. Senna then proceeded to pester Williams and Patrick Head for almost a year until they finally relented and agreed to a test session at Donington. He drove just twenty laps, but by the tenth lap had bettered the time of the young Williams' protégé Jonathan Palmer by almost 1.5 seconds.

Further tests with top teams followed before he signed a three-year contract with Toleman. He finished sixth in South Africa, but it was at Monaco where he gave notice of his superb driving skills in wet conditions. He was closing on Alain Prost's leading McLaren before the race was halted early. He then finished third in the British and Portuguese Grands Prix during an impressive maiden campaign, although he was dropped for the Italian Grand Prix when he announced that he would be reneging on his Toleman contract and would move to John Player Team Lotus for the 1985 F1 World Championship.

His decision was justified within two races when his car dominated the wet Portuguese Grand Prix as he scored his breakthrough victory. Seven pole positions were more than any other driver that year but poor reliability initially hindered his cause. However, five podium finishes in a row included another victory at Spa-Francorchamps and helped Senna to fourth in the final championship standings.

It was a similar story in 1986 with Senna again dominant in qualifying with eight poles. He beat Nigel Mansell's Williams by just 0.014 seconds in the Spanish Grand Prix at Jerez and assumed the points lead with victory on the streets of Detroit. However, mechanical failures restricted Senna to fourth overall once more. Lotus switched to Honda engines in 1987 with the team experimenting with computer-controlled suspension. Senna and Mansell clashed during the Belgian Grand Prix before the former won back-to-back street races in Monaco and Detroit to finish third in the final standings.

Senna defected to McLaren for the 1988 season with Honda replacing Porsche as engine supplier. Teamed with Prost for the first time, they dominated proceedings like no combination had done previously. Their cars won fifteen of the sixteen races, only losing the Italian Grand Prix when Senna collided with Jean-Louis Schlesser's Williams-Judd while lapping the French debutant. On pole position for thirteen races that year, Senna won eight times and clinched the World Championship for the first time after a dramatic comeback drive in the Japanese Grand Prix at Suzuka. Only fourteenth after a poor start, Senna drove back through the field to claim a famous victory and the title itself.

The McLarens were not as dominant in 1989, but Senna still won six races. However, mechanical failures meant that Prost was ahead in the points as they headed to Suzuka for the penultimate race of the year. In need of victory to keep his title hopes alive, Senna attempted to pass the Frenchman with seven laps to go. The two cars collided and appeared out of the race. Senna resumed, however, and overtook Alessandro Nannini's Benetton to win the race. Ironically, Senna was disqualified for not re-joining the track at the point he had left it – which handed the World Championship to Prost.

Prost moved to Ferrari rather than remain as Senna's teammate, but the 1990 World Championship was once more between the two rivals. They arrived in Japan with roles reversed – Prost needing to win to prevent Senna from regaining the championship. Senna qualified on pole position but when the race started, the second-placed Prost made the better start. Senna was having none of it though – he kept his foot on the throttle all the way into turn 1 and when Prost turned in on his normal line, the two collided. Both were instantly out of the race and Senna was champion once more.

Four consecutive victories at the start of 1991 included an emotional first win in his home race but Williams-Renault and Nigel Mansell grew ever-more competitive as they improved their car. The Williams was also more technologically sophisticated, but teething troubles with the semi-automatic gearbox saw Mansell score zero points in the first three races. Senna eventually won three more times and clinched his third title when Mansell spun off in Japan.

With his car now fully sorted, Mansell dominated the 1992 World Championship. In contrast, Senna was restricted to three victories and fourth overall. The following year, Prost returned from a year away to lead the Williams-Renault line-up, Mansell having defected to drive Indy Cars in America. Senna won in Brazil and, famously, at Donington Park to take an early championship lead. He won the Monaco Grand Prix for a sixth time and the final two races of the year but could only finish as runner-up behind Prost's technically superior Williams-Renault.

Having tested for Williams a decade earlier, Senna now signed for them for a reported $20 million – prompting Prost into permanent retirement. Overwhelming pre-season favourite for the 1994 title, Senna initially struggled and he was outpaced by Michael Schumacher's Benetton-Ford in the early races. He spun out of the opening two races and arrived at the San Marino Grand Prix at Imola without a point to his name.

Senna qualified on pole position but a serious accident to Rubens Barrichello and the death of Roland Ratzenberger meant there was a dark cloud looming over the race even before it had even started. Senna was leading Schumacher when he crashed at 190mph at the Tamburello corner at the start of lap six. Part of the suspension struck Senna's helmet and he was airlifted to the Maggiore Hospital in Bologna with serious head injuries, only to be pronounced dead later that afternoon.

Motor sport had lost one of its greatest drivers at the peak of his powers and Brazil declared three days of national mourning. Disliked and admired in equal quantities, there was no denying that he was one of the – if not *the* – greatest motor racers of his generation.

Michael Jordan (USA) 1991–1993

Arguably the greatest player in NBA history, Michael Jordan transcended sport in a way few athletes could, combining his ability to perform aerobatics on the court with inspiring an entire range of athletic shoes, which are still top-sellers to this day.

Michael Jordan was born on 17 February 1963 in Brooklyn. His parents, James Jordan and Deloris Peoples, grew up on eastern North Carolina farms and met after a basketball game in 1956. In 1970, the Jordans obtained better jobs in Wilmington, North Carolina, near where James had grown up. The young Michael shared a special bond with his father, which included baseball being both of their first loves. However, following in the footsteps of his older brother Larry, Michael began to play basketball and their father accommodated their love by building them a full-size court at their home.

He attended Laney High school in Wilmington, but as a sophomore, he failed to make the basketball team. However, after growing 4 inches in a year and improving his skills he was able to play alongside his brother. His talent attracted the University of North Carolina, and he spent his freshman year mainly playing in the shadow of James Worthy and Sam Perkins. He shone in the spotlight of the College Championship game against Georgetown, however, and scored sixteen points, including the winning basket with eighteen seconds left in the game, to give his team a 63–62 victory. His college career continued to go from strength to strength; he was named 'College Player of the Year' after his sophomore year and as a junior he won the award again.

The 1984 NBA draft was one of the greatest ever, with four future Hall of Famers drafted within the first sixteen picks. The Houston Rockets selected Hakeem Olajuwon with the first pick, which most expected. The Portland Trail Blazers, however, with the second overall pick chose Sam Bowie from Kentucky, which came as a surprise. Not quite believing their luck, the Chicago Bulls selected Jordan third overall, and a love affair began.

In 1984, the penultimate time an amateur US team travelled to the Olympic Games to play basketball, Jordan was part of that Los Angeles gold-winning squad. He carried that form into a fabulous first season, earning the NBA Rookie of the Year Award after averaging more than twenty-eight points per game. The Bulls won eleven more games than in the season prior to his arrival and made it to the playoffs, where they lost to the Milwaukee Bucks.

The Bulls' crowds swelled both at home and on the road and Jordan's own personal style became as notable as his basketball skills. He signed a major shoe deal with Nike which propelled him to superstardom as demand for the Air Jordan line was unprecedented. He also wore his North Carolina shorts under his Bulls outfit, starting the trend towards baggy shorts across the entire sport.

Three games into his second season, he broke a bone in his left foot. He was voted on to the All-Star team but could not play. However, he returned late in the year to score an NBA play-off-record sixty-three points in a first-round game against the Celtics. The 1986/87 season was the first of seven consecutive seasons in which he led the league in scoring.

That off-season, the Bulls began assembling a potential championship team by drafting power forward Horace Grant and acquiring the versatile small forward Scottie Pippen from tiny Central Arkansas in a draft day trade with the Seattle SuperSonics. In 1987/88, Jordan won every major award including MVP (Most Valuable Player), Defensive Player of the Year and All-Star MVP. He also helped the Bulls to a first-round play-off win over the Cleveland Cavaliers before falling to the Detroit Pistons in five games in the conference semi-finals.

In 1989, the Bulls hired Phil Jackson as their head coach, who instituted the 'triangle offense' – a fluid passing system that created opportunities for all five players on the floor to score. The Bulls went 55–27 that season, their best record since 1971/72, but again fell short against the Pistons who defeated them in a tough seven-game series. Those who doubted Jordan could ever lead his team to a title would be silenced the following season.

Jordan led the Bulls as the team lost only two post-season games on the way to the franchise's first NBA title. After losing the first game at home to the Los Angeles Lakers in the NBA finals, the Bulls won four straight games with Jordan earning the first of six NBA finals' MVP awards. The Bulls would go on to successfully defend their title in each of the next two seasons, defeating the Blazers and the Suns in six games.

Jordan was the key figure in forming the Dream Team that competed in the 1992 Olympics in Barcelona. The squad were treated like basketball royalty by their opponents, whom they outclassed on the way to the gold medal.

By the end of that three-year run, Jordan had achieved folk-hero status. However, he was rocked by the murder of his father in July 1993 during an armed robbery. Emotionally drained, Jordan stunned the basketball world by announcing his retirement. Attempting to fulfil a dream inspired by his father, the younger Jordan set his sights on Major League Baseball. He spent the 1994 baseball season playing for the Birmingham Barons, an affiliate of the Chicago White Sox in the Class AA Southern League.

He was a competent if unspectacular performer, but any hopes he had of reaching the Major Leagues appeared dim, and with baseball stuck in a labour dispute, he decided to focus on returning to the NBA. Late in the 1994/95 NBA season, he came out of retirement with the two-word press release which said simply: 'I'm Back.' However, despite Jordan's presence in the line-up in the playoffs, the Bulls didn't have quite enough to get past Shaquille O'Neal's Orlando Magic in the conference semi-finals.

Jordan didn't have long to wait to rekindle the championship fire, this time with almost an entirely new band of players, with just Pippen remaining from the first three championship-winning teams. The Bulls added Dennis Rodman, an unpredictable player but a rebounding and defensive phenomenon and the team went on to enjoy one of the most remarkable years ever posted by any club. The Bulls won a record seventy-two victories during the regular season, then stormed through the playoffs ending in a six-game finals win over the Sonics.

In the 1996/97 season, the Bulls again advanced to the finals, where they faced the Utah Jazz, which included Karl Malone, who had beaten Jordan for the NBA MVP award. Determined to show who was the true MVP, Jordan won Game 1 for the Bulls with a buzzer-beating jump shot and in Game 5, with the series tied at 2-2, Jordan played despite being feverish and dehydrated from a stomach virus. He scored thirty-eight points, including the game-deciding 3-pointer with just twenty-five seconds remaining, and the Bulls won the series in six games to retain their title.

The Bulls faced the Jazz again in the finals the following year, and Jordan's performance solidified his exalted status in sport. With the Bulls trailing by a point in Game 6 with seconds to go and the ball in Malone's hands, the Bulls appeared to be doomed. However, Jordan stripped Malone of the ball before calmly making the climactic shot of his Bulls' career, giving Chicago an 87–86 victory, and with it a second "three-peat" in the decade. He ended up with forty-five points in the game – which still has the highest television rating of any NBA game in history – and promptly retired again.

Unable to stay out of basketball for long, Jordan became president of the Washington Wizards in January 2000, but the team struggled and in 2001 he again shocked the basketball world by announcing he would play for the team himself. After a difficult start, Jordan managed to guide the team back to respectability and in 2003, at the age of 40, he scored forty-three points against the New Jersey Nets. He retired for good at the end of the season, widely regarded as the finest – and probably the most-recognised – basketball player ever.

Pete Sampras (USA) 1993–1996

Few players have dominated a tournament in the way that Pete Sampras swept all before him at Wimbledon in the 1990s. He was far from just a one-trick pony, as it was he who first bettered Roy Emerson's haul of twelve Grand Slam titles which had stood for more than thirty years.

Pete Sampras was born on 12 August 1971 in Potomac, Maryland, the third of four children to Sam and Georgia. Sam was of Greek extraction and worked as a mechanical engineer for the Defense Department as well as part-owning a local restaurant and delicatessen. Young Pete found a tennis racquet in the house when he was just 3 years old and started hitting a ball against anything that was solid enough to bounce it back.

At the age of 7, the family moved with Sam's work to Los Angeles, which also had the additional advantage of being the focal point for tennis in the US. They settled in Palos Verdes, where they discovered the Jack Kramer Tennis Club, which had helped to develop many fine players, such as Tracey Austin. Pete started lessons with Robert Lansdorp and also met Peter Fischer – a friend of his father's – who was to become his first full-time coach.

At the age of 14, Sampras took Fischer's advice and switched from a two-handed to one-handed backhand. He also changed his style from a defensive baseliner to a serve-and-volleyer. Fischer told him that these changes would one day help him to win Wimbledon and the US Open. Sampras was part of a thriving junior scene in California which also featured Michael Chang and Jeff Tarango and, despite the fact that he was not winning national titles, he was still a target for recruitment for UCLA. However, he decided to turn professional at the age of 16, following his junior year in high school and by the end of the year he stood at No. 97 in the world rankings, which he improved to No, 61 by the end of 1989.

Sampras' breakthrough year was 1990. He defeated world number eight Tim Mayotte at the Australian Open and John McEnroe at the Canadian Open. He also won his first professional tournament at the Indoor Championships at Philadelphia, which propelled him into the top twenty in the world for the first time. Entering the US Open as the twelfth seed, he stunned Ivan Lendl, McEnroe and Andre Agassi in the final three rounds, to become the youngest man to win the title.

Perhaps understandably, the following year was to prove an anti-climax, with defeat in the quarter-finals of the US Open to Jim Courier, after which he claimed that he was more relieved than disappointed and felt a huge weight had been lifted from his shoulders. He bounced back in 1992, winning five tournaments and helping the US win the Davis Cup. However, it was defeat to Stefan Edberg in the US Open final that year that proved to Sampras how much he wanted to win.

New coach Tim Gullikson showed Sampras the value of playing percentage tennis – going for smart, makable shots rather than flashy, difficult ones. In April 1993, Sampras reached the number one ranking for the first time. He won eight tournaments that year, including his first Wimbledon – over Jim Courier in the final – and second US Open. When he won the 1994 Australian Open, he became the first player since Rod Laver in 1969 to win three consecutive Grand Slam titles. After losing at the French Open on his least favourite surface of clay, he quickly made amends by defeating Goran Ivanisevic to win his second Wimbledon.

In 1995, a year that was to prove an emotional roller-coaster for Sampras, his coach and long-term friend Tim Gullikson collapsed during the Australian Open and was forced to return home. Soon after Sampras lost in the final to Agassi, Gullikson was diagnosed with brain cancer, and Paul Annacone took over as Sampras' full-time coach. Sampras did not let his visible upset affect him on the court as he became the first American to win three consecutive Wimbledon titles; he also regained his US Open title. He ended 1995 by accounting for all three points as the US defeated Russia in the Davis Cup final.

Gullikson died on 3 May 1996 and Sampras failed to reach the final in any of the first three Grand Slam tournaments that year, including defeat in the Wimbledon quarter-finals to eventual champion Richard Krajicek. That would be his only defeat on the grass of SW19 between 1993 and 2000. He did manage to retain his US Open title, recovering from dehydration, against Alex Corretja in a four-hour and nine-minute quarter-final before victory over old rival Michael Chang in the final.

Sampras won his second Australian Open title in 1997, defeating Carlos Moya in the final, and he rekindled his love affair with Wimbledon, defeating Cédric Pioline in the final. He was to win three more Wimbledon crowns in the next three years, with his straight-sets defeat of Agassi in the 1999 final often held to be his finest achievement, coming as it did with him suffering from back pain, which was later diagnosed as a herniated disc. That injury forced him to withdraw from the US Open and also cost him the number one position in the rankings.

His rivalry with Agassi would continue in 2000, losing to his American compatriot in the semi-finals of the Australian Open, before Sampras defeated Pat Rafter in four sets in the Wimbledon final to tie Willie Renshaw's then-record of seven Wimbledon titles set in the 1880s. That victory was also a thirteenth Grand Slam title, which bettered Ken Rosewall's previous record. However, after Wimbledon, Sampras didn't win any of his next thirty-three tournaments, covering twenty-six months, and many considered him a spent force.

The following year at Wimbledon, Sampras was drawn against 19-year-old Swiss player Roger Federer in the fourth round. In what can now be viewed as a symbolic passing of the baton, Federer emerged victorious in five sets. Eight years later it would be Federer who overtook Sampras' then-record number of Grand Slam titles.

Sampras continued to play on the tour for the rest of 2001 and in 2002 but was increasingly troubled by injuries. He lost in the second round of Wimbledon in 2002 to George Bastl of Switzerland. He continued to struggle throughout the summer, losing at Cincinnati to No. 70-ranked Wayne Arthurs in the second round, and then was beaten in the first round at Long Island by Paul-Henri Mathieu.

Seeded seventeenth for the US Open, and supposedly 'a step and a half slower' – according to Greg Rusedski – Sampras defeated Andy Roddick in the quarter-finals and Sjeng Schalken in the semi-finals to reach his eighth US Open final overall. This time he met Agassi again and after a captivating, four-set battle, Sampras claimed the title – his fourteenth and final Grand Slam victory, and also matched Jimmy Connors' Open Era record of five US Open singles championships.

Sampras was expected to announce his retirement following his victory, thereby enabling him to leave the game on top, but it was not until the following year that he did so, on the first night of the 2003 US Open. The trio of Federer, Rafael Nadal and Novak Djokovic may have surpassed his tally of Grand Slam titles, but to many, Pete Sampras remains the greatest serve-and-volleyer of all time.

Ronaldo (Brazil) 1996–1999

The 'original' Ronaldo burst upon the scene in the mid-1990s as one of football's most talented players, combining child-like enthusiasm with strength, speed and skill. His play continues to influence strikers to this day, and he remains the second-highest scorer of all time in FIFA World Cup tournaments.

Ronaldo Luís Nazário de Lima was born on 18 September 1976 in Rio de Janeiro, Brazil. Named after the doctor who delivered him, he was the third child of Nélio Nazário de Lima, Snr and Sônia dos Santos Barata. His father was an alcoholic and his parents separated when Ronaldo was just 11 years old, by which time he had already started kicking a ball around Bento Ribeiro – the poor suburb of Rio in which he lived.

He started playing futsal (a form of football) as a junior for the local Social Ramos Club, and scored 166 goals in the indoor league in his first season when he was just 12. The smaller ball and playing area helped him improve his close control and within two years he had left home and started playing for the São Cristóvão youth team, having been spotted by former Brazilian World Cup star Jairzinho. He had hoped to play for Flamengo, but he could not afford the bus fare to the practice.

He progressed rapidly at São Cristóvão, where it was apparent that he was a childhood prodigy, comfortably playing at Under-20 level when just 15 years old. Understandably attracting attention from larger clubs, he was sold for $50,000 to Jairzinho's former club Cruzeiro, based in the city of Belo Horizonte.

An instant hit at Cruzeiro, he scored fifty-eight goals in sixty games for the club, and helped them win the Copa do Brasil in 1993 and the Minas Gerais State Championship the following year. At the age of just 17, he made his international debut for Brazil against Argentina, and his first goal for the national team came in a May 1994 victory over Iceland. He was the youngest member of the World Cup squad that year in the US, but spent the entire tournament on the bench as Brazil emerged as champions. Despite not featuring on the pitch, he attracted the attention of several European clubs, and he signed for PSV Eindhoven in the Netherlands, on the advice of his teammate Romário, who had played for the Dutch club with great distinction.

He continued his goal-scoring feats in Eindhoven, notching up thirty league goals in his first season to lead the Eredivisie, and added a hat-trick in the 1994/95 UEFA Cup against Bayer Leverkeusen. At the age of just 18 he already looked like a complete player, and he added nineteen goals in twenty-one games in a second season in which he was troubled by a knee injury. His quality of play attracted the attention of both Inter Milan and Barcelona, and it was to the latter that he moved for a world record fee of $19.5 million, having just helped PSV win the Dutch Cup.

After helping Brazil win the bronze medal at the 1996 Atlanta Olympics, Ronaldo made himself at home with his new club. Few players could have ever had a better first year with a club, as he led all European goal-scorers with thirty-four goals and helped the team win the 1997 European Cup Winners Cup, scoring the only goal in the victory over Paris Saint-Germain at Rotterdam. However, despite having been named World Footballer of the Year, that was to be his only season with the Catalan giants, as contract negotiations broke down, and Inter Milan signed him for another world record fee – this time $27 million.

He adjusted well to life in Serie A, ending as the league's top scorer in his first season with twenty-five goals in thirty-two matches to earn the nickname 'Il Fenomino' – the phenomenon – from Inter's fans. He won a second European title in two years as Inter defeated Lazio 3–0 in the UEFA Cup Final at Parc des Princes in Paris, scoring the final goal. As the world gathered for the 1998 World Cup in France, he was already acclaimed as the greatest player in the world at the tender age of 21.

It all started so well for him and the Brazilian team too, as Ronaldo contributed four goals and three assists as the defending champions progressed to the final. He scored in the 3–0 win against Morocco, twice more against Chile and scored Brazil's only goal in their 1–1 semi-final draw with the Netherlands, as well as netting his spot kick in the subsequent penalty shoot-out. However, come the final against the hosts, something went terribly wrong.

Just hours before the final, Ronaldo suffered convulsions and was rushed to a Paris hospital. He was evaluated, released and arrived just before the start of the game. The Brazilian team sheet was submitted to FIFA showing Edmundo as his replacement up front, and the news was soon broken to a stunned world media amid chaotic scenes. However, Ronaldo pleaded his case to Brazilian coach Mário Zagallo, stating that he felt fine, and he was duly reinstated to the starting line-up. The damage had been done though, and Ronaldo was ineffective as France won the match 3–0. Conspiracy theories abounded over what had caused the problem, and many thought it was a reaction to the intense emotional pressure of his situation, combined with physical exhaustion and a possible reaction to his pain medication. It remains one of the great sporting mysteries.

He returned to Inter and scored fifteen goals in all competitions in the 1998/99 season and was named club captain going into the following season. However, playing against Lecce on 21 November 1999, Ronaldo limped off the field with a knee injury. It was confirmed that he had ruptured a tendon in his knee and would require surgery. When he returned to the team five months later, he lasted only six minutes before rupturing his kneecap tendons. That injury ruled him out of the entire 2000/01 season, most of the following season, and all of Brazil's qualification campaign for the 2002 World Cup – for which they were fortunate to qualify having lost six of their eighteen qualifying matches.

When he finally returned, he was forced to adjust from relying on his earlier athletic flair to combining skill with opportunistic guile. Once he returned to the line-up for the tournament in South Korea and Japan, Brazil were a different team. He scored against every opponent in the competition, except England in the quarter-finals. He scored the winning goal in the semi-final against Turkey and both Brazil's goals in the 2–0 final victory against Germany. Ronaldo was able to celebrate with both Brazil's fifth World Cup win and the Golden Boot as the tournament's top scorer with eight goals. It was a remarkable comeback and granted him some redemption for the shambolic way his 1998 tournament had ended. He was subsequently named FIFA World Player of the Year for the third time.

That same year, Ronaldo signed for Real Madrid as part of the Galácticos, which also included Zinedine Zidane, Luís Figo, Roberto Carlos and David Beckham. Although older and slower than in his earlier career, he scored within a minute of making his debut and ended his first league campaign with the Spanish giants with twenty-three goals and a league winners' medal. He also scored a memorable Champions League hat-trick against Manchester United at Old Trafford, but injury kept him out of the defeat in the semi-finals to Juventus.

He scored consistently in the 2003/04 and 2004/05 seasons, but Real Madrid failed to win the league. He added a further fourteen goals the following year and, despite Brazil winning their first two games at the 2006 World Cup against Croatia and Australia, Ronaldo appeared overweight and much slower than he had been in the past. Coach Carlos Alberto Parreira kept him in the starting line-up and was rewarded with two goals against Japan, before scoring a record-breaking fifteenth World Cup goal against Ghana, breaking Gerd Müller's record.

Brazil were defeated by France in the World Cup quarter-finals and, once back in Milan, injuries started to catch up with Ronaldo again and manager Fabio Capello also preferred new signing Ruud van Nistelrooy up front. The writing was on the wall, and in January 2007 he signed for AC Milan, and scored seven goals in fourteen games before the end of the season.

Due to recurring injuries, Ronaldo only played 300 minutes in the 2007/08 season and his only goals came in a 5–2 victory against Napoli at the San Siro. On 13 February 2008, he jumped for a cross against Livorno and had to be stretchered off with another ruptured kneecap – this time his left knee. He was released by Milan at the end of the season, as his contract expired and was not renewed, and returned home to Brazil.

After recovering from his injury, he signed for Corinthians and helped them win the Campeonato Paulista in São Paulo with eleven goals in fourteen games. He also scored as his side won the 2009 Copa do Brasil. That proved to be his last hurrah on the pitch, as he retired in February 2011 admitting defeat to his long line of injuries.

Tiger Woods (USA) 1999–2002

Such was his dominance over his competitors, Tiger Woods can lay claim to being the greatest player ever to pick up a club. He may still trail Jack Nicklaus in terms of Major wins, but he has completely transformed the sport since he turned professional in 1996.

Eldrick Woods was born on 30 December 1975, in Cypress, California, the only child of Earl and Kultida Woods. His parents had met in Bangkok where Lieutenant Earl had been stationed. A few months before Earl left the army in 1974 another officer introduced him to golf, and he continued to practise his game after taking a job with McDonnell Douglas in California. His son's nickname 'Tiger' came from Earl's wartime friendship with Lieutenant Colonel Vuong Dang 'Tiger' Phong, an officer who served in the army of the Republic of Vietnam.

The young boy's talent was spotted at an unusually early age, and he possessed not only exceptional playing abilities but also a passion for the sport. Young Tiger first gained national attention on a talk show at the age of 3 when he beat the famed comedian and avid golfer Bob Hope in a putting contest. Woods was quickly hailed as a prodigy, and when he was 5 years old, he was featured on the television show 'That's Incredible!'

Earl was single-minded in devoting his energies to developing his son's talent and to furthering the boy's career as a golfer. During practice sessions, Tiger learned to maintain his composure and to hold his concentration while his father made loud noises in an attempt to distract him. At the same time, his mother passed on to her son the ideals of Buddhism. His father had playing privileges at the navy's golf course beside the Joint Forces Training Base in Los Alamitos, and Tiger also played at the Heartwell golf course in Long Beach.

In 1984, at the age of 8, he won the Under-10 boys' event at the Junior World Golf Championships and went on to win six Junior World Golf titles. As a 15-year-old student at Western High School in Anaheim, he became the youngest US Junior Amateur champion in 1991 and defended his title the following two years. In 1994, he won the US Amateur title and entered Stanford University on a full golf scholarship.

During Woods' first year of college, he won the US Amateur title and qualified to play in the Masters tournament in Augusta, Georgia, in the spring of 1995. By 1996, Woods had won three US Amateur titles in succession, and in August 1996 he decided to quit college in order to play professional golf. There were only seven events left in 1996 for him to finish among the top 125 money winners and earn a player's card for the PGA Tour for the following year. However, he won the Las Vegas Invitational and the Walt Disney World/Oldsmobile Classic and ended among the top thirty money winners.

In April 1997, only eight months into Woods' professional career, he participated in the Masters tournament at Augusta National for the third time. By the time the tournament was completed, Woods had made history as the youngest person ever to win the Masters title. His score was an unprecedented 270 strokes and his victory margin of 12 strokes set another record. He also became the first man of colour ever to win the title and he gave tribute to the African American golfers who came before him and helped pave the way for his success. On 15 June, after just forty-two weeks as a professional, he became the youngest ever player to be ranked number one in the world, at the age of just 21 years 24 weeks.

He failed to win a Major in 1998 despite leading the Open Championship after a first-round 65, but after having successful laser eye surgery the following year he was soon back to winning ways. He had led the PGA Championship for most of the tournament but lost his lead on the last day – before recovering to record a 1-stroke victory over Sergio Garcia. His success continued when he led the US to victory in the World Cup and was named the PGA Tour Player of the Year, after earning more than $6.6 million in prize money during the season.

On 7 February 2000, Woods won the Pebble Beach National Pro-Am to become the first player since Ben Hogan in 1948 to win six straight tour events. The streak was broken in his following tournament, but he roared back with a 15-stroke victory in the US Open, which equalled Old Tom Morris' 1862 record for the largest victory margin in a Major. He then won the 2000 Open Championship at St Andrews by 8 strokes, setting a record for the lowest score to par (-19) in any Major tournament, and completing his set of all four Majors at the age of just 24.

Bob May was a serious threat to Woods in the PGA Championship later that year, but Woods completed his final twelve holes in seven under par to force a three-hole play-off. Woods then carried that form into the play-off, birdying the first hole and parring the next two to claim victory. He joined Hogan as the only golfers to have won three Majors in one year.

He continued to dominate in 2001 and claimed another Masters title at Augusta in April, thereby becoming the first – and so far – only golfer to hold all four Major championship titles at the same time, giving birth to the phrase 'Tiger Slam'. Despite not factoring in the three remaining Majors of the year, he still won five PGA Tour titles, and retained his Masters crown with a 3-stroke victory over Retief Goosen in early 2002.

He was the only player under par in the 2002 US Open as he claimed yet another Major title, but his career hit a relative slump over the following two years. He remained one of the top competitors on tour, but failed to win a Major in either 2003 or 2004 and lost top spot in the world rankings when Vijay Singh moved ahead of him in September 2004. Attempting to recapture some of his magic, he changed coaches from Butch Harmon to Hank Haney. The change appeared to work as Woods quickly returned to his winning ways and broke his relative 'drought' in Majors by winning the 2005 Masters, thus regaining top spot in the world rankings. He also won the Open at St Andrews by 5 strokes from Colin Montgomerie to become the youngest player to win each of the four Major championships twice.

On 3 May 2006, Earl Woods died after a battle with cancer, prompting Tiger to take a two-month break from the tour. Understandably rusty when he returned, he missed the cut in the US Open but retained his British Open title in emotional fashion at Hoylake. Missing just four fairways all week, he shot 18-under, just one stroke off his then Major championship record. A month later at the PGA Championship, he again won in dominating fashion, finishing 18 strokes under par.

Woods began 2007 with his seventh consecutive PGA Tour victory and ended the year with a second consecutive PGA Championship, his thirteenth Major title. However, injury was to catch up with him the following year when he was forced to have surgery on his left knee after finishing second in the Masters; it kept him away from the course for two months. He returned in time for the US Open where he struggled early on but eventually won a play-off victory over Rocco Mediate at Torrey Pines. Two days after his victory, he announced that he would have further surgery and that he had played the tournament with a torn anterior cruciate ligament in his left knee and a double stress fracture in the same leg.

In November 2009, Woods was involved in a car accident near his home in Florida. What followed was a very public unravelling of his personal life and resulted in Woods taking a lengthy break from golf. He eventually returned to competition, but he struggled on the course, failing to win a tournament in 2010 for the first time in fifteen years.

He started to win again in December 2011 and carried that form into the following two years, and he managed to recapture the world number one ranking from Rory McIlroy in early 2013. Majors would continue to prove elusive, however, and he would be plagued by back injuries, necessitating surgeries in September 2015 and April 2017.

Woods arrived at the 2019 Masters at Augusta without a Major win for eleven years, but shot 70 and 68 to enter the weekend just one behind the leaders. He made 67 in his third round to finish the day tied for second, 2 strokes behind leader Francesco Molinari. The Italian held on to his lead on the front nine of the last round but the tide swung in Woods' favour at the twelfth hole when Molinari put his tee shot in the water, consequently double-bogeying. Woods moved 2 strokes ahead following birdies at 15 and 16 and held on to complete a 1-stroke victory. It was his fifteenth Major victory, just three short of Jack Nicklaus' record and has its place in the list of greatest sporting comebacks of all time.

In 2020, Woods won his eighty-second tour title, to equal Sam Snead's record, but he was hospitalised in February 2021 after a car accident in which he sustained open fractures in his right leg and additional injuries in his right foot and ankle. It remains to be seen whether he has another comeback for the ages in him.

Michael Schumacher (Germany)
2002–2004

Juan Manuel Fangio's record of five Formula One World Drivers' Titles stood for five decades until it was passed by seven-times champion Michael Schumacher, who many consider the greatest driver to ever step into a racing car.

He was born on 3 January 1969 in Hürth, near Cologne, six years before his brother Ralf, who would also become a Formula One driver of note. Their father Rolf, a bricklayer, ran the local kart track, at Kerpen, where Mrs Schumacher operated the canteen. Rolf built young Michael his first kart at the age of 4, but when he fitted it with a motorcycle engine, the young Michael crashed it into a lamppost. Keen to avoid a repeat, Rolf enrolled him in the local kart club, but in Germany the regulations stated the minimum age to obtain a kart licence was 14. Michael managed to circumvent that rule by obtaining a licence from Luxembourg, where you only had to be 12! In 1983, he obtained his German licence and the following year won the German Junior Kart Championship.

By 1987 he was European kart champion and had left school to work as an apprentice car mechanic, a job that was soon replaced by full-time employment as a race driver. In 1989, Michael signed with Willi Weber, whose team WTS he would drive for in the German Formula Three Championship. In the 1989 season, Schumacher finished third behind Karl Wendlinger, but the following year he won the championship and was hired by Mercedes to drive sportscars. Weber believed that exposure to professional press conferences and dealing with the cars of 700bhp would be more beneficial.

The Belgian Grand Prix of 1991 at Spa was Michael's debut in the world's top racing series. His lucky break came as a result of Bertrand Gachot being imprisoned for spraying CS gas into a London taxi driver's face. Qualifying seventh, he unfortunately retired on the first lap from the race with clutch failure of his Jordan-Ford. That performance was enough to earn a deal with the Benetton team for 1992, for whom he won his first race, in wet conditions at Spa. He was to finish third in the Drivers' Championship that year. The Williams cars of Damon Hill and Alain Prost dominated the 1993 season, but the following year was to prove different for all manner of reasons.

The 1994 Formula One season started tragically with the deaths of Roland Ratzenberger and Ayrton Senna in the San Marino Grand Prix and later became marred with allegations that several teams had broken the sport's technical regulations. Schumacher let his driving speak for him, as he won six of the first seven races to build up a lead in the standings. However, he was to fall foul of the authorities as he was disqualified from the British Grand Prix and again from the Belgian race – after having finished first. Schumacher led Hill by a point going into the final race in Australia, but both drivers were forced to retire after a collision, giving Schumacher his first world title.

For the 1995 season Schumacher now had Renault power, to match the Williams, and he dominated the season, winning nine races. Again, the season was marred by collisions between Schumacher and Hill, most notably in the British and Italian Grands Prix. Together with teammate Johnny Herbert, he led the Benetton team to their first Constructors' Championship before announcing he was to leave and join Ferrari for 1996.

Stating his desire to return Ferrari to the pinnacle of motorsport, as well as signing an annual contract worth a reported $30 million, Schumacher found the F310 car to have poor handling and it was a testament to his ability that he managed to steer it to three wins, including a masterful drive in the rain in Spain. He won five more races in 1997, but his season ended in humiliation when in the final race, at Jerez in Spain, Schumacher tried unsuccessfully to ram the Williams of his title rival Jacques Villeneuve off the road. As punishment for his misdemeanour, Schumacher's points and his second place in the championship were struck from the record books he would thereafter begin to rewrite.

After finishing second overall in 1998, Schumacher's 1999 season was interrupted by a broken leg suffered in a crash at the British Grand Prix. However, from then on, there was no stopping him as in 2000 he became Ferrari's first champion in twenty-one years. He won the first three races but mid-season failures gave Finland's Mika Häkkinen the chance to successfully defend his title he had won in the previous two years. Schumacher, however, won the crucial Japanese Grand Prix to clinch the title.

Schumacher won a record-equalling eleven races in 2001 and finished on the podium in all seventeen of the year's races, winning the title with four races to spare. The Schumacher brothers finished first and second in the Canadian

Grand Prix, with Ralf winning the race, and Michael's victory in Belgium was his fifty-second in Formula One racing, breaking Alain Prost's record.

He was arguably even more dominant in 2002, a season in which Ferrari won fifteen of the seventeen races, and was crowned champion with six races yet to be run. Controversy was never too far away though and it reared its head at the Austrian Grand Prix. His Ferrari teammate, Rubens Barrichello, was leading, but in the final metres of the race, under team orders, slowed down to allow Schumacher to win the race. The tactic – although not illegal – angered fans but it mattered not to Schumacher, who won the title by 67 points.

Before the 2003 season started, the FIA introduced a new points system in an attempt to make the championship more competitive. It worked to some degree as McLaren's Kimi Räikkönen opened up a 16-point lead on Schumacher early in the season. The German then reeled off three victories in a row to put himself right in the mix and he headed for the final race of the season in Japan needing just a solitary point to win the title. He finished eighth to win his sixth world driving crown and overtook Fangio's previous record of five. In 2004, he won thirteen of the eighteen races to take a seventh title by a massive margin.

Schumacher's qualities included confidence, dedication and determination as well as a passion for racing and an endless desire to improve. His racing brain enabled him to make split-second decisions, adapt to changing circumstances and plan ahead while driving on the limit. He trained harder than any other driver and possessed an astute knowledge of all the cars he drove, which his teammates in the pits always found invaluable.

Rule changes for the 2005 season meant that tyres had to last for an entire race, partly to counter Ferrari's continuing dominance. Schumacher only won one race and ended up third in the driver standings, a long way behind champion Fernando Alonso. The German won seven races in the 2006 championship to take his career total to ninety-one, but Alonso again won the title and Schumacher – tired of the effort required to continue to excel behind the wheel – decided to retire from driving.

He spent two years as Jean Todt's assistant at Ferrari, but his retirement from the wheel would prove only to be temporary as the lure of a return to driving would be irresistible. In 2010, at the age of 41, he joined the new Mercedes team headed by Ross Brawn. He finished sixth in the first race in Bahrain and continued the season without a win, a podium, a pole position or even a fastest lap, ending up ninth in the World Drivers' Championship, which he improved to eighth in 2011. He achieved his last podium finish in the

European Grand Prix in 2012, but at the end of the season, his indecision as to whether to continue led to Mercedes signing Lewis Hamilton, which hastened Schumacher into retirement for the second – and final time.

Sadly, he was not to enjoy a long and active retirement. His first year away from Formula One ended with him suffering a very serious head injury while on a family skiing holiday. He was in a coma for several months before being taken home for a lengthy rehabilitation, where he remains to this day.

Roger Federer (Switzerland) 2004–2008, 2017–2018

Those who lived through the first quarter of the twenty-first century were treated to watching three of the greatest tennis players who ever lived perform wondrous feats on the court. They dominated men's singles, with all of them winning at least twenty Grand Slam titles, leaving Pete Sampras' previous record of fourteen trailing in their wake. Rafael Nadal and Novak Djokovic both have valid claims to be the greatest, but it has been Roger Federer who has most captured the imagination and has been more universally acclaimed as a true genius of the court.

Roger's father, Robert, grew up in Berneck and at the age of 20 he headed for Basel, where he found his first job at Ciba, a leading chemical company. After four years in Basel, he decided to emigrate to South Africa, taking a new job with his same employer in Kempton Park, near Johannesburg. It was there he met Lynette Durand, with whom he returned to Switzerland in 1973, and two years after their daughter Diana was born in 1979, a son, whom they named Roger, followed on 8 August 1981.

Robert was a keen tennis player and Lynette would often take the young Roger to the tennis courts; at 4 he could already hit twenty balls in a row over the net. When he was not at the court, he would hit balls against anything – a wall, a garage door or even cupboards at home. Idolising Boris Becker, he quickly became the best in his age group and participated in special training sessions three times a week. Federer trained with Adolf Kacovsky, who soon recognised that the young boy had a natural talent. In 1993 at the age of 11, Roger won the Swiss 12-and-under indoor championships and six months later, he won the equivalent outdoor title.

In March 1995, he passed the entrance exam for the Swiss National Tennis Centre at Ecublens, but he found it difficult to be away from home and he was the youngest boy on the programme. However, after a difficult start, his tennis continued to improve and in 1997 he won both the indoor and outdoor Swiss national junior championships in the 18-and-under division. The following year, he narrowly missed reaching the junior singles final at the Australian Open, but he made amends at Wimbledon, defeating Irakli Labadze to win the Junior Singles Championship.

Turning professional, he made his ATP (Association of Tennis Professionals) debut in his home Swiss Open but lost in the first round. His first victory came later that year against Guillaume Raoux in Toulouse, and he reached the final of the Junior US Open where he lost to David Nalbandian. He started to make steady progress up the world rankings, taking advantage of wild card entries where he could, and he won the 2001 Hopman Cup for Switzerland playing with Martina Hingis. His first singles victory came in the Milan Indoor tournament the same year, before he caused a sensation at Wimbledon by defeating the four-time defending champion Pete Sampras in the fourth round. He may have lost to Tim Henman in the quarter-finals, but he ended the year ranked thirteen and at the end of 2002 he had risen to number six.

The floodgates finally opened at Wimbledon in 2003, when he beat Mark Philippoussis in the final to claim his first Grand Slam title. In all, he won seven ATP tour titles, including the year-end championships over Andre Agassi. He started 2004 by defeating Marat Safin in the final of the Australian Open to become world number one for the first time. He successfully defended his Wimbledon title – this time against Andy Roddick – before beating Lleyton Hewitt in the US Open final to become the first man to win three Grand Slams in the same year since Mats Wilander in 1988.

He would lose in the French Open semi-final in 2005 to Rafael Nadal, who would become his biggest rival on the red clay, but once he was on the grass it was a different story, as he won Wimbledon for the third year running. He also claimed the US Open crown, although his season came to a premature end due to a foot injury.

Federer swept all before him again in 2006, winning three Grand Slam titles, with the only blot on his copybook being a loss to Nadal in the French Open final. Regardless, Federer became the first man to reach all four finals in the same year since Rod Laver's second Grand Slam year of 1969. He also enjoyed an emotional first victory in the Swiss Indoor Open in Basel towards the end of the season. He repeated the trick in 2007, again winning three Grand Slams and only falling short in Paris against Nadal.

Federer's all-court style transcended tennis. In the past, players had been considered either clay, grass or hard-court specialist. He was able to play comfortably from the baseline, but could also volley proficiently, oozing style from every pore. It was the combination of his off- and on-court appeal which led him to become the world's highest-paid athlete, as well as one of the most admired.

Roger Federer (Switzerland) 2004–2008, 2017–2018

The 2008 Wimbledon final against Nadal is considered by many to have been the greatest tennis match ever played, and it was Federer who came up short on that occasion, losing in five sets to Nadal and ending his five-year winning streak at the tournament. Overcoming a back injury, he claimed the US Open for the fifth time before making the most of Nadal's early exit in the 2009 French Open to win his first title. A few weeks later, he defeated Andy Roddick in another epic Wimbledon final – this time 16–14 in the final set – to win a fifteenth Grand Slam title and overtake Pete Sampras' previous record.

After winning his fourth Australian Open in early 2010, his younger rivals Nadal and Djokovic started to close the gap on him, and Federer failed to win any of the subsequent nine Grand Slam tournaments, suffering surprising upset defeats to Tomáš Berdych and Jo-Wilfried Tsonga at Wimbledon. He finally came good in the 2012 Wimbledon championship, defeating local favourite Andy Murray in the final. Murray had revenge in the Olympic final, taking the gold medal in front of his adoring home fans in London.

Injuries started to catch up with him in the 2013 season, when a back injury prevented him from playing his best tennis and he also experimented with increasing the size of his racquet. The following year, he helped Switzerland beat France to win the Davis Cup for the first time, but Grand Slam titles continued to prove elusive for four long years as Nadal and Djokovic dominated the scene.

With many experts believing his career was coming to an end, Federer enjoyed a renaissance in 2017 when he started by winning the Australian Open, defeating Nadal despite trailing 3–1 in the final set. After deciding to miss the entire clay-court season, he travelled to Wimbledon, where he became the first player to win the title without dropping a set since Björn Borg in 1976. It was his eighth title at Wimbledon, setting a new record, and he became the oldest male player to win the title.

He successfully defended his Australian Open title in early 2018 to become the first man to win twenty Grand Slam titles, but lost in the quarter-finals at Wimbledon against South African Kevin Anderson in five sets, despite winning the first two sets and having a match point in the third set. He defeated Nadal the following year to set up a Centre Court final with Djokovic, but in another thrilling encounter, it was Djokovic who prevailed in five sets.

Knee surgery prevented him playing much at all in the 2020 season and following defeat by Hubert Hurkacz in the 2021 Wimbledon quarter-finals, Federer announced that he would be undergoing further surgery on his knee, and would not appear again on the tour until 2022.

Michael Phelps (USA) 2008

The most-decorated Olympian in history, Michael Phelps was born on 30 June 1985, in Baltimore, Maryland. The youngest of three children, Phelps grew up in the neighbourhood of Rodgers Forge. His father, Fred was a fine all-around athlete and a state trooper and his mother, Debbie, was a middle-school principal. When Phelps' parents divorced in 1994, he and his sisters lived with their mother, to whom Phelps grew very close.

Phelps began swimming at the age of 7 when his two older sisters, Whitney and Hilary, joined a local swimming team. He was still rather nervous of putting his head underwater, so his instructors allowed him to float around on his back and so the first stroke he mastered was backstroke.

The swimming competition at the 1996 Summer Olympics made a huge impression on the 11-year-old Phelps and he met his coach, Bob Bowman, when he started training at the North Baltimore Aquatic Club. Bowman immediately recognised Phelps' talents and fierce sense of competition and began an intense training regime with him. By 1999, Phelps had made the US National B Team and the following year he became the youngest man to be selected for the US Olympic swimming team for sixty-eight years. He finished fifth in the 200-metre butterfly, but it would not be long before he would be achieving greater honours.

In the spring of 2001, Phelps set a world record in the same event, becoming the youngest male swimmer in history, at 15 years and 9 months, to set a world swimming record. He then broke his own record at the 2001 World Championships in Fukuoka, Japan, earning his first international gold medal.

He continued to excel in the 2002 US Summer National Championships in Fort Lauderdale, setting a world record for the 400-metre individual medley, and US records in the 100-metre butterfly and the 200-metre individual medley. The following year, at the same event, he broke his own world record in the 400-metre individual medley with a time of 4:09.09. He graduated from

Towson High School in 2003 and celebrated by winning four gold medals at the 2003 World Championships at Barcelona. He then became the first US swimmer to qualify for six individual events in the same Olympic Games, but decided not to compete in the 200-metre backstroke.

Phelps became a sensation at the 2004 Athens Olympics, at which he won six gold medals, and eight medals in all, equalling Soviet gymnast Aleksandr Dityatin's 1980 record for the most medals in a single Olympic Games. He won the first of his gold medals when he broke his own world record in the 400-metre individual medley and went on to triumph in the 100-metre butterfly, 200-metre butterfly, 200-metre individual medley, 4 x 200-metre freestyle relay and 4 x 100-metre medley relay. He also took home bronze medals in the 200-metre freestyle and the 4 x 100-metre freestyle relay.

He continued to dominate in the pool, winning five gold medals at the 2005 World Aquatics Championships in Montreal and five more in the 2006 Pan Pacific Championships in Victoria, Canada. He did even better in the 2007 World Championships in Melbourne, in which he won seven gold medals, setting five world records in the process. He therefore equalled Mark Spitz's record set in the 1972 Olympics for the most gold medals in one major swimming competition. After a successful 2008 Olympics Trial in Omaha, Nebraska, Phelps set his sights on winning an unprecedented eight gold medals at the games themselves in Beijing.

In China he won gold in each of his first three events: the 400-metre individual medley; the 4 x 100-metre freestyle relay; and the 200-metre freestyle. Each victory came in world record time. On 13 August he won golds in the 200-metre butterfly and the 4 x 200-metre freestyle relay to give him eleven Olympic gold medals – a new Olympic record. He then won a sixth gold of the games by breaking his own world record in the 200-metre individual medley. He tied Spitz's seven golds by winning the 100-metre butterfly final by 0.01 seconds from Milorad Čavić and broke the mark as a member of the victorious American 4 x 100-metre medley relay team. In all, Phelps set world records in all but one (the 100-metre butterfly) of his eight gold medal-winning events.

Much of Phelps' success can be attributed to his work ethic, but his physiology also played a part. His wingspan (the distance from fingertip to fingertip when arms are stretched out to the side) was 6 feet 7 inches, which was 3 inches longer than his height. That difference allowed him to generate more power with each stroke, reaping the benefits of a large wingspan without the increase in weight that it typically comes with.

He also had disproportionately small legs and a long torso. According to sports biographer Colleen de Bellefonds, 'Phelps has the torso of a man who's 6 feet 8 inches tall ... and the legs of a man 8 inches shorter.' This meant that his legs produced less drag than other swimmers of similar stature. In addition, his size 14 feet acted as flippers, propelling him through the water efficiently.

Phelps was hit with a three-month ban in early 2009 after a photograph appeared of him smoking marijuana at a party, but once he had completed the ban the gold rush continued at the 2009 World Championships, with five victories. He did miss out in the 200-metre freestyle to Germany's Paul Biedermann, which was his first defeat in a race in four years. That defeat was not without its controversy; Biedermann was wearing a full polyurethane swimsuit, which drew some unfavourable comments from coach Bowman.

Phelps made amends the following year with five golds at the Pan Pacific Championships, but finished second twice to his teammate Ryan Lochte in the 2011 World Championships – in the 200-metre freestyle and 200-metre individual medley. He did take home four more golds from the meeting in Shanghai, but it was the first sign that his aura of invincibility was starting to slip. Nonetheless, he still won four races in the Olympics trials and headed for London looking to set more records in the pool.

At the ripe old age of 27, Phelps had a disappointing start to the London Olympics, failing to gain a medal in his first event, the 400-metre individual medley. However, he subsequently won silver medals in both the 4 x 100-metre freestyle relay and the 200-metre butterfly and a gold medal in the 4 x 200-metre freestyle relay. With that last victory, he captured an unprecedented nineteenth career Olympic medal, surpassing the record set by Soviet gymnast Larisa Latynina. He then went on to claim gold in the 200-metre individual medley, becoming the first male swimmer to win the same individual event at three consecutive Olympics, and later repeated that feat in the 100-metre butterfly. His final event was the 4 x 100-metre medley relay, in which he won yet another gold medal, before announcing his retirement from the sport.

His retirement proved to be short-lived, as he announced his return to competitive swimming in April 2014, but the plan was soon derailed by a six-month suspension after he was charged with driving under the influence. As a result, he was dropped from the US team for the 2015 World Championships in Kazan, but was still chosen as the flag-bearer at the opening ceremonies of the Rio de Janeiro 2016 Olympic Games, after he had won three individual events at the trials.

He then proceeded to add to his medal count by winning golds in the 200-metre individual medley, 4 x 100 metre medley relay, 4 x 100-metre freestyle relay, and 4 x 200-metre freestyle relay as well as a silver in the 100-metre butterfly. It was his gold in the 200-metre butterfly that captured the most international attention after he gained revenge for his 2012 defeat by South African Chad le Clos. Having nothing else to prove and with a record twenty-eight Olympic medals to his name – of which twenty-three were gold – he retired for a second time – this time for good.

However, the gold medals are just the start of Phelps' legacy. He was named World Swimmer of the Year on seven occasions, and claimed twenty-seven World Championship gold medals in addition to his Olympic tally. He set thirty-nine world records over the course of his career and his dominance over all four strokes have meant that he has few rivals who can justifiably claim to be the greatest swimmer of all time.

Usain Bolt (Jamaica) 2008–2010, 2012–2013

In another lifetime, he could have opened the bowling for the West Indies cricket team or played as goalkeeper for Manchester United, but fate turned his feet to sprinting, and he ended his track career as the fastest man the world had ever seen.

Usain St Leo Bolt was born on 21 August 1986 in Coxeath in the Trelawny District in the north of Jamaica. He grew up in a small two-bedroom house with his older sister, Sherine, and younger brother, Sadiki. His father, Wellesley, worked for a coffee company and – together with his mother – they instilled solid values in all their children, regularly attending church and ensuring they were courteous and polite at all times.

As an outstanding cricket player and a sprinter early on, Bolt's natural speed was noticed by coaches at school, and he began to focus solely on sprinting under the tutelage of Pablo McNeil, a former Olympic sprint athlete. He won his first high-school championship medal in 2001 at the age of 14, taking silver in the 200 metres and went on to win gold at both 200 and 400 metres in the Caribbean CARIFTA Games in March 2002.

Bolt first marked himself as a track prodigy at the 2002 World Junior Championships, which were held in his home country. Racing before a crowd of 36,000 in Jamaica's National Stadium in Kingston, the 15-year-old Bolt won gold in the 200 metres, clocking 20.61 seconds to become the youngest world junior gold medallist. At the age of 17, he ran the event in 19.93 seconds, becoming the first teenager to break 20 seconds in the race.

With the help of a tutor, he passed his school exams, but after he won the 200 and 400 metres at the 2003 Jamaican High School Championships it was clear that a career in athletics beckoned. Heading into the 2003 World Championships, he was ready to make his debut on the world stage, but conjunctivitis ruined his training schedule, and although he recovered in time, the Jamaican selectors refused to let him compete on the grounds that he was too young and inexperienced.

Bolt turned professional in 2004, but a hamstring injury ruled him out of most of the season. He made the Olympic team, but failed to progress past the first round of the 200 metres in Athens after struggling with a leg injury. He was offered several scholarships to American colleges, but Bolt turned them down, adamant that he wanted to stay in Jamaica. A change of coach to Glen Mills and a new focused Bolt saw him qualify easily for the 200 metres final at the 2005 World Championships in Helsinki, but he suffered cramp and finished last.

After treatment in Germany, he prepared for a lower-key 2006 season, and ran a career-best 19.88 seconds for the 200 metres in Lausanne. Desperate to try his hand at the shortest sprint, Bolt was told by Mills that he would only allow him to do so once he had broken the Jamaican 200 metres record. In early 2007, he ran 19.75 seconds to break Don Quarrie's 36-year-old mark and debuted over 100 metres in Crete, where he ran 10.03 seconds to prove he could be a contender over the shorter distance.

He first made his mark on the senior international stage in the 2007 World Championships in Osaka, where he won a silver medal in the 200 metres behind Tyson Gay of the US. Another silver would follow in the sprint relay, and he entered his winter training confident that he could make progress in both events before the following year's Olympics in Beijing.

In May 2008, on his home track in Kingston, Bolt ran the 100 metres in an astonishing 9.76 seconds, only two-hundredths of a second outside Asafa Powell's world record. Just four weeks later he travelled to New York City to compete in the Reebok Grand Prix, where would have the opportunity to face Gay over the shorter distance. On a sodden track, Bolt burst out of the blocks and was never headed, slowing down as he crossed the line in 9.72 seconds, a new world record, striking a psychological blow over his main rival. Bolt's 6-inch height advantage over Gay translated to his completing the race in just forty-one strides to Gay's forty-five.

It was in Beijing that Bolt became an overnight global superstar. He became the first man since Carl Lewis in 1984 to win the 100 metres, 200 metres, and 4 x 100-metre relay in a single Olympics and the first ever to set world records (9.69 seconds, 19.30 seconds, and 37.10 seconds, respectively) in all three events. However, a failed drug test by one of his relay teammates Nesta Carter led to Bolt having his gold medal in that event taken back. His 0.66-second winning margin in the 200-metre race was the largest in Olympic history, and his 0.20-second edge over the second-place finisher in the 100 metres, despite beginning his victory celebration about 80 metres into the race, was the largest since Lewis won by the same margin.

After recovering from a foot injury suffered when he crashed his BMW in April 2009, Bolt won both the 100 metres and the 200 metres at the Jamaican national championships, despite still not being at full fitness. He was the firm favourite to repeat his Olympic double at the World Championship in Berlin, where he didn't disappoint, storming to the 100 metres title in 9.58 seconds, breaking his own world record by over a tenth of a second. Then, in the 200 metres, he won by a huge margin, the biggest in World Championship history, and set a new world record of 19.19 seconds.

Bolt was the heavy favourite in the sprint events heading into the 2011 World Championships in Daegu, South Korea, but a false start disqualified him from the 100-metre final as his friend and training partner Yohan Blake claimed the gold medal. Despite failing to win a medal in his signature race, Bolt recovered to capture golds in the 200 metres and the 4 x 100-metre relay, helping to set a new world record in the latter event.

There were some concerns over Bolt's form heading into the 2012 Summer Olympic Games in London, but he silenced his critics in style, running the second-fastest race of all time to become only the second man to successfully defend his Olympic 100-metre crown. He went on to claim his second consecutive gold medal in the 200 metres, becoming the first man to win both the 100 and 200 in consecutive Olympic Games. Although he did not break any world records in his individual events, the Jamaican 4 x 100-metre relay team smashed their own world record en route to defending their title.

He repeated the 100/200 double in the 2013 World Athletics Championships in Moscow, but a hamstring injury meant that he only raced once in the 2014 season in an individual race, before deciding to concentrate on the following year's World Championship in Beijing. In the 100-metre final, his late lean at the line gave him the 100-metre title by just one-hundredth of a second from Justin Gatlin. The 200-metre final was more one-sided, with Bolt finishing in 19.55 seconds, the fifth-fastest run in history to give him a fourth successive World gold in the event.

Bolt returned to Olympic glory at the 2016 Summer Olympic Games when he won gold in the 100-metre race, making him the first athlete to win three successive titles in the event. He finished the race in 9.81 seconds with Gatlin 0.08 seconds behind him. His winning streak continued in the 200 metres, taking gold in 19.78 seconds. He rounded off his Olympic career by running the final leg as the Jamaican relay team sprinted to another gold medal.

Alas Bolt was unable to round off his career in a blaze of glory at the 2017 World Championships in London. He won the bronze medal in the 100 metres behind Christian Coleman and, in what was scheduled to be his final competitive race, he pulled up with a hamstring injury in the final of the 4 x 100-metre relay and could only cross the line with help from his teammates.

Never one to shun the limelight, he captained the World XI in Soccer Aid 2018 at Old Trafford in Manchester and even played some football in Australia for Central Coast Mariners. He owns several restaurants and has opened an electric car business. However, for all his extra-curricular activities, he will always be remembered as one of the greatest athletes of all time, and one whose 'lightning bolt' victory celebration was imitated worldwide.

Lionel Messi (Argentina) 2010–2012, 2013–2015, 2021–2022

Argentina had been waiting to find a successor to Diego Maradona, and in the first decade of the twenty-first century they finally found him, in the diminutive form of Lionel Messi.

He was born on 24 June 1987 in the industrial city of Rosario – also the birthplace of Che Guevara – the son of a father who worked in a steel factory and a mother who cleaned part-time. Looking for a player to make up the numbers for a friendly game between two local teams of 5-year-olds, a friend of the family – Salvador Aparicio – asked Celia Messi, Lionel's mother, if her son would like to join. With his second touch of the ball, the young Messi started going past the opposing team's players as if they weren't there – as if he had been playing football all his life.

As a result, soon afterwards he was snapped up by Newell's Old Boys, one of Rosario's two professional clubs. Aged 6, Messi was joining the club that had provided more players for the Argentina national team than any other. However, in spite of its glorious achievements, Newell's Old Boys' facilities were relatively modest: two mini-pitches and only four full-sized ones, all of which had seen better days.

Aged 9, El Pulga ('The Flea') as he was known – was 10cm shorter than average. The Newell's establishment didn't immediately consider his size a handicap, but around Christmas 1996 the directors of the club suggested that Lionel and his family meet for a consultation with Doctor Diego Schwarzstein, a leading endocrinologist. On 31 January 1997, Lionel and his father, Jorge, went to see the specialist in his office in Rosario and they agreed that Lionel should undergo a year-long battery of tests to ascertain how best to treat his condition.

They discovered he was suffering from a partial growth hormone deficit, which enabled the medical team to devise a treatment involving daily injections of a biosynthetic growth hormone. The treatment was expensive, however, and Newell's were unable to afford the medical costs. Even the wealthiest

Argentine teams, such as River Plate, refused to foot the bill, and so the Messi family had to look elsewhere.

They had relatives in Catalonia, so they tried to arrange a trial with Barcelona in September 2000. It was unusual for European clubs to sign a player at such a young age, but finally a deal was done – signed on a paper napkin – and the family moved to Barcelona in February 2001 with the club agreeing to pay the medical bills. Messi found it difficult to adjust to his new surroundings, and he suffered from homesickness after his mother moved back to Rosario with his brothers and little sister, while he stayed in Barcelona with his father.

Messi spent a year at Barcelona's youth academy and completed his course of growth hormone treatment when he was 14 years old. He was now more outgoing, and became friends with his teammates, among whom were Cesc Fàbregas and Gerard Piqué, fellow stars in Barcelona's great youth side. In the 2002/03 season the youth side won an unprecedented treble of the league and both the Spanish and Catalan cups. A week before the final of the Copa Cataluna, Messi broke his cheekbone and had to wear a mask for the game. Hindered by the mask, he removed it and scored two goals before being substituted.

He made his first-team debut on 16 October 2004, against Espanyol, becoming the youngest Barcelona player since Paulino Alcántara made his debut in 1912. The following year, on his eighteenth birthday, he signed his first senior contract and helped Argentina win the FIFA World Youth Championship in the Netherlands, scoring two penalties in the 2–1 final victory over Nigeria.

Promoted to a regular in the 2005/06 season, he helped Barcelona reach the Champions League final, but his season ended prematurely when he tore a hamstring against Chelsea in March. Unfortunately, he was unable to play in the final against Arsenal, which Barcelona won, but he recovered in time to play in the World Cup that summer in Germany.

He scored Argentina's final goal in their 6–0 victory over Serbia & Montenegro, but had a goal against Mexico controversially ruled out for offside. He was left out for Argentina's eventual quarter-final defeat to Germany, a decision which was greeted with widespread criticism from fans back home.

Following the decline in form of Ronaldinho and several other key players, at the age of 20 Messi became Barcelona's new star after standout performances domestically, including a hat-trick against Real Madrid in March 2007. In Pep Guardiola's first season as Barcelona manager in 2008/09, Messi formed a superb partnership with Thierry Henry and Samuel Eto'o, guiding the club to a historic treble by winning La Liga, the Copa del Rey and UEFA Champions League. Messi also scored the second goal in the Champions League final against Manchester United, and won the Ballon D'Or (World Footballer of the Year) for the first time.

Despite the departures of Henry and Eto'o soon afterwards, Xavi and Andrés Iniesta, together with Pedro Rodriguez, David Villa and Sergio Busquets helped create one of the greatest sides of all time. The team was triumphant in Europe two years later with a 3–1 victory over Manchester United at Wembley and Messi was the tournament's top goal-scorer with twelve goals.

In 2012, Messi became the first player to score five goals in a single Champions League match when he performed the feat against Bayer Leverkusen. A few weeks later, he surpassed César Rodriguez Álvarez's club-record 232 goals to become Barcelona's all-time leading scorer at the age of just 24. By the end of the calendar year, he had scored ninety-one goals in all club and international play – eclipsing the eighty-five netted in a single calendar year by Gerd Müller in 1972. Fittingly, he won his fourth Ballon d'Or in January 2013.

Under new manager Luis Enrique, Barcelona completed another 'treble' in the 2014/15 season – the season in which Messi, Suárez and Neymar ('MSN') – proved too strong for all-comers. Messi's scoring prowess guided Barcelona to triumphs in La Liga and the Copa del Rey before claiming another Champions League victory with a 3–1 win over Juventus in Berlin.

Barcelona retained their domestic title the following year, but in July 2016, Messi suffered a blow off the soccer field when a Barcelona court found him and his father guilty of three counts of tax fraud. During a four-day trial, Messi and his father denied breaking the law and claimed they were unaware of any tax illegalities that were committed. Both were sentenced to twenty-one months in prison, but under Spanish law, first offences under two years are suspended. Messi was ordered to pay a fine of €2 million with his father required to pay €1.5 million.

The team added further triumphs in 2017/18 and 2018/19 – Messi's tenth title – but those achievements were somewhat overshadowed by Real Madrid's hat-trick of Champions League victories. However, the team's performances had started to decline, especially in Europe, where they surrendered a 3–0 first-leg lead to Liverpool in the quarter-final of the 2019 Champions League.

It was worse the following season, when they lost 8–2 to Bayern Munich at the quarter-final stage, Barcelona's heaviest defeat for sixty-nine years.

During the summer of 2020, Messi handed in a transfer request after sharing his dissatisfaction of Barcelona's progress on the pitch and behind the scenes. His request was turned down and he was forced to remain with the club. Things changed the following summer when he became a free agent. On 6 August 2021, Barcelona announced he would be leaving the club, having scored 672 goals in 778 games, and four days later Messi signed a two-year deal with French side Paris Saint-Germain.

For all his domestic success in Spain and despite being Argentina's record goal-scorer, Messi was criticised for being unable to lead his nation to victory in either the World Cup or Copa America. After a penalty shoot-out defeat to Chile in the 2016 Copa America final, Messi announced his international retirement. However, following words from Argentina's President Mauricio Macri and a national call for him to return, Messi's retirement lasted just a week. He won an international trophy in 2021 when Argentina beat host nation Brazil 1–0 in the final of the Copa America and Messi was named Player of the Tournament having scored four goals. He rounded off the year by winning a seventh Ballon D'Or, two more than his closest rival Cristiano Ronaldo.

Serena Williams (USA) 2015

The winner of more Grand Slam singles titles than anyone else in the Open Era, and the highest-earning female athlete of all time, Serena Williams started her career in the shadow of her older sister Venus. However, she went on to not only overtake her sister's achievements but helped to usher in a new era of athleticism on the women's tennis tour.

Serena's father, Richard, grew up in Shreveport, Louisiana, the son of a cotton-picker, where he experienced racial segregation first-hand throughout the 1940s and 1950s. He moved to Los Angeles in 1979 and met Oracene Price, a widow with three daughters. They married and shortly after daughter Venus was born in 1980 the family moved to Oracene's home town of Saginaw, Michigan, where Serena was born on 26 September 1981.

The family moved to Compton, a neighbourhood of Los Angeles ruled by gangs, with even the police avoiding some areas. Richard claimed that he wanted his daughters to grow up in a tough environment which would prepare them for their future lives. Having been inspired by watching Romanian player Virginia Ruzici win $20,000 for winning the 1978 French Open, Richard produced a seventy-eight-page plan for Venus and Serena to make it out of Compton and conquer the tennis world. Although he had never played tennis and had no formal training – aside from the tennis magazines that he read – he and Oracene home-schooled and coached their daughters themselves. Eventually, Williams quit his job as a security guard to coach Venus and Serena full-time while Oracene supported the family.

Richard gave Venus her first tennis racquet when she was 4 years old, and soon afterwards, the two sisters would be found hitting the ball to each other with an equal mix of fun and competition which was to spill over to their professional careers years later. They were both natural athletes, excelling in softball, soccer, gymnastics and on the track.

Serena entered her first tournament at the age of 4½, and by the time she turned 10 she had won forty-six of the forty-nine tournaments in which she participated. However, her parents realised that for the girls to progress to the next level they would need some outside help. That help came in the form of Rick Macci, who had helped guide the career of Jennifer Capriati, and was one of the foremost tennis coaches in the country. After watching the girls play, Macci was suitably excited, and invited the girls to join his academy. So, the Williams family upped sticks and headed east to Florida.

The girls spent four years training with Macci before Richard Williams decided they would be better served with him acting as their coach again and opted out of letting them compete on the junior circuit. Serena's first professional event was the 1995 Bell Challenge in Quebec City in which she lost in under an hour to Annie Miller 6–1, 6–1. She spent all of 1996 working on her game at home with Richard and fellow coach Dave Rineberg, entering no professional events, but, due to her training, improving dramatically on the court.

That improvement was clear to see at the 1997 Ameritech Cup, where she upset Mary Pierce and Monica Seles – results that catapulted her into the world's top 100 – and after graduating from high school she signed a five-year $12 million shoe contract with Puma.

In 1998, she won the mixed doubles titles at Wimbledon and the US Open partnering Max Mirnyi, and the following year the sisters won the women's doubles crown at the French Open. Just three months later, Serena beat Venus in their race to the family's first Grand Slam win when she captured the US Open title. She became the first African American woman to win a Major in the Open Era and it propelled her to superstardom, with an appearance on the cover of *Sports Illustrated*.

It would be Venus' turn in 2000 to claim her first Grand Slam titles, with victories at Wimbledon and the US Open but controversy was to rear its head the following year at Indian Wells. The sisters were due to play each other in the semi-finals, but Venus withdrew, citing tendonitis in her knee. The crowd for the final were incensed, suggesting that the withdrawal was deliberate, and proceeded to boo when Serena defeated Kim Clijsters. Later the same year, the sisters met in the final of the US Open with Venus emerging victorious in straight sets.

After withdrawing from the 2002 Australian Open with an ankle sprain, Serena quickly made up for lost time. She won the French Open, her first Wimbledon title and the US Open before she returned to the Australian Open in 2003 and won that to complete what became known as the 'Serena Slam' – holding all four Major titles simultaneously but not in the same calendar year. Remarkably, all four of the victories came against Venus in the final.

Tragedy struck in September 2003 when Serena's older half-sister and assistant, Yetunde, was caught in gang crossfire in Compton and killed. Serena was the first to learn of the murder, and had to inform her mother. At the end of that year, Serena underwent knee surgery and spent eight months away from the tour.

She reached the final of Wimbledon in 2004, where she lost to Maria Sharapova, and won a second Australian Open title in early 2005, but she spent most of the following two years struggling with knee injuries, poor fitness and depression after Yetunde's death. She started to rekindle her love of the game thanks to several charity trips to Africa and stunned the tennis world with a 6–1, 6–2 victory over Sharapova in the 2007 Australian Open final. Determined to improve her fitness, she started to work with renowned fitness trainer Mackie Shilstone, and the Williams sisters went on to claim the gold medal in the women's doubles at the 2008 Beijing Olympics. Just a few weeks later, Serena won the US Open for the third time.

Following victory at Wimbledon in 2009, Serena reached the semi-finals of the US Open where she was called for a foot fault in the second set of her semi-final against Clijsters. She argued the call, and was assessed a point penalty which cost her the match. She made amends with a three-set win over Justine Henin in the 2010 Australian Open and went on to retain her Wimbledon crown. However, four days after winning Wimbledon, she stepped on a piece of glass and lacerated a tendon in her right foot. In January 2011, a pulmonary embolism was detected in her lungs for which she underwent emergency treatment and only returned to the court in June, after a year away.

She lost in the fourth round at Wimbledon in 2011, and her losing streak continued into 2012 when she lost in the fourth round of the Australian Open in January and in the first round of the French Open in May. That proved to be the final straw for Serena, who reached out to French tennis coach Patrick Mouratoglou for help.

The move paid off almost immediately. After extensive work on her serve, as well as on her confidence and conditioning, she won Wimbledon for the fifth time. She followed that performance by winning two Olympic gold medals, in singles and doubles, at the London Games. She rounded off her year by winning her fourth US Open title and became the oldest woman – at 31 – to be ranked number one.

She won both the French Open and US Open titles in 2013 and clinched her third straight and sixth overall US Open singles title the following year by defeating her good friend Caroline Wozniacki. Her winning ways carried over into the new year as she beat Sharapova to claim the 2015 Australian Open championship. At the French Open in June, Serena managed to overcome flu to win the tournament for the third time and claim her twentieth Grand Slam singles title.

She was not finished; victory over Garbine Muguruza brought her a sixth Wimbledon title to earn her second 'Serena Slam' by holding all four Major titles at once. Trying to become the first woman since Steffi Graf in 1988 to complete the calendar-year Grand Slam, she suffered a shock defeat in the semi-finals of the US Open to unseeded Roberta Vinci. A week later, she presented her collection at New York Fashion Week, demonstrating the other love in her life – clothing design.

Serena opened 2016 by advancing to the Australian Open final, where she lost in three sets to Angelique Kerber. She also reached the French Open final, but this time succumbed to Muguruza in straight sets. On 9 July she again tasted victory, defeating Kerber 7–5, 6–3 at Wimbledon and winning her twenty-second Grand Slam title. With her historic win, Serena tied Steffi Graf's record twenty-two Grand Slam victories in the Open Era. In that year's US Open, Serena suffered a surprising defeat to Karolina Pliskova in their semi-final match. With the loss, she also gave up the No. 1 ranking that she'd held for 186 weeks.

Perhaps fittingly, her Open Era record twenty-third Major victory came against her sister Venus, in the 2017 Australian Open. Later that year, she revealed she was two months pregnant during the match, and she gave birth to her daughter in September.

That was her most recent Grand Slam victory, as injuries have troubled her and she has lost in each of her last four Grand Slam finals. However, even as she turned 40, she was still as fierce a competitor as ever, so few people would totally dismiss her ability to add to her titles.

Cristiano Ronaldo (Portugal) 2015–2017, 2018–2021

The man who would become the world's highest-paid athlete was born on 5 February 1985 in Santo Antonio, a mountainous neighbourhood and one of the poorest communities of the capital Funchal in Madeira. The youngest child of a humble family, he was the son of Dolores, a cook, and Dinis, a municipal gardener. He was named Cristiano Ronaldo dos Santos Aveiro – the Ronaldo part in honour of the then-president of the US, Ronald Reagan.

Dinis also worked as a kitman at local club Andorinha and he asked Fernao Barros Sousa, one of the players who had earlier represented the island's biggest club, Nacional, if he would be Ronaldo's godfather. Later on, the boy would accompany his father and from the age of around 8, he started representing Andorinha's youth team in seven-a-side matches, where his talent soon became evident. It was not long before other clubs started to show an interest in him, including Nacional.

He arrived at Nacional at the age of 10 already a gifted footballer. He was adept with both feet and always tried to score beautiful goals, a trait he continues to this day. He soon graduated to playing eleven-a-side matches, often competing against boys who were up to three years older than he was. He soon became the outstanding talent in Madeira and he started to look farther afield in order to progress his career.

Barros Sousa introduced Cristiano to local magistrate João Marques de Freitas, who had connections at Sporting Lisbon and arranged for him to have a trial with the club. Sporting were impressed and, at the age of 12, Ronaldo moved to the Portuguese capital all on his own. He found it difficult to adjust at first, but eventually he started to make friends and settled into life in one of football's great academies, under the tutelage of Osvaldo Silva.

He made his first-team debut at the age of 17 but it was a 3–1 pre-season victory over Manchester United in August 2003 which was to shape his future career. He so impressed visiting manager Alex Ferguson, that immediately after the game he offered to buy the 18-year-old for £12.24 million, stating that he was one of the most exciting young players he had ever seen. Ronaldo ended his first season in English football by scoring Manchester United's opening goal in their 3–0 win over Millwall in the FA Cup final, winning his first trophy in the process. He subsequently helped the Portuguese national side reach the final of Euro 2004 on home soil, but they were surprisingly defeated by Greece in Lisbon.

Originally starting his career a right-winger, under Ferguson he developed into a forward who could bamboozle defenders with his dribbling and flair, not to mention his step-overs, which delighted and frustrated to the same degree. His second season didn't quite live up to the promise of his first and his 2005/06 season was also plagued with inconsistencies before he headed off for the World Cup in Germany. In the quarter-finals, Portugal faced England and Ronaldo became the pantomime villain after Wayne Rooney was sent off.

Determined to counter the boos from the crowd by his performance on the pitch, he played the lead role as Manchester United won the Premier League title in the 2006/07 season. He improved still further the following season, scoring forty-two goals in all competitions, including a decisive penalty on the final day of the league campaign and a powerful header against Chelsea in the Champions League final in Moscow. His individual performances earned him his first FIFA World Player of the Year award.

The following season was not quite as dominant, but his team were still able to complete a hat-trick of league titles, and reached the Champions League final, where they were beaten by Lionel Messi's Barcelona. Despite constant rumours that he wanted to move on from the club, it still came as some surprise when news broke on 11 June 2009 that Manchester United had accepted a world record £80 million offer from Real Madrid; less than a month later, the transfer was completed.

He got off to a great start in Madrid, scoring in each of his first four league games, but an ankle injury sustained while playing for Portugal kept him on the sidelines for seven weeks. He recovered to finish the season with thirty-three goals in all competitions, but his first season in the Spanish capital ended without a trophy.

Inheriting the number 7 shirt from Raúl in advance of the 2010/11 Spanish season, he scored the match-winning goal in the Copa del Rey final to earn his first trophy in Spain. His total of forty league goals won him the European Golden Boot for a second time, becoming the first player to win the award in different leagues. Real Madrid won their first league title in four years in the 2011/12 season but the team again bowed out at the semi-final stage of the Champions League, the standard by which Real Madrid seasons are measured.

He helped Portugal to the semi-final of Euro 2012, where they were beaten by Spain in a penalty shoot-out, but back in Madrid his goal-scoring exploits continued to set new records, with sixty-nine goals in the calendar year of 2013 earning him the FIFA Ballon D'Or. He also managed to help Real Madrid overcome their semi-final bogey to win 'La Décima' – their tenth European Cup with a 4–1 victory over city rivals Atlético in early 2014, a match in which Ronaldo became the first player to score in the final for two different European Cup winning teams. However, despite his domestic and European success, he was unable to inspire his national side in the 2014 World Cup in Brazil and Portugal suffered an early elimination.

In 2014/15, he netted forty-eight goals to lead La Liga in scoring again and a landmark came against Levante in October 2015 when he scored his 324th goal to become Real Madrid's all-time leading goal-scorer. He was also the top scorer in the 2015/16 Champions League, but despite a poor performance in the final – again facing Atlético – he was still able to convert the winning penalty in the shoot-out to win another European title for the club.

He went from strength to strength as he helped Portugal win the 2016 European Championship in France, the country's first major international tournament title. Ronaldo contributed three goals and three assists although he only played the first twenty-five minutes of the final due to a knee injury sustained early in the match. He rounded off one of the greatest years any footballer has had by winning another Ballon D'Or trophy – his fourth.

In the 2016/17 season, he helped Real Madrid reclaim the La Liga title for the first time in five years and his two goals against Bayern Munich made him the first player to score 100 goals in European club competition. His European form continued with two goals as his club retained the Champions League trophy with a 4–1 victory over Juventus, and Ronaldo went on to retain his Ballon D'Or trophy.

In May 2018, Real won their third Champions League final in a row, defeating Liverpool 3–1, with Ronaldo top-scoring in the tournament for the sixth successive season. However, soon after winning his fifth winner's medal, negotiations to sign a new contract broke down, and he completed a €100 million transfer to Juventus, citing the need for a new challenge and ending his Real Madrid career with 451 goals in 438 competitive appearances. He put the distraction behind him as he played brilliantly at the 2018 World Cup, scoring four goals before Portugal lost to a strong, defensive Uruguay team.

He scored ten goals in his first fourteen games for Juventus, and his header won the Supercoppa Italiana against AC Milan. His team went on to win their eighth successive Serie A title, and Ronaldo's twenty-one league goals led to him being named the competition's Most Valuable Player. Juventus retained their title in the 2019/20 season and in what would prove his final season in Italy in 2020/21, he scored twenty-nine league goals to win the 'Capocannoniere' award as the highest goal-scorer.

Despite winning two league titles in his three seasons in Italy, Juventus failed to make it beyond the quarter-finals of the Champions League. Adding to the frustration was the fact that none of their defeats came against the game's modern heavyweights, instead losing out to Ajax, Lyon and Porto.

Manchester City pulled out of a potential deal with Juventus due to the overall cost of the transfer and the following day his former employers Manchester United stunned the football world by announcing that Ronaldo would be re-joining the team for £12.85 million. He scored two goals on his second debut for the club, but it remains to be seen if his signing is enough to bring a first Premier League title to the Reds since Alex Ferguson's departure in 2013.

Rafael Nadal (Spain) 2022

In 2003 it was Roger Federer who made most of the headlines at Wimbledon, losing only one set as he cruised to his first Grand Slam title. However, the youngest player in the main draw that year was a 17-year-old, who won his first two matches before falling to twelfth seed Paradorn Srichaphan in the third round. Two years later, Novak Djokovic would debut at the Australian Open and the men's tennis scene was set for the next two decades.

Rafael Nadal was born on 3 June 1986 in Manacor, on the Balearic Island of Majorca. One of his uncles – Miguel – represented Spain in three football World Cups – and another – Toni – a top amateur tennis player and coach – introduced the youngster to the sport at the age of just 3. There was no hint of nepotism, as Rafa had to sweep the red clay court after every practice and was forced to dodge balls hurled at him if his attention wavered.

The young Nadal was also a talented footballer, but by the time he turned 8 he was forced to choose between the two sports in his life. However, despite opting to pursue a tennis career, he made sure to find time for his weekly kickabout with his friends. Another decision he made early in his career was to switch from a double-handed forehand to a single-handed stroke. Even though he used his right hand for all his everyday tasks, such as writing, eating, throwing or anything else, his uncle Toni identified that he had a stronger left hand while playing tennis.

Having reached the semi-finals of the Spanish Under-14 National Championship at the age of 11, he returned the following year determined to win the title. In the first round, however, he slipped on the court and broke the little finger on his left hand. Undeterred, and using just four fingers to grip the racquet, he went on to win the tournament. It was this refusal to give up which was to so characterise his career from then onwards.

Despite requests from the Spanish Tennis Federation to move to the mainland, the Nadal family always turned them down, insisting that his education would suffer and, under uncle Toni's guidance, Rafa turned professional at the age of 15.

In 2002, he helped Spain win the Junior Davis Cup and the following year he won his first two Challenger titles as well as becoming the youngest player to reach the third round at Wimbledon since Boris Becker in 1984. In 2004, he won his first ATP singles title at the Prokom Open before helping Spain win the Davis Cup, the first of five such titles he would help bring to his country.

He dominated the 2005 clay-court season, which culminated in a triumph in the French Open, the start of his love affair with the red clay of Roland Garros. He celebrated his nineteenth birthday by breaking Roger Federer's serve nine times in their semi-final match before defeating Mariano Puerta in the final to claim his first Grand Slam singles title. He was unable to continue his winning streak at Wimbledon though, crashing out to Gilles Müller in the second round, fuelling talk that he was a one-trick pony.

He started to chip away at those doubters over the following couple of years, in which he successfully defended his Paris title and reached the final at Wimbledon, where he lost to Federer both times. However, on 7 July 2008 he finally laid those ghosts to rest with a five-set triumph, ending Federer's sixty-five-match unbeaten streak on grass, in a Wimbledon final widely considered to be one of the greatest matches ever played. He went on to win the gold medal at the Beijing Olympics and ended the year ranked number one in the world. He started 2009 by winning his first Australian Open title – again in a five-set classic against Federer – but he suffered a surprising loss to Robin Söderling in the fourth round at Paris, ending his thirty-one-match unbeaten streak in the event. Injury forced him out of that year's Wimbledon, but he bounced back in 2010 with what he still considers to be his greatest season.

It didn't start particularly well. A knee injury, which would require a month off the court, forced him to pull out of his quarter-final match with Andy Murray at the Australian Open. Nadal returned in time for the clay-court season and gained revenge for his previous year's defeat by beating Söderling to reclaim his French Open crown. Crossing the Channel, he defeated Tomáš Berdych to win his second Wimbledon title and later in the year defeated Novak Djokovic in four sets to win his first US Open title. This meant he had clinched Major titles on clay, grass and hard courts in the same calendar year.

It was Djokovic's turn to claim three Grand Slams in 2011 as he improved his training regime and became the player to beat on the men's tour. Nadal continued to hold court at Roland Garros, winning each time from 2011–2014, but over that period his only other Grand Slam title was the US Open in 2013.

Nadal saw his run of thirty-nine consecutive victories in Paris ended by Djokovic in 2015 and injuries started to catch up with him as he saw his run of ten years with at least one Major title come to an end. It was a similar story the following year as a wrist injury brought his French Open to a premature end and ruled him out of Wimbledon. His renowned killer instinct was being questioned and it was feared that he had started the long decline towards retirement. People also doubted that he would add to his tally of Grand Slam titles, which stood at fourteen, alongside Pete Sampras.

Nadal made a major change at the end of 2016 by adding childhood hero and former world number one Carlos Moya to his coaching staff, with a specific focus on his serve. The move paid immediate dividends as Nadal claimed a tenth French Open win and added another US Open to his resumé. His career was kick-started, and he won at Roland Garros in each of the following three years to give him an astonishing thirteen French titles. He added a fourth US Open title in 2019, the same year he helped Spain win their sixth Davis Cup title.

After suffering a surprising defeat in the 2021 Australian Open to Stefanos Tsitsipas, having held a two-set lead, he reached Paris as the hot favourite to become the first player to win twenty-one Grand Slam titles. Things seemed to be going to plan as he reached the semi-finals, but he met an inspired Djokovic, who won in four sets, inflicting only Nadal's third defeat at the venue. The rest of his season was plagued by a foot injury, and, after he was only able to compete in one tournament in the last seven months of 2021, his critics were again starting to write his career off.

However, the stars aligned at the Australian Open in early 2022. With Federer missing the tournament after surgery on his right knee and Djokovic making headlines for all the wrong reasons as his visa to enter Australia was cancelled, Nadal progressed through the draw to reach the final against Daniil Medvedev. The Russian was attempting to win successive Grand Slams after his triumph in the 2021 US Open and he opened up a two-set lead. Conceding ten years to his opponent, Nadal had to dig deeper than ever before into his reserves of fitness and technique in an attempt to claw his way back.

But claw his way back he did, and he found the form which had made him such a warrior over the previous two decades. He won the next three sets to complete a 5-hour, 24-minute victory to move to twenty-one Grand Slam titles, one ahead of his rivals Federer and Djokovic. He may not have the ethereal grace of Federer or the unpredictable brilliance of Djokovic, but when it comes to fighting qualities, there has possibly never been a player like Nadal.